TITAN SINKING

TITAN SINKING

THE DECLINE OF THE WWF IN 1995

James Dixon

www.historyofwrestling.info

Published by lulu.com

This book is set in Garamond, Calibri and Courier New.

10 9 8 7 6 5 4 3 2 1

This book was printed and bound in the United Kingdom.

ISBN 978-1-291-99637-1

In 1995, I lost $6 million out of my ass.

- Vince McMahon

FOREWORD
by Jim Cornette

A S YOU WILL SOON READ, 1995 was the worst year - financially, creatively, artistically - in the hundred years of the professional wrestling/sports entertainment industry up until that point in time. Vince McMahon's WWF bled over $5 million, the only loss in company history to this day that wasn't caused by outside business endeavours. Vince himself was free and clear from his legal tangles with the government, but the effects on his operation were still being felt. WCW was entering its seventh year of ownership by Turner Broadcasting, having lost millions in each of those years, and showing little sign of changing that as 1995 began. The more than two dozen regional territories that existed in the United States and Canada in the early eighties had boiled down to one: Jerry Jarrett's Memphis. One territory had been *started* in the nineties, my Smoky Mountain Wrestling on the other end of Tennessee opposite Memphis, and we closed down at the end of 1995. ECW, not really a territory but a "pioneer" Northeastern independent, was still in its early days and not setting the box offices on fire. Fewer fans than ever were watching wrestling on TV, or going to live matches, of which there were less being run - at least on a major scale - than at any other point in the sport's history. As a talent - wrestler, manager, referee, announcer, booker - it was harder than it had ever been to make money in wrestling, and a few were making big money, while the vast majority could barely pay rent.

SO, WHY write a fucking book about 1995?

BECAUSE, BASICALLY, it's a dividing point--a tipping point, if you will, between the dying days of the pro wrestling business, killed by outsiders, egos, exposure and parody, and the takeover of sports entertainment. It's also the year where both businesses sowed the seeds of what could ultimately be the death of the entire genre. For each different fear of, and reaction to, the horrible business of that year by different promotions and personalities, led to the most egregious period of "hotshotting" ever seen before, the effects of which last to this day nearly twenty years later and which can never be fully recovered from.

VINCE MCMAHON'S reaction at the horrible business in 1995, followed by his drubbing at the hands of WCW just a few years later, was to make the A.D.D-ridden editor of his magazine his head writer, and the excesses of the Attitude Era left a legacy of the most trite show business cliché in history: after going as far as you can possibly go, how do you follow it? WCW's reaction to 1995 was to finally open up the check-book of TBS, but it was given to Verne Gagne's former coffee boy, whose complete lack of knowledge of history caused him to take an unprofitable wrestling promotion, make it the most profitable one ever, then one that lost more money than any promotion ever, then one that went out of business, all in five years. Paul Heyman's reaction was to "innovate" himself into a promotion that broke all the rules, then found out why there *were* rules, with ECW going bankrupt just after it immuned fans to the most extreme violence ever presented in a wrestling ring, leaving many of its top stars crippled or with substance abuse problems. And no one in the bunch followed the most important concept of hotshotting: pull back before you start losing the people while still hotshotting, because if you don't, you risk never getting them back.

IT ALL stems from 1995, and James Dixon and the staff at History of Wrestling have made the utmost effort to bring you the story of the chaos, confusion, drama, tantrums, prima donnas, mishaps and outright silliness that engulfed the sport during that year. They've made every effort to be both factual and impartial, talking to people who were there and lived it. But after all; it's still wrestling, so one never fully knows the truth. Still, most of this stuff *is* true - because as you'll soon see, there's no way you could make most of this shit up!

Jim Cornette
Louisville, Ky.
July 2014

ONE

VINCE MCMAHON BUILT A WRESTLING empire in the eighties, and his kingdom was the World Wrestling Federation.

In 1982 at the age of thirty-seven, he bought the promotion from his father Vincent James McMahon when it was still a modest but successful North East regional group based in New York. The company had the added benefit of exclusive access to the wrestling equivalent of Mecca: Madison Square Garden. This wasn't enough for the man old-timers disparagingly nicknamed Vinnie; he wanted to go national. Vince Junior had far grander plans that called for the WWF to barge in on other already well-established territories and take advantage of what he surmised were crotchety, out-of-touch promoters.

He had realised most would rather die or watch their own business fail than sell up to him or change their archaic methods, so he undercut them all with the local television stations and secured syndication rights that helped build the WWF a national patchwork. In the space of just a few months Vince had already become a widely reviled figure, having violated countless long-standing principles the industry had adhered to for decades. In doing so he managed to undo the lifetime of goodwill his father had amassed in the industry as one of few promoters that everybody respected.

McMahon was a young visionary in an age where men from a bygone era were running a business they no longer understood. Bold as brass, Vince saw himself in the mould of the great Roman emperor Augustus, a man who had once bragged about how he wanted Rome to, "rule the world," and who was responsible for a significant expansion of the Empire. The parallels were certainly striking. Like Augustus, McMahon felt no sense of immorality when he began his own aggressive expansion, only it was local wrestling territories rather than political geographic territories that he conquered.

"It's just business," McMahon would say dismissively, as he tore livelihoods away from men and crushed family businesses that had been built over generations. Just as numerous civilisations fell before Augustus to be claimed under an all-powerful Roman rule, Vince demolished the regional groups across the country and soon presided over an empire of his own. The WWF became an unstoppable juggernaut.

Thanks to an expensively assembled cast of characters led by the charismatic, larger-than-life Hulk Hogan, a man who could virtually print money at the height of his popularity, the WWF was the hottest ticket in town wherever it went. In the mid-to-late-eighties they sold out arenas nationwide, often in two or three different cities in a single day. At the peak of the Hulkamania-led wave, the WWF ran over eight-hundred events annually and routinely broke attendance and television records. A prime time special that aired on *NBC* in February 1988 called *The Main Event*, headlined by WWF Champion Hogan against Andre the Giant, scored an historic 15.2 television rating, which translated to an almost incomprehensible 33,000,000 (thirty-three million) viewers. As a comparison, the number was on par with the final ever broadcasts of *Dallas*, *Frasier*, and *Everybody Loves Raymond*, and in wrestling terms was considerably higher than even the highest rated episode of WWE flagship program *Monday Night Raw*, or any other wrestling show aired since.[1]

The nineties had been far less kind to McMahon and the WWF, as years of excess and extravagance began to take their toll. Perennial champion Hogan's veneer had started to crack a little, and though he remained a huge draw he had begun to cast longing glances towards Hollywood and a life after wrestling. Realising that he needed to build for the future, McMahon searched for a man to replace Hogan and carry the company's flagship title, but it proved much harder than he had anticipated.

But that was the least of Vince's worries between 1991 and 1994, a period besieged with damaging stories and allegations that arraigned his company. The most damning came in 1993 when he was indicted by the United States government, accused of buying steroids and supplying them to his wrestlers in order to advance their unnatural physiques. The investigation into the WWF's practices had first started in 1989 when Dr. George Zahorian was charged on fifteen counts of distribution of controlled substances, which included steroids. Zahorian was the state athletic commission doctor in the state of Pennsylvania, and was known amongst the boys as, "The Candy Man." At shows in Hamburg and Allentown he would show up and set up shop, selling steroids ("candy") to members of the roster. In late 1990, Zahorian was found guilty and jailed, and the government decided to go after McMahon next. They spent the next few years compiling reams of evidence against him, before the case eventually went to trial in 1994.

THERE WERE other public relations nightmares to deal with too, such as a 1992 sex scandal that rocked the WWF and caused the immediate

---

[1] The highest rated episode of Monday Night Raw pulled an 8.1 rating in May, 1999 which equated to around 9.2 million viewers.

resignations of behind the scenes staffers Pat Patterson and Terry Garvin. In addition, ring announcer Mel Phillips was fired by the company. The allegations against them were numerous, but all involved the exploitation of young ring boys, and promises of more lucrative positions (*pushes)* for opening act wrestlers in exchange for sexual favours. One of the accusers was Barry Orton (the uncle of future multiple-time WWE Champion Randy Orton and brother to 'Cowboy' Bob Orton), who performed as Barry O. He claimed that Garvin had accosted him when he was just starting out in the business as a twenty-year-old kid (though not while he was in the WWF), and that he tried to lure him into his perverse web with the promise of success in the industry.

Mel Phillips preferred them even younger according to former ring boy Tom Cole, who accused the announcer of molesting him when he was in his early teens. Phillips was infamous in the locker-room for having a foot fetish, which everyone knew about but no one paid much attention to. The boys were well aware of Phillips' perversity, but it was the decadent eighties so few particularly cared. But the national press *were* paying attention when Cole outed Phillips as a paedophile, and used it as another bullet in the increasingly loaded gun they were aiming towards the WWF.

Pat Patterson didn't do anything wrong other than being openly gay, not exactly a criminal offence but still seemingly bordering the line in some states in the early nineties. Patterson was tarred with the same brush as the other two accused, partly due to his well-known friendship with Garvin but also because he never made secret of his homosexual lifestyle. Political correctness wasn't as highly touted on the social agenda as in more modern times, and the WWF worried that people would hear that Patterson was gay and assume he was behaving in the same manner as Garvin.

Vince told Pat to take a few months out for things to cool off and then he would be brought back, which ironically incriminated him far more than remaining would have done. By August, less than six months after the accusations were first made public, Patterson was back under the umbrella. No one said a word about it when he returned. The boys just pretended like he had never left and he played along with the charade. It was a case of don't ask, don't tell, and of the ever guarded business protecting one of their own.

But the deluge continued when Vince himself was accused of sexual harassment by ex-employee Rita Chatterton. Chatterton had worked for McMahon in the eighties as Rita Marie, the WWF's first female referee, and she came out of the woodwork in April 1992 as the swell of hostility against the WWF was at its most fervent. When she appeared on a special episode of Geraldo Rivera's sensationalist social commentary show *Now It Can Be Told* subtitled *Wrestling's Ring of Vice,* Chatterton delineated the tale for the world.

Speaking in a sombre, submissive tone, she told how McMahon had promised that her face would appear on *Time* magazine and how she would be given a contract of half a million dollars per year. Onlookers in the know immediately sensed that the exposé they were watching was going to be just another smear campaign against the WWF; Vince did not have guaranteed contracts, and even if he had done the figure would still be absurdly high for a referee. The majority of the boys hadn't earned anything close to that kind of money, even at the company's peak when they worked several hundred dates per year.

Chatterton continued, and sharp ears in Stamford pricked up when she contradicted herself by first saying how well her career had gone by citing appearances at Madison Square Garden and a lengthy feature about her in *WWF Magazine,* but then talked about how she had struggled for work and so met with Vince in his limousine to ask for more dates. If this part of her story was obviously untrue, they argued, then it stood to reason that it all was.

According to Chatterton, the limousine was where the assault occurred. She recalled, "I got into the limo and we started talking, and he started telling me that he had really neglected doing something with my career and it was really time that Rita Marie came to be, and the next thing I know..." At that point, she stopped talking and closed her eyes for dramatic effect, before detailing how Vince unzipped his pants and forced her to touch his penis.

Rivera's director loved that; it was just the kind of overly-dramatic recollection of accounts that the trashy show courted. He instructed the cameraman to zoom in on a tissue that Chatterton was grasping tightly in her hands, which she then used to wipe away tears before going into detail about how McMahon had forced her to give him oral sex. Chatterton claimed to have pulled away at that point, apparently angering him.

She rocked her head back gently and closed her eyes, almost, some observers noted, as if trying to remember pre-scripted lines. Then, she dropped the bombshell that would result in Vince filing a lawsuit against her, "When I said no, he said that I had better satisfy him and he started pulling my pants, and he pulled me on top of him and he satisfied himself through intercourse." Chatterton might not have used the exact words, but her message was crystal clear; she was accusing McMahon of rape.[2]

It soon became apparent that in appearing on the show and making the claims, Chatterton hadn't acted of her own volition. While at least part of her story may well have been true, she had clearly been coerced into spinning her yarn by exploitative media sharks who wanted further McMahon blood in their already frenzied anti-WWF waters. She wondered to herself if she had taken things too far. Rivera's show was obviously designed as a hatchet piece against McMahon, and everyone who watched could see that it was presented from a very one-sided, agenda-driven perspective. Whether it was the right forum for her to have gone public on, she couldn't be sure.

When Vince was shown a tape of Chatterton's damning attack on his character, he couldn't believe the words that had come out of her mouth. Like most others, he too suspected that she had been put up to the appearance, probably, he guessed, in return for being well compensated. After he first placated his wife Linda and swore blind to her that no such incident had ever occurred, Vince picked up the phone and called his already overworked lawyers. Like him, they assumed Chatterton was involved in a conspiracy.

The timing of Chatterton's accusations were no coincidence to Vince or his legal team. It was a shakedown. Numerous obscure ex-employees with an axe to grind joined forces and jumped on the anti-WWF bandwagon, all of them willing to sell their souls for a quick buck. Ex-employees like former presenter Murray Hodgson, an immaculately coiffured but inherently insincere character who was also involved in the Rivera piece. After he heard Tom Cole and Barry Orton had gone public with stories of sexual harassment in the WWF, he suddenly came out with his own claims, declaring that he had been fired for refusing Pat Patterson's sexual advances.

McMahon had little time for Murray Hodgson. He saw him as a con-man looking to make some easy money by latching onto a media-driven scandal, and had smelled a rat immediately when Hodgson's legal team demanded hush money in advance of his multiple television appearances. On an episode of *Donahue*, McMahon made a rare public appearance in an attempt to tell his side of the story and defend himself. He took great pleasure in cutting Hodgson down when he sneered directly to his face, "You were fired because you were terrible at your job."

While Hodgson was barely enough of an annoyance to register on McMahon's radar, he knew that the Chatterton claims were serious and

---

[2] The show was very careful not to use the word "rape", reediting the original interview with Chatterton and changing the original voiceovers to remove the term.

needed to be squashed. A year later in March, 1993 on the grounds of having been caused, "severe emotional distress," Vince and Linda sued Chatterton, Rivera and also former performer David Schultz, who was named as a conspirator.

Schultz had been fired by McMahon back in 1985 for trying to fight Mr. T in Los Angeles and nearly killing *WrestleMania,* but had also garnered significant notoriety for slapping reporter John Stossel when he provocatively asked if the business was "fake." Schultz still harboured a grudge against McMahon for firing him, and claimed he was put up to both incidents by his superiors under orders from Vince himself.

WWF holding company Titan Sports alleged that Schultz and Chatterton had colluded in 1992 with the intention of making an audio tape where they would discuss the alleged limo incident, and would then try and pass it off as having been recorded in the eighties. The case was eventually dropped as the WWF's legal team instead channelled all of its resources into getting McMahon acquitted, but the stigma of the accusations lingered.

VINCE'S LAWYERS were already busy. On top of the ongoing criminal trial they had a lawsuit from former performer and commentator, and future governor of Minnesota, Jesse Ventura to deal with. Ventura had filed against Titan because he believed he was owed a backlog in unpaid royalties from video tapes featuring his commentary, which he had unwittingly waived the rights to when he first signed his contract.

Ventura had been told that company policy was to only pay royalties to feature performers, and the advisement of his agent Barry Bloom was that it may be unwise to try and challenge that if he wanted to retain his job. He later found out that there was no such policy and demanded to be recompensed for the ninety plus tapes that had been released containing his work. The courts agreed, and on April 13, 1994 they ordered restitution, awarding Ventura $810,000 in unpaid royalties. McMahon was incensed by the decision, growling, "That's my *fucking* money!" at Ventura when he learned of the verdict.

Little over two weeks later his company was in court again, this time stemming from an incident that occurred back in 1990. On December 11th of that year in Tampa, Florida, Marty Jannetty wrestled in what was supposed to be a bog-standard television bout alongside Rockers tag partner Shawn Michaels, where they *worked* (competed) against Lanny 'The Genius' Poffo and an hitherto unknown debutante called Charles Austin.

Austin, a former college footballer, had only completed six weeks of wrestling training prior to the match, and was dangerously unprepared to wrestle at all, let alone compete on television. Austin expressed reservations to Jannetty about him performing his "Rocker Dropper" finishing move, telling him that he had never been shown how to take the *bump* (fall) for it and that he was worried about getting hurt. Jannetty, not realising just how inexperienced Austin was, assured him it was, "A piece of cake."

Austin's reservations were proven to be justified. When Jannetty wrapped his leg around the rookie's neck and dropped to the mat for the move, Austin panicked and tried to flip over rather than land flat, which caused his spine to break with a sickening snap. The accident left Austin semi-paralysed, and he sued both Jannetty and Titan Sports on the grounds of assault and battery, negligence, and misrepresentation.

The case dragged on for over three years. The WWF argued that all performers knew the risks of potential injury when they got into the ring, due to the nature of what they were doing. Still, they stressed that Jannetty had not acted recklessly, and even had him perform the move in the courtroom to show how safe it was. Their downfall was the conduct of the chosen witnesses. Walter 'Killer' Kowalski and Robert 'Gorilla Monsoon' Marella were both from a different era where *kayfabe*[3] was law, and they refused to deviate from that even under oath. They both came off as cold and heartless as they clung onto the same fabricated tales they had recounted as fact for years, which cast the wrestling business in a disingenuous light.

The jury were not impressed with Titan's performance, and felt like they were being deceived. They ruled in favour of Austin, who they had immense sympathy for, and awarded him an enormous compensation payout of $26.7 million. It was the biggest judgement ever awarded in a Tampa Bay court room and an unprecedented six times higher than what Austin's lawyers had originally asked for. Titan were responsible for $23.5 million of that, which could hardly have come at a worse time for McMahon what with the millions being pumped into his own trial, business across the board being at its lowest ebb, and the company having just paid Jesse Ventura nearly $1 million. The verdict threatened to sink the entire operation, and potentially the entire business if other enhancement talent[4] injured on the job would have followed suit.

---

[3] Archaic wrestling terminology for the practice of keeping the secrets of the wrestling business on the inside only. That extended to rivalries, storylines, relationships, etc. In real terms, "kayfabe" was just another term for lying.

[4] Also known colloquially within the business as "jobbers". Enhancement talent were performers brought in on a date-by-date basis to work on television against the contracted stars, with their only job being to get beat and make the star look good in

AWAY FROM the courtroom, Vince hated being labelled a "wrestling promoter". To McMahon, it was a term to describe a carnie shyster, an unflattering individual with an image he didn't want to be associated with. Vince didn't see himself that way, he saw himself as more than that; he was a purveyor of *sports entertainment*. He also believed that he could transfer his success promoting the WWF into other avenues, so that eventually he could become an all-encompassing entertainment godfather.

During the dark years of the early nineties, Vince tried to distract himself from the sex scandals, allegations, legal trials and his declining wrestling business by channelling his energies into other ventures. He had fingers in many pies, but unfortunately each one turned out to be more half-baked than the last. ICOPRO was one of them, a bodybuilding supplement that McMahon marketed from 1992 to 1995 that once caused Curt Hennig's son Joe (better known as third generation wrestler Curtis Axel) to develop the runs during a pee-wee football game.

In a similar vein, the World Bodybuilding Federation, McMahon's farcical attempt at combining bodybuilding contests with the overblown theatrics and performances associated with wrestling, was another flop. Bodybuilding fans and wrestling fans viewed the WBF with derision, and the amalgamation of the two worlds was enough to turn off both potential audiences. It was no surprise when the group folded in 1992, but the timing was no coincidence. McMahon had needed to get the over-muscled bodybuilders out of his employ as his business practices came under increased scrutiny from the federal prosecutors. A roster full of inflated muscle-heads was the last thing he needed them to see.

By that token and somewhat more pressingly, McMahon realised that he also had to reduce the physical mass of the roster in his wrestling company. He scanned his ragtag crew of oversized monsters, many one of them walking advertisements for the effects of Dianabol and Deca Durabolin, and knew that drastic action was required immediately. He needed to get his house in order fast and be seen as proactive in reacting to Zahorian's jailing. Vince wanted to show that while steroids had been used by WWF wrestlers in the past when they supposedly didn't know any better, they were now strictly outlawed.

It was a canny move, because Vince knew that by the time he went on trial his roster would be far smaller, and he could dismiss the previous use of steroids as mere innocent ignorance. Still, thanks to Zahorian and the

the process.

pages of bad press devoted to the other internal scandals, McMahon knew that he needed to terminate anyone who was identified as a potential problem, steroid user or not. In 1991 and 1992, Vince underwent a spring cleaning every bit as aggressive as his expansion and talent acquisition drive had been in the eighties.

Among the first to go was Terry Szopinski who wrestled as The Warlord. Szopinski was so pumped that his real-life physique looked less realistic and of human form than that of his plastic action figure. He was unceremoniously dumped after a four year stint with the company. Raymond Fernandez was similarly inflated, something he had felt was vital in order for his Hercules character to be a success. If he was playing a divine hero from classical mythology, then he figured he had to at least look the part. Fernandez was huge, appearing almost as wide as his six-foot frame was tall. He had to go.

Then there was James Reihcr, known worldwide as 'Superfly' Jimmy Snuka, a huge star for McMahon in the eighties who had been used infrequently in the nineties as he approached his fiftieth birthday. Reiher was abruptly cut after the publication of an article from vocal anti-wrestling columnist Irving Muchnick called *Superfly Snuka and the Groupie*, which detailed Reiher's alleged murder of girlfriend Nancy Argentino in 1983. The controversy and outrage over the incident had peaked nearly a decade prior, but McMahon was determined not to have any more skeletons in the WWF closet for the bloodthirsty press and sensationalist TV journalists to exploit.

Marty Jannetty was another headache. While the WWF sided with him in the Charles Austin case, they were not so quick to defend him in early 1992 when he attacked a police officer and was placed under house arrest for six months. McMahon couldn't risk further incidents that might potentially shame the company and so released Jannetty, which scuppered plans for a long-awaited match between he and former tag team partner Shawn Michaels at *WrestleMania VIII*.

Aurelian Smith, Jr.'s consummately performed Jake 'The Snake' Roberts character was one of the WWF's most recognisable of the eighties. Roberts was a captivating, gravel-throated talker who compensated for his rough-around-the-edges ring style with engrossing interviews and an unmatched grasp of wrestling psychology. The way he excelled as a performer was starkly contrasted by the way he handled his personal life, which was ruined by vices: drugs and alcohol. Like so many others in the industry, Roberts became dependant on them and it soon caused his career to spiral. As he later admitted, "I was given an innate amount of talent by God a long time ago. People saw some of it, I'm ashamed that I wasted a lot of it."

In early 1992, Jake was enjoying a run near the top of the card as a baleful *heel*,[5] but he yearned for a position behind the cameras so that his screaming body could take a break following years of punishment on the road. Vince had previously told Roberts that he would use him on the writing team when the time came for him to wind down his in-ring career, so when a position became available due to Pat Patterson's post-sex scandal resignation, Roberts saw it as an opportunity to get what he sought. When he finally caught up with McMahon during a television taping, he told him, "Vince, Pat's gone, now is the time. I'm ready." McMahon declined, telling Roberts that, "Out of due respect to Pat, we're not going to hire anyone for that position." In truth, Vince knew that Pat would soon be back - he was on hiatus rather than gone - and didn't want to replace him, but Jake was non-the-wiser and treated the snub as a personal affront. Feeling slighted, Jake told Vince that he wanted to leave, and opened talks with Kip Frye over at Atlanta-based WCW, Vince's main competitor.

Vince was in a difficult position. On one hand he needed to trim his roster and Roberts was a well-paid member of the crew, but he was also almost a WWF institution. Not only that, but Jake was one of the few of his remaining big name stars who wasn't on the *gas*[6]. Vince decided he didn't want Roberts to leave and rejected his resignation, but Jake had a plan to counter that. Minutes before he was set to walk out of the curtain to wrestle Mark Calaway's ghoulish Undertaker persona at *WrestleMania VIII*, Roberts told Vince that he wanted him to sign his release or he wouldn't wrestle in his heavily hyped match. Incensed but left with little choice, McMahon was forced to comply. After Roberts let Calaway *go over* (beat him), he was through with the company.

Roberts had negotiated a lucrative seven figure per annum contract with Frye to join WCW as the promotion's top heel, but Frye didn't last through to his debut. Bill Watts had been hired to replace him and was tasked with slashing the wage bill almost in half. Watts took one look at Jake's gigantic contract and ripped it up, sneering, "You've got to be *kidding* me," before he threw it in the horrified wrestler's face and laughed. With his bridges burned with Vince, Jake had no choice but to settle for a $200,000 per annum deal that was actually inferior to what he had been making with Titan, and without anywhere near the same royalty potential from merchandise.

Roberts bemoaned his bad luck, and realised that he would have been well positioned if he had stayed on with the WWF. In all likelihood he would have been a bona fide headliner later in the year, as Vince further

---

[5] A villain or bad guy
[6] A slang term used amongst the boys and those within the industry for steroids

downsized his roster. He wasn't a body guy; he didn't have that distinctive steroid look that McMahon's prosecutors were interested in. He did, however, have a crippling drug and alcohol addiction that he constantly battled, but that wasn't a concern to the Feds. Jake knew he would have been perfectly suited for the role of chief antagonist, but he had allowed his pride and ego to rule his head. Filled with regret, he cursed his own stubbornness and poor timing.

LATER IN 1992, McMahon was forced to release two more top stars from his crew. The first was Jim 'The Ultimate Warrior' Hellwig, a superhero incarnate who McMahon had used to try and replace Hogan in 1990. Resplendent in neon, with a painted face, hyperactive ring entrance and the rippling muscles of He-Man, most assumed that Hellwig was using something to enhance his physique. He was; Human Growth Hormone, which was not technically illegal under the WWF's steroid testing policy because there was no actual test developed to trace it, but, "It seemed wrong," according to McMahon.

British star Davey Boy Smith was using the hormone too. It had helped him go from being one-hundred-and-fifty pounds soaking wet when he broke into the business to carrying around over a hundred pounds of extra mass when he worked for the WWF. Davey became so unnaturally massive that he struggled to walk with a normal gait due to the extra muscle he had piled on.

Upon discovering that the pair were using the drug, McMahon mined them for one last major house[7] at *SummerSlam* then made the decision to fire them both. Hellwig was pulled from the *Survivor Series* event, even though he was part of a scheduled bout towards the top of the card, whereas Smith was made to drop the Intercontinental Title that he had won at *SummerSlam* to the much trimmer and more naturally athletic Shawn Michaels. McMahon hadn't wanted to let them go, but if he had retained them then questions would have surely been asked of their physiques by the federal prosecutors that were currently putting together a case against him, and about how seriously Vince was taking his drug testing policy.

KERRY ADKISSON had been one of the biggest stars in the wrestling world during the eighties as Kerry Von Erich, not for Vince but rather his promoter father Jack (Fritz Von Erich) and his World Class Championship Wrestling promotion out of Texas. McMahon had been desperate to sign

---

[7] Wrestling's (and other live performance shows) term for the *gate* or attendance of a show. The *house* is simply the audience.

Kerry and his brother David (who died in 1984 while on tour in Japan) during his expansion, but they were both committed to their father and addicted to the adoration afforded to them by the Texan fans.

When World Class imploded thanks to a series of untimely deaths caused by suicide (Mike Von Erich), drug overdose (Gino Hernandez) and murder (Bruiser Brody, who was stabbed to death in the locker-room by booker and wrestler José Huertas González (who worked as 'Invader #1') in Puerto Rico in 1988), Kerry finally made his way to the WWF. Sadly, Adkisson was a shell of the performer he once was, and now wrestled on a prosthetic limb that he had been forced to wear following a motorcycle crash in 1986, that had caused him to lose his foot and very nearly his life.

The accident would have more far-reaching consequences. Kerry struggled to come to terms with the injury and deal with the enormous pain he suffered through each day, and he became addicted to the pain medication prescribed to deal with it. Everyone who knew Kerry could see that he was a risk to have around with the government sniffing about, and his status was gradually reduced to that of elevated enhancement talent before he was quietly released in 1992. The next year, he followed in the footsteps of two of his brothers and took his own life with a self-inflicted gunshot wound to the heart, aged just thirty-three years old.

The news troubled Vince, who was still grieving over the death of one of his closest friends, André 'the Giant' Roussimoff, an international megastar and genuine wrestling icon. Roussimoff had been a loyal disciple for Vince's father prior to the takeover, and he played a significant role in Junior's expansion. A larger-than-life special attraction born in a small village in France, Andre was billed as seven-foot-four and weighed over five-hundred pounds. He was one of the biggest draws in wrestling, but he suffered from a life-shortening syndrome called acromegaly. The disease caused his extremities to swell far beyond their normal size, and disfigured his once handsome face into that of an ogre, something McMahon had capitalised on in 1987 by turning him heel, leading to his historic and box office-shattering run with Hogan.

The ever-increasing severity of Roussimoff's condition caused him around-the-clock pain and relentless back problems, but he worked through it in order to help McMahon in his quest to take over the wrestling world. Andre was defiant about his illness, and refused to listen to doctors who told him he wouldn't live past forty, and instead decided to enjoy life to its fullest. He eventually died in solitude in his home country aged forty-six, in January of 1993. Towards the end Andre had known he was on borrowed time, and even walking had become a major struggle for him. He had made peace with his mortality, but that didn't make the news any less tragic to McMahon, who was devastated that one of the most celebrated and faithful soldiers of his empire had passed.

Unfortunately, he would be far from the last. Just two months later, and a month following Von Erich's suicide, Adolfo Bresciano who performed as Dino Bravo, was gunned down in a mob hit at his Montreal home. Bresciano, a native Quebecoise bleached blonde heel with the chiselled physique of a power-lifter, had last worked for the WWF in April 1992. In his time out of the business, he became involved in a cigarette smuggling syndicate, and used his notoriety from wrestling to make the racket a well-paid endeavour. While his murder case remained officially unsolved, the widespread belief was that his new vocation didn't sit well with the Mafia, who hunted him down for encroaching on their turf.

In the years that followed, a sudden spate of deaths in the industry would cause Vince further consternation. He was saddened to learn that Buddy Rodgers, the first ever WWWF[8] Champion, died in June 1992 after a series of strokes. Art Barr, who had never worked for Vince but was an established name in Mexico and had worked in WCW, died of a drug overdose in 1994. Robert 'Gino' Marella, one of McMahon's most trusted employees, lost his son Joey in July 1994 when he died in a car accident on his way home from refereeing matches at a WWF house show in Maryland. Each one of these deaths brought with it an amount of heartache for Vince, but more pertinently, further bad publicity for his company.

THE BIGGEST loss to McMahon was not a death but a departure: the man he had built his empire around, Hulk Hogan. Problems between the pair had really started to escalate in 1991 when Hogan went on the Arsenio Hall Show and denied using steroids other than to rehabilitate a bicep injury. The claims caused an immediate backlash against him from people who knew he was lying, which served as the catalyst for the WWF's decline. Vince was furious, because he had told Hogan to tell the truth. As McMahon had suspected would happen, fans soon began to turn on Hogan, so the pair collectively decided the best thing for Hulk to do would be take time off until things had settled down and the controversy had blown over. After *WrestleMania VIII* in April 1992, Hogan departed, and didn't return for nearly a year.

---

[8] The WWF was originally known as the World Wide Wrestling Federation, or WWWF, but the third "W" was dropped in 1979 to make the name flow better when spoken and in marketing.

Hogan's return in 1993 was underwhelming. He was employed to win the WWF title from the super-heavyweight Rodney Anoa'i at *WrestleMania IX*. Anoa'i, who was born in California, was part of the famous Samoan Anoa'i wrestling family that had spawned (and would later spawn) the likes of The Rock, The Headshrinkers, Roman Reigns, Umaga, The Usos, The Wild Samoans and countless others. Weighing over eight-hundred-pounds at his peak, Anoa'i was signed by the WWF in 1992 on the recommendation of Pat Patterson. Despite his Samoan heritage, Vince clad him in a mawashi and gave him a Japanese sumo wrestler gimmick, renaming him Yokozuna. With Vince wanting a big guy on top but unable to use anyone that looked like they might be using steroids, Yokozuna was the perfect fit for his top new heel.

Putting the title back on Hogan was a case of Vince trying desperately to recapture the glory days, but it didn't work. Fans had still not forgave Hogan for deceiving them, and didn't respond to his title run. Hogan hardly helped the cause, rarely working house shows or appearing on television. Behind the scenes, tensions between Hogan and McMahon grew, with Hogan unwilling to be cast in the role of the veteran used to pass the torch, and he rejected proposals for him to put over Bret Hart at *SummerSlam*.

Annoyed, Vince decided to take the belt off Hogan in his first title defence, and had him lose to Yokozuna courtesy of his own legdrop finishing move at *King of the Ring* in June 1993. After he fulfilled local dates that he was already advertised for, and a European tour built around him, he left the company. It ended a near-decade relationship that had made both he and McMahon into multi-millionaires, and had caused the wrestling business to boom on scales never before seen.

Even though Vince hadn't worked with Hogan in over a year and their split had been less than amicable, McMahon was still rocked in June 1994 when he was forced to sit and watch helplessly as his former champion, one-time close friend and untouchable WWF icon, signed with fierce rival Ted Turner to work for WCW - his competition. Hogan leaving disappointed Vince because he had wanted him to be the WWF's answer to Babe Ruth if and when they reconciled. As disappointed as the news made him, he wasn't too surprised by Hogan's defection to Turner. Money had always been his primary motivation, and Turner was paying him an unprecedented sum that Vince could no longer afford to match.

HAVING SPENT the last few years systematically dismantling the roster that had served him so well during the times of prosperity, by 1994 Vince looked at his talent pool and found himself surrounded by increasingly unfamiliar faces. He had been forced to part ways with several performers that had become household names; men who had helped him build the WWF into an international powerhouse.

He had assembled an almost entirely new troupe, but his creative edge was blunted, and attempts to make new stars failed more often than they succeeded. Goofy, unmarketable characters started to appear more frequently (such as The Repo Man, a petty thief in a Hamburgler mask who used to steal his opponent's entrance gear; Ludvig Borga, a Finnish environmentalist whose portrayer Tony Halme went on to become a shoot fighter, musician and politician before taking his own life; and Papa Shango, a voodoo practitioner who supposedly cursed his opponents by setting fire to their boots, making them vomit or causing black slime to ooze from their faces), and all were greeted with indifference. Vince had killed the territories that had once been breeding grounds for him to cherry-pick fresh, already marketable stars, and there was nowhere left to harvest. In many ways he had been the architect of his own downfall.

As Vince pooled all of his resources into battling the U.S. government, his scripted on-screen battles suffered as a result. The stress of the trial had caused his usual razor-sharp judgement to become impaired, and his product waned. That, combined with the company's battered image from the volume of bad press, resulted in ludicrous storylines (*angles*). One such notorious fiasco took place at the *Royal Rumble* in 1994, when The Undertaker character was subject to a ten-on-one beat down from a raft of midcard heels, who then stuffed him in a coffin and seemingly "killed" him before he ascended to "Heaven". When Vince brought the character back in August at *SummerSlam*, it was opposite another creatively bankrupt idea: an Undertaker doppelgänger, portrayed by Brian Lee Harris. The match between the two headlined the show, and was criticised from all quarters. If that was the best McMahon could come up with, commented people within the company, then the well had run dry and the future looked bleak.

McMahon's attempts at replacing the icon Hulk Hogan had also been unsuccessful. NWA legend Ric Flair, a veteran multiple time World Champion with a distinctive shock of pure white hair and a tremendous reputation amongst his peers for his ability to work a one-hour *Broadway*[9] with near enough anyone, proved not to be the answer. Flair's achievements

---

[9] Wrestle-speak for an hour-long draw. The NWA World Champion would tour the regional territories that made up the group and defend the title against the top local talent. As the local promoters didn't want their top guy to get beat and thus hurt them as a draw within the territory, and as the champion couldn't get beat unless losing the title, a time-limit draw or *Broadway* would often be the best solution for all parties.

away from Titan were unmatched, but he was a wrestler, not a sports entertainer, and WWF fans were reluctant to accept someone who was so closely associated with the company's rivals. Vince had programmed them for years to think that WCW was inferior to the WWF in every way, and the impressionable fans had taken that to heart and believed the propaganda. Flair's high standards didn't drop, but his name made surprisingly little difference to the bottom line upon his 1991 arrival.

After a mixed year, Flair came to Vince in late 1992 and told him that he wasn't happy in the WWF. McMahon had previously told him that if he was ever unsatisfied with his spot in the company then he could leave, and Flair wanted to call him on that promise and return to WCW. McMahon wasn't all that surprised, and if anything he was a little relieved. He had recently told Flair that he was going with a younger roster and his role would be reduced, so the veteran's decision was not unexpected.

Hiring Flair in 1991 while he was the reigning WCW Champion had been a novel opportunity for Vince that he couldn't turn down, but he had little faith in him as his top guy. Vince's mindset was different to that of his competitors; he liked a good-looking *babyface* (good guy) with strong genetics as his champion, not a middle-aged villain with a forehead covered in tiny blading scars. He respected Flair's in-ring work and his contributions to the business, but he felt uneasy pushing someone who had been such a key figure for his competition. Vince theorised that it damaged the credibility of his roster to have the top guy from somewhere else come in and quickly win his prestigious title, and conveyed the wrong message about his long-established WWF acts.

Vince still agreed to put the title on Flair in early 1992, but that was partly to deflect the steroid allegations, as 'the Nature Boy' was obviously not a heavy user. But Flair's failure to move business as McMahon had hoped meant that he was willing to let him leave. The two shook hands on an entirely amicable split, a rarity in the business, with the proviso that Flair put over the man Vince had chosen to be his next babyface hero: Bret 'Hitman' Hart.

Hart was Vince's latest flirtation. The eighth of twelve children (all of whom either became wrestlers or married them) to veteran wrestler and promoter Stu Hart, Bret had worked for Vince since 1985 when McMahon had bought out Stu's Calgary-based Stampede Wrestling territory. Bret had always been a solid hand, professional and easy to deal with. He took his ring work and reputation very seriously, but pride was a character trait that Vince could deal with. He knew he could rely on Hart, and decided that he was the man to carry the company forward. Hart was nowhere close to the size of Hogan or Warrior and their ilk, but he wasn't small either, and the key was he didn't *look* like he was on the juice.

Going with Hart wasn't a spur of the moment decision. Vince had put together a list of names containing potential candidates who were in contention for the top babyface spot, and had discussed them all at length with his creative team. His criteria simply called for the man chosen to not be too old or too jacked up, everything else they could work on.

Age ruled out Randy Savage, who on the cusp of forty was deemed to be too old. The Undertaker fit the criteria, but he was a side-show attraction and didn't need the title. Merced Solis, better known as Tito Santana, had, like Hart, been a consistent and reliable performer for Vince over the years, but he too was past his best and his mainstream run was drawing to a close. Plus, he had spent the previous year having his popularity and appeal neutered by being saddled with a matador gimmick. Five years earlier in the same scenario, Santana would have been a perfect fit, but the business had passed him by and he too was fast approaching forty. The same applied to Rick Martel, Santana's former tag partner who was also an option. Former Rockers member Shawn Michaels, the last man on the list, was still finding his feet as a heel and wasn't ready to turn babyface.

That only left Bret Hart, who had been loyal to Vince for the better part of eight years, had a marketable look without the excessive physique, and was a craftsman in the ring. Hart had delivered consistently excellent performances for McMahon since he had finally pulled the trigger on him as a singles star in 1991 (after Hart had spent seven years as part of The Hart Foundation tag team alongside brother-in-law Jim Neidhart), and he had a loyal and committed fan base. Once Vince had made his decision, he didn't want to wait to be talked out of it by doubters or locker-room politicians, and decided to rush the belt onto Hart on a house show in Saskatoon, the same city in which Hart had wrestled his first ever match. Flair had no problem dropping the strap to Hart, and did the honours clean in the middle of the ring to an emotional response from the Canadian audience.

EVEN THOUGH McMahon had told Hart that he wanted him to have a long reign with the title, he took it off him just five months later. He just didn't see Bret as the top guy, even if his reactions were twice that of anyone else that worked for him. Instead of being the long-term champion, for the next three years Hart was the constant, the man whom Vince turned to for dependably good performances or to put the belt back on when his other experiments failed. Experiments like Lex Luger.

Vince had been desperately searching for the next Hulk Hogan since as far back as 1990, and as good and popular as Hart was, Vince didn't see him as larger-than-life like Hogan had been, nor possessing the same charisma. He was more the working man's champion than a superhero. In 1993, Vince decided to try Lex Luger in the Hogan role. Luger, known away from the ring as Larry Pfohl, was a former WCW Champion with an incredible physique, who had originally signed a lucrative contract to be part of the WBF in 1992 due to a non compete clause in his previous WCW deal that prevented him wrestling for a year. Luger had the kind of sculpted body that McMahon just couldn't help but push, steroid trial or not. Lex was a diet and gym obsessive, so Vince figured he could justify his push by pointing to those attributes as the reasons Lex looked the way he did.

McMahon poured money into Luger, sending him on an expensive meet and greet tour around the country like a presidential candidate seeking voter approval. Dubbed "The Lex Express", Vince hoped the unprecedented marketing campaign would cause a swell of fan support for Luger, and he would be accepted as the next babyface All-American hero. It was all part of the build-up to his eventual showdown with Yokozuna, who was cast as an antagonist foreign champion. USA versus the world was a premise that McMahon invariably reverted to when the chips were down, because in his mind the clean-cut patriotic hero was always the definitive depiction of what a good protagonist should be.

But times were changing. Fans had seen Hulk Hogan do the same act for a decade, yet by the end had grown tired of him, and Lex Luger was no Hulk Hogan in terms of ring ability or - more importantly - charisma. Luger flopped horribly, though wasn't helped by McMahon's lack of faith in him.

When the time came to take the plunge and make Luger the WWF Champion at *SummerSlam* in 1993 - the obvious culmination of the campaign - Vince got cold feet and refused to do it. McMahon told his perplexed staffers that he was simply holding off on Luger's eventual ascension until *WrestleMania X* at Madison Square Garden. The truth was down more to his increasingly paranoid state. Vince was worried about the possible repercussions of having another muscle guy as his champion, fearing it might seem to his would-be prosecutors that he was flaunting Luger's physique in their faces.

With that weighing on his mind, he made the call to change the logical but predictable ending of Luger walking out of *SummerSlam* as WWF Champion, and instead had him win via count out, emerging victorious sans title. It was a cheap finish that killed Luger as a viable draw, and fans hated it. "He looked like a plate full of piss when he didn't win the belt, and from that point onwards nothing they did was going to get him over," summarised renowned on-screen manager and former Titan booker Jim Cornette.

AFTER NEARLY three years of anxiety and trauma, the verdict in the steroid trial finally came in July 1994. *Not guilty*. Vince felt a wave of relief wash over him and punched the air in celebration, as his family cried tears of joy from the dock. It was the shadowy wrestling business that had saved him. The secretive and kayfabed nature of the industry meant a number of guys were unwilling to give testimonies against Vince, whereas others were so obvious about their existing grudges against him (like Kevin 'Nailz' Wacholz who told the court that he, "Hated McMahon's guts"), that they were deemed unreliable. Ironically the ones who complained the loudest and hardest abut McMahon, ended up being the ones to inadvertently keep him out of jail.

The trial had caused a strenuous few years for Vince, who prior to hearing the words, "Not guilty," ringing around the room, had firmly believed he was going to be incarcerated. He even had plans in place for Gino Marella and Memphis promoter Jerry Jarrett to steer the ship in his absence under the auspices of wife Linda. So when the verdict came in, especially following the shocking rulings against the company in the Ventura and Austin cases earlier in the year, it was both a surprising and immensely satisfying result for him. He could finally put the taxing ordeal behind him and concentrate on rebuilding his shattered empire.

TWO

THE POSITIVE VIBE DIDN'T LAST long. The trial verdict was shortly followed by Randy Savage jumping the rapidly sinking WWF ship and pitching up with Hulk Hogan in Atlanta. Savage had been a major star for Vince in the eighties, second only to Hogan, whose unique look and trademark growling voice had made him a much-imitated mainstream star. Vince paid glowing tribute to Savage when he left, looking into the television camera and seemingly speaking directly to Randy through the lens:

> Obviously conspicuous by his absence is the Macho Man Randy Savage. I'd like to announce, unfortunately, that Randy Savage had been unable to sign a contract with the World Wrestling Federation. Not unable, but rather come to terms with the World Wrestling Federation for a new contract. But Randy, I know you're out there listening, and on behalf of all of us here in the World Wrestling Federation, all of your fans and certainly me, the number one fan, I'd like to say thank you for all of your positive contributions to the World Wrestling Federation. Thank you, Randy Savage for all of the wonderful memories for so many years here in the World Wrestling Federation. We wish you nothing but the best. Godspeed, and good luck.

Despite how Vince presented it on television, Randy's exit upset him greatly. The past few years he had grown close to Savage from the time he had spent doing commentary with him on *Monday Night Raw*, and he considered him a close friend. It was the nature of Savage's departure that hurt McMahon the most. Randy hadn't given any notice, he had just drunkenly phoned in the middle of the night and ranted at him in his intoxicated state, declaring that he was quitting. Vince simply dismissed it as just the high-strung wrestler having had one drink too many and being unable to control his mouth. He would reprimand him the next day at television for the insubordination, he thought, but he wasn't going to lose sleep over it.

He never got the chance. Randy didn't show up at the Fernwood Resort in Bushkill, Pennsylvania, the venue for that evening's *Raw* television tapings. He really had quit, he had been serious about that, and he wasn't even going to let McMahon give a counter offer to convince him to stay.

Vince thought back about how Randy had manipulated the situation so that his contract would be up, allowing him to leave in that manner, and he realised that it was pre-meditated. Savage had wanted out and nothing Vince could have said or done would have changed that.

The boys couldn't believe it. Many thought it was a *rib*[10] because they saw how close Randy was to Vince, or at least it seemed so. "They rode together," exclaimed one shocked member of the locker-room, who added, "Everyone, every single person in the building was shocked that Randy would ever leave Vince."

SAVAGE HAD become irked by McMahon relegating him to the role of announcer as he looked to establish a new, younger group of performers as stars. He was bored behind the announce desk. He understood the business was changing and he was a remnant of a dying breed of grapplers who had come through the territories when they were hot, but he wasn't asking to be Vince's top guy, he just wanted to work, and help build the next generation. Plus, he had been financially hit by his divorce from real-life and on-screen wife Elizabeth Hulette, and the lower paying salaried announcer role that Vince wanted him to take permanently - which would also mean calling time on his in-ring career- was not something he was willing to consider.

Deep down, Savage wanted that one last great match, something he could leave as his legacy. He had already achieved near perfection once, at *WrestleMania III* against Ricky Steamboat, where the two performers contested an intricate ballet of crisp counters, explosive bursts of energy and gripping near falls, in a match for the ages. That wasn't enough to satisfy Savage; he was hell-bent on topping it. Once could be perceived as a fluke, he reflected, but doing it again would prove he was still great. It was his firm belief that Shawn Michaels was the perfect opponent with whom to recapture that bottled lightning, so he proposed a program with Shawn to Vince. He envisioned a long feud which would culminate in putting Shawn over at *WrestleMania*, and as the wrestlers referred to it, "give him the rub".

McMahon refused, again citing the WWF's new youth movement, before advising Randy that he was better served behind the announce desk. Randy was left feeling slighted and he grumbled, "I didn't realise I was considered elderly, I think I will seek a second opinion."

"That would have really pissed him off," noted one of his friends from the time, "If someone had told me that I was too old, I would have wanted to show them that I could still go too." Subsequently, Randy felt like he had

---

[10] Wrestling terminology to describe practical jokes that people within the industry play on one another.

no choice but to leave the company in order to prolong his in-ring career, so he could seek that one final defining moment elsewhere.

RANDY KNEW he should have given Vince proper notice and acted more professionally towards the man who had made him into an international star, but he had an old score to settle. Back in November 1987, the WWF had held a battle royal at their monthly Meadowlands Arena house show, with the twist being that it only featured legends from a previous era. Men like Lou Thesz and Nick Bockwinkel, who had little time for Vince and his twisted carnival brand of what they knew as pro wrestling, but still appreciated the payday. In his own heyday, Savage's father Angelo Poffo had worked with a number of the veterans booked in the match, and hadn't seen several of them in years. A few had called him and said how they were looking forward to seeing him in New Jersey, but Angelo had to grudgingly admit that he wasn't booked.

Angelo confessed to Randy that he would love nothing more than to have been booked at the show to catch up with his old friends, some of whom he expected he might never see again due to their advancing ages. "Don't you worry, I'll get it done," Randy declared to his father confidently. Not long after that conversation, Savage talked to the office and asked them if they could accommodate Angelo in the bout, but as his brother Lanny Poffo would recall, "The reason was vague, but the answer was no."

Savage was fiercely loyal to his family and it had devastated him that he was not able to give his father that final swansong with his contemporaries. He mused that he was one of the biggest stars in the company and yet Vince couldn't even do him one small favour on a throwaway house show. "From now on it is just business," he told his bemused brother, "Fuck the WWF." Savage carried the resentment and bitterness about that night with him for the rest of his life, once ruminating to Lanny, "I did it like Martin Luther King, I should have done it like Malcolm X; by any means necessary." Vince had no idea what damage the slight did to Savage's psyche. He didn't even know there was a problem, it was just another one of many requests on a typically busy day that had slipped his mind.

Vince wasn't the only one that Randy held responsible; he also blamed veteran road agents 'Chief' Jay Strongbow and Pat Patterson for the rebuff. He had vowed from that day onwards to never give either of them any respect in front of the boys ever again. Strongbow actually competed in the battle royal on that fateful night. He was eliminated from the action early by Lou Thesz and he landed awkwardly on his arm and broke it. Backstage Strongbow complained to the other boys, "Thesz broke my arm!" to which

Savage instantly shot back at him, "Lou Thesz didn't break your arm, you broke your arm because you're too fat to be in the ring; you're an embarrassment."

As Lanny remembers, "From that point on, Randy intentionally became a locker-room asshole, and he was good at it. He could get away with it because of who he was, and he refused to give anyone any respect if he didn't like them."

When Savage was given the opportunity to trade in his lower paid WWF announcing gig for a high six-figure deal with WCW, he remembered the insinuation that he was old, he remembered the Meadowlands snub, and he simply walked away. McMahon tried to remain stony-faced in front of the boys, a defence mechanism he had always employed. As Jim Cornette observed, "If you were at television or pay-per-views, then unless Vince had been anally probed by aliens, you wouldn't know that anything was going on with him. Once he got to the arena he was all about the show and he always tried to no-sell everything. He would frequently give his opinions on things that pissed him off, but he would always no-sell anything that happened to him."

Despite McMahon's outwardly unflappable demeanour, Bret Hart could see the truth; losing yet another of his former headliners had truly bothered him. Hart recalled how Vince had tears in his eyes that night when he went into the chairman's office and vowed never to be disloyal to him in the same way.

A FEW weeks later, Vince was furious when officials from major sponsor Slim Jim contacted him and informed him that they were pulling out of Titan, and taking their product to Turner Entertainment along with Savage.

On many occasions, McMahon had attended NASCAR events to meet with potential advertisers, with his belief being that the fan bases were a very similar demographic, and that anyone who sponsored NASCAR could be potentially wooed into supporting the WWF. Savage frequently attended with McMahon dressed in his full Macho Man regalia, making the extra effort to bring the Macho Man character to the suits in attendance rather than simply being Randall Poffo.

After the racing had finished, Savage often wined and dined with potential partners and in particular the representatives from Slim Jim, learning their names and becoming friends with them. He was going the proverbial extra mile, whereas McMahon treated them as just another sponsor. The relationship grew and evolved as time passed, and when Randy left Vince, he went to the Slim Jim executives with a pitch.

"Here's the deal," he started in his distinctive growl, "I'm going to WCW, what I would like for you to do is un-invest the money you have put into Vince and instead invest in Ted Turner." Three days later they called up Randy and told him they were going to follow him to Atlanta. "It must have been some pitch," noted Lanny before adding, "Vince doesn't like losing even one round, so that pissed him off." Despite how much Savage's leaving and stealing Slim Jim away bothered Vince, he insisted that Randy would be welcomed back with open arms in the future.

In late 1996, his opinion of Savage suddenly underwent an unexplained shift. People who worked closely with McMahon recounted that after a few years of him having championed a potential return for Savage, he would now behave completely out of character whenever his name cropped up. On one occasion when agent Michael Hayes pitched an idea that involved Savage coming back into the company, Vince stared into the distance and forlornly stated, "I have no interest in doing business with that man," but on other occasions he would fly off the handle at the mere mention of him. Vince's staff were warned never to bring Savage's name up for any storyline, merchandise idea or feature ever again. Many years later when the Poffo family contacted the WWE after the passing of Angelo in 2010 and asked for a message of condolences from them to be recited at his funeral, McMahon repudiated the request.

Vince's dogged refusal to even consider working with Savage seemed strange to both onlookers and insiders, who couldn't understand his sudden change of heart. They knew that Vince had been furious when Savage had taken the lucrative Slim Jim endorsement over to WCW with him. It had cost the company millions in potential advertising revenue that at the time would have helped pay the mounting legal bills, but even that didn't add up as a viable reason for the sudden bitterness. After all, Vince had known about that for years; it wasn't new information that would have suddenly discoloured his opinion of Savage.

As former Heavenly Bodies grappler Tom Prichard remarked, "Out of all the guys who screwed Vince, Randy was the only one of that magnitude that he never brought back. A few people have told me over the years that Vince doesn't hold grudges, and that if it is good for business he will bring *anyone* back."

Randy was a big name who could make the company money, and McMahon had fallen out and made up with countless wrestlers who had done far worse to him than just jump ship with an endorsement deal. Down the years, people who had tried to put McMahon out of business, physically assaulted him, testified against him in court or who had sued him themselves, were always forgiven and ended up working with him again. "It's just business," was always his philosophy, yet Savage was different to the others.

THE REASON was never explained to the people who worked for Titan. Vince never spoke about it, but many had their suspicions. The belief of several in McMahon's inner circle and of many others within the industry, was that the only explanation that made any sense suggested Savage had engaged - or attempted to engage - in an illicit affair with McMahon's teenage daughter Stephanie sometime in 1993 or 1994.[11].

Others dismissed the story as fantastical because it was never brought up by any of the McMahon family, specifically Vince, but it never would have been. Vince didn't make a habit of talking about his personal, private family matters, even with the people he was around all day, every day. In later years when his writing staff came from Hollywood rather than from within the industry, he became even more distant. The turnover was so high that delicate subjects would never even be broached in the writing room.

Savage never confirmed or denied the story to anyone, but again that was not unusual. Savage was a private person, the kind of man who had high security fences surrounding his property and CCTV cameras at his gate. Not one for sharing his feelings outside of the occasional fist through a wall when he was angry, he rarely let anyone inside, or even gave interviews once his in-ring career ended. He was a recluse.[12]

No one involved ever spoke publicly about the reasons for the nuclear heat, but despite the wall of stony silence from Stephanie, Randy, and Vince, testimonies from those close to the situation strongly supported the credibility of the claims. Speaking in 2009, Dave Meltzer from *The Wrestling Observer Newsletter* added his own take:

---

[11] Making Stephanie seventeen or eighteen-years old, not fourteen as had often been repeated in rumours. Because Stephanie lived in Connecticut, the legal age for consent was sixteen-years old, so there would have been no illegality involved if any relations between her and Savage did occur.

[12] Just a few weeks before his death in 2011, Randy was reported to have appeared on *The Hitman and Groberman* radio show. In an interview he referenced Stephanie several times, noting that he wanted to wrestle Vince McMahon, with Triple H and Stephanie in his corner, and that he would give Stephanie a kiss for "old time's sake". It was later revealed to be a hoax, with the Savage voice provided by an impersonator.

I think that the reason is the same reason that everyone says. It's the reason everyone in the company says. It's the reason that is the only one that makes any sense. So I think that's the reason! I can't come up with any other reason. I mean, I've heard that reason from so many people that are not internet rumourmongers. All I know is that within the company as far as the top people, they all believe it, and nobody knows for sure, because it's never brought up. When I first heard the story I didn't believe it because I thought it was just some story, but then, and I mean even when people who are very high up in that company, after they left the company, would tell me that story I still didn't believe it. But, you know, after a certain number of years when it's just, you know, ideas are brought up for Randy Savage and the reaction - there's something real, real bad because, let's face it, I mean, I couldn't count the number of times Vince said he would never do business with Hulk Hogan, and he always does.

Bob Holly was good friends with Savage while he was in the WWF, and worked under Vince and later Stephanie for years. He too found Vince's refusal to work with Savage as completely at odds with his usual attitude towards business. In his book *The Hardcore Truth*, he wrote:

Vince is a businessman first and foremost, so even when someone screws him over, if he feels he can make money with them, he'll put his differences aside and work with them - but he never worked with Randy again. There were rumours going around for years involving Vince's daughter, Stephanie, and Randy. I won't say anything other than Randy was always pretty friendly with her.

Tom Prichard spent some time working in the office alongside Vince and Stephanie, and he too knew Randy from his run in the WWF from 1993 onwards. He said of the alleged story, "It seems plausible. I've personally seen Steph say, 'Fuck Hogan,' only to then see him back with the company six months later. There had to be something major to keep Randy away. Knowing the people involved and the culture of the business, the story wouldn't surprise me at all. Overall, it really makes a lot more sense than anything else. Vince wasn't about to have somebody around who might have got the upper hand or could humiliate him. You can't un-ring the bell..."

Savage's ex-girlfriend Stephanie Bellars, who briefly performed in WCW alongside him as Gorgeous George, added credence to the story when recounting the reason the pair broke up. "He wanted to have a three-way with me and my sister," she recalled, "He wanted us all three to live in a house together. My sister was only seventeen-years-old at the time." Bellars herself was only twenty-three when they started dating; Savage, it seemed, had a predilection for younger women.

SOME QUESTIONED whether Randy would have risked his job for the taboo of making a play for the boss's daughter, but his own vendetta against McMahon was personal and family related, so it was not unrealistic to consider that Savage might have viewed it as payback for the Meadowlands incident all those years earlier.

Lanny had his own take on what happened, "I would be willing to bet that he did something with her. When he was with Elizabeth he was loyal to her, and he was just crushed when she left him. He was hurting, so he started fucking everything that walks. The last time I checked, Stephanie walks. I think Randy parlayed her and then laid her, but it was not for revenge; it was a love affair."

It is certainly not outside of the realms of reality to suggest that Randy Savage could well have been Stephanie's first teenage crush. She was young and impressionable when she watched the on-screen wedding of Savage and Elizabeth Hulette at *SummerSlam* in 1991, one of the fondest memories of her childhood. "As a little girl, watching this romance unfold in wrestling was the greatest thing in the world for me. It was so exciting to me, because I *loved* Miss Elizabeth," Stephanie later admitted. When she was going through puberty, Stephanie looked up to Elizabeth, enamoured with her virtuousness, and fantasised about one day growing up to be just like her. "To a degree I somewhat idolised her," she confessed.

Then once she reached her late teens, Stephanie did what all teenagers do: she rebelled. Ex-college classmates later recounted how she was, "A bit of a party girl," and even Vince's close friend Pat Patterson once noted that she was, "Pretty wild," in her youth. Those combined factors, insiders noted, could have played a part in Savage being able to coerce her to engage in the suspected relations.

As the story is alleged, McMahon didn't learn of whatever transgression occurred until late 1996. At the time he was in secret negotiations to bring Savage back to the WWF, because Randy, whose contract happened to be up in Atlanta, had again fallen out with Hulk Hogan and was unhappy at playing second-fiddle to him in WCW. The WWF was in desperate need of star power, so the two parties opened talks. No one in the office knew of it, but that in itself was not uncommon. As Jim Cornette, who served on the booking team in 1996 noted, "Vince was on the phone all the time. Even in an era before cell phones, if there was a phone around with a wire, Vince was on it. In the creative team we wouldn't have known anything until discussions had reached a certain point where things were likely to happen."

One person who apparently did find out was Stephanie. The belief is that she broke down in tears, either at the prospect of seeing Savage again or because she couldn't bear living with the secret anymore, and told her father everything. With Randy out of sight he was out of mind, but it would have been much harder for her to pretend that nothing had happened with him if he was around the company regularly again.

"Stephanie was never around the buildings," people who denied the claims would state, which was accurate, though she did do intern work for the company from the age of thirteen. In the timeframe the affair is said to have taken place, she was living at home in Connecticut, preparing for college in Boston where she would take a communications course. At the time it was not uncommon for the top guys to drop by and stay at the McMahon family home when they were in town. Despite a chip on his shoulder that he carried with him from the perceived lack of respect he felt he had been given, Randy was close with the McMahons. He stayed with them many times, often socialising with the family, so the opportunity for something to happen was undoubtedly there.

As Vince presumably listened in horror at Stephanie's deeply personal tale, his heart would have sank. He wouldn't have been able to comprehend how any of what was revealed could have happened, because Stephanie was never on the road. At that point he likely would have realised that the affair must have taken place in his home. He would have been mortified. Everything that anyone else had ever done to him, said to him or had accused him of, surely paled in comparison. That was just business, he could forgive that and he always did, but this was far worse. It was personal, very personal, and Savage had transgressed abominably. The belief was that Vince vowed to Stephanie that Randy Savage would never work for the WWF again, and then he washed his hands of him forever.

IT WAS Randy who first blinked publicly. A few years into the new millennium, with Savage having been off television for years after leaving WCW in 1999[13] there was again talk of a WWF return amongst those unaware of the heat McMahon had with him. Savage was a free agent and a proven commodity, and when the likes of Ric Flair, Hulk Hogan and

---

[13] Aside from a brief one-off appearance in a throwaway battle royal on an episode of *Thunder* in 2000.

Diamond Dallas Page all turned up in the company in 2001 and 2002, Savage seemed a good bet amongst fans to join them. He had even gone so far as to say on record in 2000 that he wanted to go back to the WWF, and that for him it was, "The WWF or nothing," before ruling out renegade hardcore group ECW or a WCW return.

A few years later, a magazine interview with Paul Levesque, Stephanie's real-life and on-screen partner, put an end to any chance of that from Savage's perspective. Levesque disrespected Savage, calling him a dinosaur and talking about how the WWF had moved on from that era. Savage was offended and decided to vent his feelings. In a video filmed exclusively for members of his website, Savage ranted:

Right here's the deal Triple H, I'm talking to you. Call me a dinosaur in this business dude? Well I found that pretty disrespectful. When you duck, when you blink, I'm gonna steal your girlfriend. How's that? I'm gonna take your babe, I'm gonna take Stephanie McMahon and take her for a ride around the block. And I might give her back, but I may not, you understand that, Triple H? I'm gonna do what I wanna do because you're a punk. I might be a dinosaur, but the dinosaur is calling you a punk. This dinosaur is gonna steal your girlfriend, and I'm telling ya, I'm not gonna do it behind your back, I'm gonna do it right in front of ya. I'm gonna take Stephanie McMahon and I'm gonna take her around the block and I'm gonna show her what a real man is, the Macho Man, yeah. Stephanie McMahon; get ready for the kid.

To many already in the know and to those who suspected it, that was proof enough that something had happened previously between Randy and Stephanie. While Savage didn't say anything that hinted towards a past relationship, the few who knew him well realised that he wouldn't have mentioned Stephanie's name without a motive. "Try watching that video with fresh eyes for the first time, or through the eyes of Vince, Stephanie and Hunter," suggested Lanny cryptically.

IT WAS only after Savage's death in May 2011[14] that Vince's stance softened at all. The company finally began to acknowledge his existence

---

[14] Randy was tragically killed on May 20, 2011 whilst driving with his wife Lynn, when he suffered a heart attack and passed out at the wheel with his foot still on the gas pedal. With the car careening into incoming traffic, Lynn grabbed the wheel and diverted the car into a tree where it came to a crashing halt. Poffo was later announced dead at the hospital as a result of the heart attack.

again on its television show and in retrospective historical pieces, but even that was through gritted teeth. Soon after Randy's passing, there was a swell of support for him to be inducted into the company's annual Hall of Fame,[15] but for years Vince refused to even consider him. Dead or not, Vince still didn't want anything to do with Randy Savage.

Savage *had* been involved in some WWE projects prior to his death, which served as evidence to those that felt the Stephanie story was merely a rumour. Nevertheless, none of these endeavours had seen 'the Macho Man' work closely with the company, or more specifically, the McMahons.

In 2003, Savage had been interviewed for the launch issue of *SmackDown! Magazine*, but it was a decision made by the editor unbeknownst to Vince McMahon, the latter not having had a great deal of hands-on involvement in the content of his publications. What it proved was that Savage was willing to work with WWE, even if Vince wasn't willing to work with him.

A DVD covering Savage's career was announced in 2008, which had somehow slipped past McMahon when first pitched, but was soon cancelled when he learned of it. Eventually it was granted a release in 2010 due to a swell of support for the project, but again Vince didn't work with Savage at all, he merely marketed his name and likeness to make money. Unlike nearly all of the other career retrospective DVDs that WWE put out, Savage was not interviewed for the production or involved in the content selection, nor was there a documentary about his career featuring a host of talking heads aggrandising his triumphs. Instead it was a dry piece that covered his more famous matches, and nothing more.

Savage's name surfaced again when THQ were told to remove him from their *Legends of WrestleMania* video game, another directive issued by McMahon. Savage did later appear in the *WWE All Stars* game released two months before his death, which led some to think that Vince's stance on Savage was softening. Others went so far as to claim that Savage and McMahon had at least partly reconciled, but these were just rumours with no evidence to support them. In truth, Randy's likeness appearing in the game was simply a selling point. As with the other projects, it required no

---

[15] According to his brother Lanny, Savage told him that if the WWE ever did want him for their Hall of Fame then the only way he would be willing to go in would be as a family along with his father and brother. He was annoyed that the Von Erich family had been inducted, even the members who didn't achieve anything of note in the business, and decided that it would go some way towards making up for the Meadowlands insult all those years prior.

direct communications between Savage and the McMahons, and the deal to include him was brokered by the game's developers THQ, not WWE.

Around the time of the game's release, Savage also had an action figure produced, and via video he even provided his first WWE related promo in nearly two decades in order to promote it. Once again though, the deal had been made by a third party, with toy manufacturers Mattel rather than WWE being the ones to contact Savage.

A 'Macho Man' Randy Savage figure had long been coveted by collectors for years prior, but former manufacturers Jakks had never been allowed to produce one by WWE during their long affiliation with the company. The Jakks *Classic Superstars* line ran for twenty-eight series and exclusively featured dolls of past WWE performers, some of whom were on poor footing with the company at the time when their action figures were mooted. However, they had made their respective deals through Jakks themselves rather than the WWE. For Randy Savage, Jakks did manage to make a deal with him, but once again Vince found out and nixed the whole thing.

The decision to allow new partner Mattel to release a Savage doll was only sanctioned to prevent Jakks from including him in their new independent line of legends figures. When Mattel and WWE got wind of their intentions, they intervened with a deal of their own, because they knew the first Savage figure in a decade would be a huge seller. Only when the WWE's bottom line was going to be affected did they take action, so it was no indication of any cooling in the tension between McMahon and Savage.

BACK IN 1994, Vince would have known nothing of the ostensible Savage-Stephanie situation and was deeply wounded by the treachery of Randy's exit. After enduring a long and troubled evening following his departure, Vince finally found a rare few moments to himself and mused about how he had made both Savage and Hulk Hogan into superstars, global icons, and very wealthy men, yet they had both betrayed him and left when the chips were down. "Fuck them both," he snarled to himself stubbornly, but deep down he wasn't angry, he was melancholy. He realised that the WWF was no longer the powerhouse it once was, and that he was losing his iron grip on both the industry and his own talent base. He also knew it was not the time to be downhearted or show any signs of weakness; that was not the Vince McMahon way. Instead, he was determined to rebuild his company brick by brick and get the glory days back. He was going to raise the sinking Titan ship, he was sure of it, because he was Vince McMahon, *dammit.*

THREE

BY 1995, A YEAR THAT would be remembered for the Oklahoma bombing, O.J. Simpson being declared not guilty of murder and the formation of eBay, the WWF was the most fragile it had been in the decade since Vince McMahon took over the reins. All one had to do was look at the houses the group were attracting to Madison Square Garden to see that. They hadn't sold out the famous arena for a live event (with the exception of pay-per-views) since 1989, and in the years since the numbers had dwindled significantly, dropping to an all-time low of 4,300 on August 25, 1994. Previous to that, the building was always attracting a minimum of 9,000 spectators, so the drop-off was significant. The number was even worse than it seemed because a lot of the tickets were given away for free (*papered*) in order to boost the size of the crowd, with the hope being that those additional fans would then spend money on the various items available at the merchandise stand. When the Garden's $85,000 rent was factored in, the August card had cost McMahon thousands.

Attendance across the board was drastically down from the boom years to an average of around 3,000 for 'A' shows and sometimes as low as three figures for 'B' cards. The amount of events Titan were running had nearly halved from just three years earlier, as nearly every house show was losing money. The group could only afford to run the bare minimum, which they did simply to placate local television partners in the respective areas.

Whilst the numbers were still holding up for pay-per-view events, the fallout from the steroid trial had made the WWF an entity that other companies didn't want to be associated with. Toy manufacturers Hasbro were one of many to pull out of their deal with the WWF amidst the controversy surrounding the company, which put an end to a popular action figure line that was a lucrative source of income for both the WWF and its wrestlers. In the eighties, royalties from the product had netted some performers in excess of $100,000 so it was a major blow for the talent to lose that vital supplementary income, especially during a time when pay-offs were already reduced due to the bad houses.

Vince knew he couldn't acknowledge the WWF's problems to the boys, but even so, everyone could see the numbers steadily dropping. He knew people no longer looked at him as omnipotent, and even if they would never dare admit it to his face, he noticed minor changes in the way people acted towards him. In the past no one would have been brave enough to answer back to him or even question any of his decisions, but now he was being challenged on them more than at any other time he could remember.

McMahon was no longer untouchable, and one enterprising group of wrestlers looked to take full advantage of his waning state, bandying together and adopting a moniker for themselves: The Kliq. In the past, McMahon had been willing to listen to his top performers and tweak things to accommodate their requests, but his weakened mindset from the tribulations of the nineties had caused his otherwise authoritative and domineering presence to slightly fade. The loss of Hogan and Savage to Atlanta weighed heavily on Vince's mind when dealing with The Kliq, and alienating them was something he simply couldn't afford to do.

THE GROUP was initially made up of four gifted performers; Michael 'Shawn Michaels' Hickenbottom, Kevin 'Diesel' Nash, Scott 'Razor Ramon' Hall and Sean '1-2-3 Kid' Waltman, who had become friends after riding together from town to town. They soon bonded when they discovered that they all shared a similar passion for the business and a yearning to make it better. They also had a desire to protect their own interests, namely their spots at the top of the card where the money was better and the glory greater, and using strength in numbers they were able to exert pressure on McMahon to comply to their whims.

Shawn Michaels was the undisputed leader of the group. He had been with the WWF full-time since 1988, and after splitting from Rockers tag partner Marty Jannetty in 1991 he embarked upon a singles run, routinely putting in some of the best performances on the show. Michaels had an insatiable ego, and he was determined not to let his career be remembered as anything other than special. Much like his mentor Curt Hennig had realised years earlier, Shawn knew that the best way for him to get noticed was to outshine everyone else with a big bumping style. He did so with aplomb, bumping around like a speedball, flinging himself into every move and taking exaggerated falls unlike anyone else on the roster.

Michaels' undeniable charisma completed the package, but his cocky on-screen persona was barely a fabrication. Many who worked with him noted how true to reality it was, because as good as Shawn was in the ring, his attitude was bad out of it. As well as being openly vocal about whatever displeased him, he also had a reputation for his party-loving lifestyle. It was a status he had gained during his Rockers days. He and partner Marty Jannetty were so notorious that when fellow party-goers The Nasty Boys joined the WWF in the early nineties, the first thing they did was seek out the duo and tell them, "We hear you guys like to party. We like to party too and we're going to hang out with you."

It was an image Michaels was more than happy to fuel. He enjoyed his peers' incredulity that he could party as hard as he did, then still go even harder and faster than everyone in the ring. Shawn presented himself as invincible, but the reality was that his body endured constant agony on a daily basis due to his extravagant ring style. He took pills to mask the aches and niggles in his back and knees, and further blunted the pain with a potent cocktail of alcohol and other drugs. A combination of uppers and downers changed his mood drastically from day to day, making him a ticking time bomb to deal with. To his friends that was just Shawn, and because they all liked to party in a similar vein, it didn't bother them.

Shawn readily admitted that he wasn't well-liked by nearly everyone else, and he knew why, "I was a prick," he later conceded, a consensus shared by the majority of his peers. They couldn't stand his tantrums, his conveniently timed injuries that gave him annual vacations, the way he treated and spoke to talent, his lack of respect for the non-wrestlers who were so important to the company, and his reluctance to *job* (lose) to anyone outside of his group of friends.

Shawn didn't care, because he knew that even his most embittered detractors couldn't doubt his ability between the ropes. If they didn't like him outside the ring, that was fine, he didn't care. He already had close allies; he didn't need any more.

KEVIN NASH was in many ways the exact opposite of Shawn. He was well-liked by nearly everyone he met due to his infectious sense of humour. He was seen by many as the voice of reason in The Kliq, almost a bridge between the group and the rest of the roster.

Standing at a legitimate seven-feet tall, the former basketball player had been forced to quit the court due to a knee injury and found himself contemplating his next move. Around that time, he just so happened to be at a WWF show during Hogan's run, and the closer he studied Hulk perform, the more the highly intelligent Nash could see the business for what it was: *a work* (predetermined). Realising that he had the genetics and athleticism for it, he decided to pursue a job in the industry.

Nash's imposing size opened doors for him quickly, and he had little trouble getting noticed by potential employers. He soon snared a job with WCW, but was given an unsuitable and ludicrous set of gimmicks that didn't play to his strengths, namely his size, at all. One was Oz, a silver-haired character based on *The Wizard of Oz*, which called for him to don all-green attire that made him look like David Bowie in his *Ziggy Stardust* pomp, complete with an entourage of eccentric hangers-on to complete the bizarre ensemble. When that failed to *get him over* (make the fans care about him) he was repackaged as the wisecracking mobster Vinnie Vegas, but he struggled to gain any traction or support from the office.

One man was paying attention though: Shawn Michaels, who got a kick out of Nash's act every time he caught him on WCW television. Despite being presented as a heel, Michaels at the time was finding it difficult to prevent cheers, largely owing to his exciting style. He had been contemplating pitching to Vince the idea of having a bodyguard to accompany him to the ring, which he reasoned would make it easier for him to build heat, and would stop him looking like so much of an underdog against generally larger opponents. An extra body in his corner would give him a numbers advantage in his favour, and thus make his smaller size less of a problem. He thought that Nash fit the bill perfectly.

Shawn asked around the locker-room to find out if anyone was acquainted with Nash, telling them that he was considering talking to Vince about bringing the big man in. Rick Steiner, who had recently arrived from WCW, told Shawn that he knew Nash and that he was right; he would be perfect in the WWF. His stamp of approval was all Shawn needed to hear, and despite having never met or even spoken to Nash, he went to Vince with the proposal. Ever the stickler for larger-than-life performers, McMahon agreed, and Nash started on television under the guise of 'Diesel' within a week of Shawn having suggested the idea.

Nash was immensely grateful to Shawn for the opportunity, later saying that, "I felt like I owed him. He gave me my freedom." Nash had an instant kinship with Michaels, though he recalled being surprised when he first met him at how tall he was (six-foot-one) compared to how he appeared on television in the land of the giants, and by how gruff and deep his voice sounded.

Nash already knew one of Shawn's locker-room allies, Scott Hall, from the brief time they had spent together in WCW (where both were at one time members of Diamond Dallas Page's *Diamond Mine* stable). He was allowed into the circle of friends and immediately taken under the pair's wings. They educated Nash on the intricacies of the business, both on the road and with the matches they were putting on each night in the ring. Nash, who realised that the Diesel character might be his last chance at the big time following his woeful WCW run, was a perfect student and absorbed as much information as he could.

SCOTT HALL was a good man to learn from. He had been bending bones since 1984 and was a well-seasoned veteran by the time he made it to the WWF in 1992. Deceptively tall at six-foot-seven, Hall wasn't what would be considered in the business as a body guy, but he looked the part with a hairy chest, stubble adorning his chiselled chin, slicked back black hair and a penchant for chewing toothpicks.

A mainstay for Verne Gagne's American Wrestling Association in the mid-to-late eighties, Hall's striking resemblance to TV icon Tom Selleck, who was immensely popular for his role in *Magnum P.I,* led to Hall renaming himself 'Magnum' Scott Hall. When the TV show ended, Hall adopted the generic moniker 'Big' and was in line for a run with the AWA World Title, but he declined the offer and left the company because he believed it to be a sinking ship. He was right, and within a year the AWA had folded.

Hall bounced around between the NWA, Puerto Rico and then WCW, but struggled to get over past a certain level. When he finally made it into the WWF in 1992 it was at the tail-end of the company's boom period, but he was given a sustained run as one of the top guys in the territory. For Vince McMahon, Scott Hall was an ideal choice to push in his new steroid-free WWF, because he was tall and well put-together, but wasn't the bodybuilder type.

Hall was repackaged as Razor Ramon, a rugged thug from the streets of Miami whose origins were purportedly Cuban. The character was actually created by Hall himself, who proposed the idea to Vince McMahon after seeing the Al Pacino movie *Scarface.* Vince didn't watch movies; he didn't have the time or the inclination. To Vince, if he wasn't working then he wasn't being productive, so when Hall went to him and laid out intricate plans for the gimmick, all of which were lifted directly from the movie, Vince thought he was a creative genius.

Hall's performances in the ring were exemplary, and matches against Bret Hart, Shawn Michaels and the 1-2-3 Kid were well received by critics. Kevin Nash credited Hall for being a teacher in the ring. "I knew how to wrestle," he reflected, "But Scott taught me how to work." Away from the ring, Hall had problems with a drink and drug dependency that would ultimately shorten his career, preventing him from becoming an enduring main event performer like Levesque, Michaels and Nash became. Even so, many credited Hall with having a great mind for the business and for being far wiser than his behaviour suggested.

THE FINAL member of the initial incarnation of the group was the gifted twenty-one-year-old Sean Waltman, who had endeared himself to Hall and Nash with a rib. The legend goes that Curt Hennig had shaved Waltman's eyebrows while he was sleeping on the day before a photo shoot, and as a result the 1-2-3 Kid Hasbro action figure had a backing card that featured an image of Waltman sans eyebrows in the background. Waltman knew that the only people around while he was asleep were Curt and The Smoking Gunns, and he didn't suspect Curt - despite Hennig's notorious reputation for being a serial ribber - because they had been friends for years. Waltman deduced that The Smoking Gunns were to blame, so made plans for revenge.

One night in El Paso, Texas he sat focused in the corner of the dressing room, with a tube of glue in one hand and the Gunns' cowboy hats in another. With his mind set on payback, he worked assiduously putting the glue delicately around the rims of the head-wear. When the Gunns went to the ring and tried to take the hats off but couldn't because they were stuck to their hair, he clapped his hands together and nodded, satisfied at a job well done.

Kevin Nash, who had watched the whole thing unfold, was amused by Waltman's audacity and wanted his personality around to keep him entertained on the road. He turned to him and simply said, "Dude, you're gonna need some protection. You need to get in our car." Once they started riding together, Waltman turned out to be a perfect fit for the group. Like the rest he was supremely talented in the ring, liked to party outside of it, and loved talking about the business. Similar to Michaels, he had no issue running his mouth to anyone he felt was disrespecting him or the business, irrespective of his size.

FOUR BECAME five when The Kliq allowed another official member into their exclusive club; newcomer Paul 'Hunter Hearst Helmsley' Levesque, who would go on to bigger fame as Triple H. A hooked-nosed former teenage bodybuilder, Levesque was a student of the business and a perfectionist when it came to honing both his craft and his physique. Having graduated from Killer Kowalski's wrestling school, he was quickly signed by WCW in 1994 and given the name Terra Ryzing, before having his gimmick changed mid-way through the year to snooty Frenchman, Jean-Paul Levesque.

Unhappy with the limited schedule WCW was offering him and realising there was little chance he would go beyond the lower midcard while Hulk Hogan and his friends were calling the shots, Levesque left for the WWF in early 1995 to be repackaged as Hunter Hearst Helmsley. The character was similar to Jean-Paul Levesque in that he was still portraying an aristocrat, only he was now billed as being from Connecticut rather than France. Vince had created Hunter in his own image like God had created Adam, giving him the surname Helmsley as a spoof on notorious business couple Harry and Leona Helmsley. Fittingly, Levesque would in later years become the real-life son-in-law to Vince when he married his daughter Stephanie in 2003.

When Diamond Dallas Page got word of Levesque's defection to the WWF, the first thing he did was get on the phone to his good friend Kevin Nash. "You've got a good kid coming in there," he told him, and Nash's ears pricked up even more when he found out that Levesque didn't drink, smoke, or do drugs. He was just what The Kliq needed; someone sober who could drive them from town to town and take care of them when they were too inebriated to take care of themselves.

Levesque was unaware of Page's call to Nash, but he was very well aware that The Kliq were the power-brokers in the WWF. He was told by his friend Terry Taylor prior to arriving in the company that if he wanted to get over and move ahead in the business, then they were the ones to be riding with. As it happened The Kliq had already heard of Levesque, because they used to get a kick out of his gimmick when they saw him on WCW's *Main Event* program. When he turned up for his debut match with Titan, they all made sure to pay close attention. Levesque had already grabbed their interest in a different way as it was, having gone up to Shawn Michaels and told him brazenly and confidently that he had heard he and his friends were the guys to hang out with, and that he wanted to ride with them. "Well, that's great kid," replied Michaels, slightly taken aback and more than a little dismissive in tone. No one had ever been brave enough to do that before, and with DDP's appraisal in mind, The Kliq were willing to consider accommodating him in the group.

Having sat at the monitor to watch Levesque's match, Scott Hall summed up the performance in his own succinct way, "Motherfucker's money," he said to Nash with a wry smile. Hall followed Levesque around in the back after the contest, clowning about to get his attention, then told him that from then on he was riding with them. It was the perfect marriage. Levesque did take care of them on the road, willingly taking the wheel while also making sure he had their backs if any situations arose. Some would later disparage his position in the group as being that of a baggage carrier, but Levesque saw himself more as a babysitter. If taking the bags of his buddies to the car got them out of the building quicker and on the road to the next town, that's what he would do. Riding with The Kliq gave Levesque the chance to learn the business from the top guys in the company, much like Nash had when he first came in, and he soaked the knowledge up like a sponge. His on-screen character was helped by the association too, with Hunter Hearst Helmsley winning the majority of matches for the first six months of his career with the WWF, which gave him instant credibility with the fans.

There was nearly another member in the posse; Shawn Michaels' eventual nemesis Bret Hart. During a tour of Germany in September 1994, Bret was still on good terms with Shawn, Scott and Kevin, and was enjoying a beer with the three in Hamburg a few days into the trip. With drinks flowing and guards lowered, the trio floated to Hart the idea of forming a union of just the top guys in the company. The aim was to monopolise the top spots on the card and with it the money. According to Hart, the trio wanted him to be the leader of the backstage group and the man who would voice concerns regarding issues in the company to Vince. Bret had seen similar unions in the past and knew it could work, but he had no interest in being around the three every night because of their increasing abuse of pills and alcohol. Plus, Bret was already the top guy and he didn't think he needed back-up to retain his spot.

THE KLIQ contained the premier talent in the WWF, and such was their camaraderie, Vince realised that if he lost one he would likely lose them all. With business at its nadir and houses vastly diminished from the time of the company's apex a decade ago, alienating any of them wasn't a risk he was willing to take. Hogan had done good business for Turner since he signed on with them, and he was convinced that The Kliq would do likewise if they left him. The group took full advantage of Vince's concerns, using their collective political clout to ensure they remained favourably positioned at the top of the card where the real money was made, while the guys on the bottom rung of the ladder near enough starved. They also made sure that no-one outside of their ordained group would be allowed access into that upper echelon, which caused bitterness towards them within the locker-room.

Cliques were not a new thing to the business. In the seventies Vince had watched as his father was strong-armed by Ernie Ladd, Ivan Koloff and Superstar Billy Graham, his three top heels, into giving them all the same main event pay-off regardless of their position on the card. With room for only one top heel per show, the other two who weren't headlining would end up working for less, and that didn't sit right with them. "We are the three top heels you have got," they told Vince Senior, "You can't do this without us." They simply wanted paying the same because they were all equally over, and they bandied together to achieve that. But all three were great, long-time professionals who were happy to put people over, and often suggested as such. "That was the difference between them and Shawn's Kliq in the nineties," cogitated Jim Cornette, "But Vince saw those guys controlling his dad like that and figured it was okay. He let Shawn and his friends get away with everything they did because he thought that they were stars too, and that was how he thought stars were supposed to act."

TO SID Eudy, whose snarling, often error-laced on-screen interviews suggested that he was less than an intellectual powerhouse, the reason for Vince's willingness to accede to the whims of Shawn and company was obvious. He could see how much Vince had invested into the group's respective pushes, building them up each week on television and marketing them as superstars. They were branded commodities, so it made no sense to risk losing them at a time when top level talents who could shift tickets were increasingly rare.

Sid was well aware that The Kliq exploited McMahon's predicament, and for all their constant badgering of the chairman to do things their way irritated him, he realised it was in his career's best interests to stay on their good side. He was already friends with Nash from their WCW days, but he was careful to keep his cards close to his chest and not get too close that others would think he was a stooge.

It was a hazardous political minefield for all of the boys to negotiate, but it was hardly anything new to Sid. He had seen groups like this form throughout his time in the business. That was just how things worked. The difference this time was that the grievances were louder because of the current ill-health of the industry, which meant grumblings were amplified against anything the boys perceived as negative towards their careers.

Lex Luger was used to it too. He had come through WCW at a time when the respective factions of Dusty Rhodes and Ric Flair had jockeyed for position, and he had been caught in the middle of it. Rhodes had pushed Luger quickly to the top, but was often met with resistance from Flair. Like Sid, Luger realised that having a powerful set of enemies would torpedo his career.

Despite his best efforts to stay friendly with The Kliq, Lex still found himself a source of ridicule for the group to prod at. Michaels would gleefully rip into Luger during stints as guest commentator on *Monday Night Raw*, referring to him as, "The biggest piece of baggage in the WWF," less then subtly implying that he needed to be carried by better workers in his matches.

Luger decided that the best course of action was no action. He recognised that if he responded things would only get worse for him, and he also knew that there was a modicum of truth to what Michaels was saying; he did need guys like The Kliq to get the best out of him.

Others, like Peter Polaco, were not as discreet in their pandering as Eudy and Luger. Polaco made no secret of the fact he admired The Kliq, the members of which he considered to be the best in the business. As a twenty-one-year-old rookie, he yearned to learn from the group and went out of his way to defend their behaviour.

His view of The Kliq was that they were the scapegoats for everything the rest of the roster were unhappy with in the company, and were an easy target to lay the blame on. If they were as all-powerful as people claimed, he argued, then he would have been in a better spot on the card. Instead he was on the bottom rung of the ladder, used in opening matches to put over anyone that the WWF was pushing. The myth that they controlled wrestling was, to him, ridiculous.

Others who had been around for a while and were friends with all of the guys in the group, saw things the same way. Jeff Jarrett was among the first in The Kliq car if someone from the unit was on a different loop, and to him they were just a very close group of friends who had a strong love of the business. Like Polaco, he believed that guys wanted someone to blame for their terrible pay-offs and lack of dates, and The Kliq were an easy target because they were the top guys who weren't shy about voicing their opinions on everything, both in the locker-room and to Vince.

Tom Prichard was part of the undercard during The Kliq's perceived reign of terror. Unlike many, he never had any problems with the group. His brother Bruce Prichard was part of the office, so he went out of his way to stay out of trouble as much as he could, sticking to himself and not making waves. As he remembers, "There were only issues with The Kliq if you were a threat to them... they were gonna keep their spots no matter what. It had always been that way in wrestling, there was always groups. The Kliq guys were just more high profile. Could they be pains in the ass? No doubt. But, I had no problem with them personally because I wasn't a threat to them."

Years later, even guys who had notorious altercations with The Kliq would be forced to concede that perhaps they were afforded greater opprobrium than they deserved, and had incidents attributed to them which they played no part in. Chris Candido, who had more issues than most with

The Kliq - Shawn Michaels in particular - admitted that at the time people blamed everything wrong in the business on the group. When he viewed things with the benefit of hindsight years later, he conceded that they were just guys on top who happened to be friends, not guys who were friends in order to stay on top.

This was not a viewpoint shared by Bob Holly. He thought business was down *because* of The Kliq, as Diesel failed to attract crowds and move pay-per-view numbers as the WWF Champion, and the rest of his crew, similarly elevated, equally failed to improve the numbers. He had watched as Vince allowed them to manipulate programs and dictate which wrestlers worked at the top of the card. It made no sense to him. If business was booming then maybe he could have understood it, but it had rarely been worse. Holly remained convinced that Shawn had something over Vince, perhaps a secret that could potentially ruin him. It was the only thing he could think of to explain why Vince remained compliant.

It was a somewhat outlandish theory, but not an uncommon one amongst the boys. Of course, that was dismissed by The Kliq as being the delusions of bitter and jaded guys who had a problem with Shawn personally. They resented him because he was so good, and one of very few men in history able to barge into Vince's office and pepper him with a tirade of expletives and face no consequences. Shawn acknowledged and thrived on the resentment; he knew that people didn't like him, but it just made him even more determined to push their buttons. He was always thrilled when he saw his name in the dirt sheets listed as one of the powers in the company, because he knew how much it riled the other boys. To Shawn, everyone else was just paranoid, unable to look in the mirror and take ownership of their own shortcomings. Instead, they wanted to blame him because he was more talented.

Shawn didn't see what made his group so notorious, because there were numerous cliques around at the time. There always had been since he started with the WWF. He viewed the business as like being at war; they were all in the foxhole, he just picked who he wanted to be in it with. He didn't believe the group were doing anything wrong by going to Vince with ideas, and more often than not McMahon would come to them *asking* for advice. They were just trying to improve the business for everyone, Shawn argued. He further attested that while The Kliq had Vince's ear and probably used their political clout to stay on top, McMahon actually encouraged that, but he continued to deny that they had used their power to bury others and derail any careers.

Tom Prichard later backed up Shawn's claims that McMahon willingly accommodated the group so much of his time. "Vince loved the chaos," he observed, "He always liked to have things going on. He can't just sit there and do nothing, he is not an easy, slow, take a break kind of guy. Those guys were non-stop, always on the phone, always talking about business, and Vince appreciated that about them. If anything he welcomed it."

After years of dealing with an uninterested Hogan, it was refreshing for Vince to have a group of talent who were twenty-four-seven about the business like he was. He had always respected and made time for performers who took initiative and weren't afraid to get their hands dirty. Like himself. McMahon used The Kliq as a sounding board, his ear on the ground. Most of the boys wouldn't tell him the truth or wouldn't tell him anything at all, so he was removed from the talk in the locker-room. The Kliq provided him that, and in return he took care of them with how they were booked. McMahon was not ignorant to how the group were viewed by the rest of his crew. He knew most of his roster perceived them as confrontational and a source of power, but he also believed they were "money". He also recognised that many of his office staff felt the same way as the boys, and struggled to deal with The Kliq's forthright, opinionated nature. "They were hell raisers," Jim Ross observed, with Pat Patterson adding, "They were not well liked. They were a pain in the ass."

Now and again, some of them would push the agents too far. One night, Kevin Nash was in a sulky mood, grumbling about the fact that he was, "The lowest paid WWF Champion in history." Jerry Brisco overheard the comment and couldn't resist biting back. "Yeah, well that's because you're the lowest *drawing* champion in WWF history," he snapped. Even though Brisco was approaching his fifties at the time, he still had a formidable reputation as a *hooker*,[16] and Nash knew better than to answer back. "One swift kick to those dodgy knees of his and Brisco would have torn him apart," laughed Jim Cornette.

Brisco wasn't the only one who felt that way. As Tom Prichard remembers it, "Agents like Tony Garea and Jack Lanza frequently grumbled about how bad the houses were, and wondered aloud if we would be, 'Diesel-fuelled,' for much longer."

Sean Waltman knew how The Kliq were perceived as well, but it didn't matter to him either that no one liked them, he just saw other guys as jealous because the group were so close. Waltman knew that Shawn could be difficult to deal with, that Scott was occasionally impossible to be

---

[16] Someone in the business with legitimate fighting ability, possessing in particular a number of holds or "hooks", many of which could be potentially career-ending if used.

around, and that people didn't like how close they all were to Vince, but he also knew that they made up for it when they performed. "There were no conspiracies to hold people back," he pointed out, "If someone was talented enough then nobody, no matter what clout they had, could stop them from succeeding."

There may have been no conspiracies, but there were occasionally dirty tricks designed to chip away at a performer's chance of thriving in the company. Tony Norris, who traded his birth name for the stage name Ahmed Johnson, was an oiled-up black muscle-head from Harlem whose calling cards were freakish strength and indecipherable promos. He was once told by Shawn not long after he debuted to stop doing flying moves. Only later did Norris realise that it was not the good advice Michaels had presented it as, but rather a way to stop himself from being overshadowed.

Then there was frequent Michaels target Chris Candido, who fluffed the finish of a match in Germany while he held the WWF Tag Team Championship with Tom 'Zip' Prichard. Shawn told him that because of that, they would be dropping the titles when they returned home, and sure enough they did. With their livelihoods seemingly at stake on the whim of Shawn Michaels' frequent mood swings or a bad match against Kid - The Kliq barometer used to judge and rate talent - the other boys felt like they were constantly tip-toeing on eggshells.

THE ONLY ones truly safe from The Kliq's machinations were veterans Bret Hart and The Undertaker. Both had Vince's ear and a significant amount of political sway due to their long tenures with the company and positions backstage as respected locker-room leaders, but they never used it to undermine other guy's careers. Both had noticed that resentment towards The Kliq in the locker-room was growing. They too were getting tired and frustrated with Vince's willingness to listen to them so readily, sometimes they felt, to the detriment of the company's best interests as a whole. They saw The Kliq as self-serving egotists, and it had become a problem. Bret recalls a lot of the boys expressed those sentiments to him, as they resented the fact that Nash as the WWF Champion was not a champion for all of them, but only for his circle of friends.

Mark Calaway, the man behind The Undertaker, was a veteran of the locker-room who had seen similar poisonous influences before and knew the damage they could cause. Calaway had been with the WWF since the Hulk Hogan and Ultimate Warrior days. He had seen and experienced the tail-end of the good times, and he knew how much the Federation's stock had fallen. The boys always liked to complain about something or other, that was nothing new, but now discontent was more rampant than at any other time he could remember.

During a typically slow evening spent driving from yet another disappointing house in the middle of nowhere, Calaway sat and listened as his running buddies complained about Shawn's gang for the umpteenth night in a row. "Thanks for the house, *Shawn*," one of them sneered. "Business is getting worse with Shawn and his boys on top," complained another, who added, "They are going to keep that belt within their little fuckin' group forever and leave everyone else with the scraps."

Calaway put his head back in his seat and sighed, contemplating the negative effect The Kliq were having on locker-room morale. Far from being just a group of friends who rode together and liked to work with each other - the same about which could be said for most of the boys - this group were dangerous. As well as trying to monopolise the money spots for themselves, he saw them intentionally going out to mess with other guys, far beyond harmless, sophomoric ribbing. When The Kliq found a target, they pounced on them and bullied them into submission, making sure their tenure with the WWF would be short and their run largely unprofitable for both the performer and the company. He had seen guys come and go, good talents, cut adrift after falling afoul of The Kliq's leanings on McMahon.

Calaway turned to Rodney 'Yokozuna' Anoa'i, one of his closest friends in the business, and muttered, "Something needs to be done about them." Anoa'i instantly agreed, "Brudda, I was thinkin' the same thing," he replied. The pair formed the Bone Street Krew, or the BSKs as they referred to themselves[17]. The idea behind the Krew was not to exert excessive political leanings on Vince McMahon or the office, but rather to keep the increasingly influential Kliq in check and stop them from derailing any more promising careers for often spurious reasons.

For Calaway, neutering The Kliq was only a part of it. To him it was more a way of having a lasting bond with his friends, people he had been drawn to. There were very few people who he let inside, but he trusted the BSKs completely and knew he could rely on them. They took care of each other and watched one another's backs, which to him just made the rigorous wrestling lifestyle that much easier to bear.

The BSKs soon evolved into the locker-room policemen, finding strength and protection in numbers and only exerting the power of their unity to force Vince's hand if absolutely necessary. Relations between the

---

[17] Other members included Charles Wright (Kama), Solofa Fatu, Jr. (Fatu), William Moody (Paul Bearer), Juan Rivera (Savio Vega), Mark Canterbury (Henry Godwinn) and later Dennis Knight (Phineas Godwinn) when he joined the promotion.

rival factions were increasingly fraught and tensions were taken to another level when the Krew started inking themselves with tattoos of the BSK initials, and The Kliq began flashing secret hand signals at one another on-screen. Kevin Nash would even compare the BSK-Kliq issue to the Five Families of New York's turf war. It was perhaps the most interesting and intense WWF rivalry in all of 1995. For Vince, it was just unfortunate that it didn't transpire on-screen where he could turn the real-life resentment into dollars.

FOUR

A FTER THE HORRENDOUS MADISON SQUARE Garden draw the previous August, the WWF came back with two more shows at the venue in 1994, which were barely half full but were a marked improvement. They returned on January 16, 1995 with a show headlined by new WWF Champion Diesel against Jeff Jarrett, but only managed to get 5,400 people into the building. Once rent, advertising costs and talent expenses had been factored in, it was another money loser.

Shows in two more traditionally well-drawing venues the Nassau Coliseum, also in New York, and the Meadowlands in New Jersey, were also unprofitable. Some pointed to the running of three venues in what was essentially the same market as the reason for the embarrassing houses, which was a decision the company had made in 1994 to cut crew travel costs, and had also been blamed for the August numbers.

A week later there was more bad news when TV station WUHF in Rochester, New York pulled long-running television show *Superstars* from their schedule. Losing syndication in the third most populous city of their "home" state was a major blow immediately following the poor draws in other areas of the city. Since its inception, the WWF had held its roots in the Big Apple, even though their offices were in Stamford, Connecticut, so much so that the boys had always referred to the McMahon territory as, "New York". Many within the company worried that if they couldn't draw there, they would struggle to draw anywhere else.

The result of losing WUHF wouldn't become evident until later in the year when the company returned to Rochester in October. They only pulled 1,200 people to a town that routinely drew 8,000 at the start of the decade. Losing the television slot had undoubtedly hurt the WWF.

AN ANNUAL tradition since 1987, the *Royal Rumble* event was one of the most celebrated creations devised by Vince McMahon's right hand man Pat Patterson. The show's eponymous centrepiece was a match in which thirty wrestlers competed in an over the top rope battle royal, with entrants joining the fray every two minutes, and the last man standing declared the winner.

Early editions of the show had seen the match contested for no other prize than the glory of victory, but that changed in 1992 when the decision was made to award the winner the vacant WWF Championship. Ric Flair won the match after entering at number three, in what was perhaps the most widely-acclaimed Rumble match ever. The next year the reward changed again, this time for good, with the winner receiving a WWF Championship match at the following *WrestleMania* from then on.

The new stakes made the Rumble match a must-see, and the pay-per-view presentation on which it featured became the undisputed number two show of the year as far as fans were concerned. 1995's card took place in Tampa, Florida in front of 10,000 people. It was a healthy crowd for the era but by some way the lowest the show had ever managed to attract, with the drop off in attendance very noticeable on camera.

On the undercard, Robert 'Bob Holly' Howard and Sean Waltman battled Scott 'Bam Bam' Bigelow and Chris 'Tatanka' Chavis for the vacant WWF Tag Team Championship. Howard and Waltman were both small by WWF standards of the past and would never have risen above the level of enhancement talent in the eighties. But with the company now no longer able to present beefy muscle-heads to the masses after the steroid trial, business had changed and men of their statures were becoming the new norm.

Waltman, thanks to his five-foot-eleven, one-hundred-and-fifty-pound frame, was cast in the role of the plucky underdog who would win against the odds, having made a name for himself in 1993 when he was booked to beat established star Razor Ramon on an episode of *Monday Night Raw*. In the intervening years he quickly established himself as one of the most talented performers in the company, and matches with the likes of Bret Hart and Shawn Michaels were considered essential viewing.

Howard on the other hand was brought in with a NASCAR driver gimmick, initially given the asinine name Thurman 'Sparky' Plugg and forced to compete in a loud spandex leotard adorned with chequered flags. His long flowing mullet and painfully forced smile only further added to the perception that his upward potential was minimal and his shelf life was limited.

Scott Bigelow was in his second run with the WWF having had a brief spell as a babyface in the eighties boom period, but left due to a knee injury and went on to have success in Jim Crockett Promotions and more notably, Japan. With Vince scrambling for new talent in 1993 to replace his departed muscle guys, Bigelow was the perfect hire due to his menacing look. At six-foot-four and three-hundred-and-fifty-pounds, and with a series of painful flame tattoos adorning his bald head, the former bounty hunter was still big, but his doughy physique meant no one would ever accuse him of using steroids. For McMahon, he ticked all the boxes. Despite his size, Bigelow moved around the ring with the agility of a cat, routinely taking big bumps and performing impressive aerial moves with the aplomb of a man half of his size, which got him over quickly.

Chris Chavis, a former bodybuilder and football player, was brought into the WWF in late 1991 after just two years in the business learning his craft. Of Native American descent, Chavis used that heritage as part of his moniker and adopted the sobriquet 'Tatanka' prior to his WWF run. At first Vince had him work under his real name, but soon changed his mind when he saw the potential for merchandising, and the chance to appeal to a minority demographic that he hadn't catered towards since they days of Chief Jay Strongbow. It was a rare divergence away from his usual policy of rebranding wrestler's gimmicks in order to secure their image rights. Three years into his tenure, Tatanka's good guy act had grown stale, so he was turned heel and aligned with Ted DiBiase's Million Dollar Corporation stable in order to freshen him up. It didn't work, with Chavis reluctant to change anything about the character's look and style, and the crowd no longer interested in the one-dimensional act.

For Howard, appearing in one of the top matches on pay-per-view was significant, as he had mostly tread water in his first year with the company and done little of note. He presumed, like everyone else, that Tatanka and Bigelow were sure-fire winners of their confrontation, but he didn't mind. He understood his role and had every intention of making his opponents look as good as possible in beating him. When he then found out that his makeshift team were winning the belts that night, he was delighted. "I thought it was fucking cool," he beamed, "Everyone in wrestling aspires to be a champion in the WWF, and here I was about to become one of the tag team champions. It was awesome, and I figured I was on my way to making some good money."

Bigelow didn't mind losing, even to two guys half his size, because he had bigger things coming his way that night. Namely, he had been instructed to get into a shoving match at ringside with NFL great Lawrence Taylor, a stunt designed to generate media interest that was being presented as a legitimate confrontation. For Bigelow, defeat to the underdogs was the storyline catalyst for him losing his cool with the football player. Backstage when the four participants were discussing the match, Bigelow was gracious and promised to do everything he could to help his opponents look good.

Pat Patterson's long-standing role in the WWF was that of a road agent, someone who helped the performers structure their matches so they complied with Vince's vision and what he wanted to see, as well as booking and overseeing house show programs. Considered by just about everyone as the best finish guy in the business, Pat was rarely questioned on his match plans. When laying out the bout in the locker-room, Pat told Waltman to get the pin on Bigelow, but Sean selflessly argued against it. Perhaps with The Kliq's reputation for having a selfish attitude in mind, he told Pat that he always won and Bob never did, so maybe Holly should be the one to get the fall. But Pat had orders to follow and that wasn't one of them, so the decision to have Waltman get the winning pinfall stood.

It didn't matter to Bob, he was just thrilled to be winning the belts. When the moment came he savoured it, soaking in the adulation and embracing the prestige of being a champion. It wasn't a title he had really gone out and fought to win, of course, it was predetermined like everything else in the business, but to Howard it was vindication that he was doing something right and that the office had faith in his abilities. The next day, he looked over at the belt and decided that he could get used to this, then he found out his team were dropping the titles that night on a live episode of *Monday Night RAW*. In keeping with his usual attitude towards the business, he didn't complain and professionally did his job, but he remained annoyed that the unit wasn't given chance to flourish and grow into their elevated role. Within a few weeks he and Waltman were broken up as a team and Holly ended up back at the bottom of the card being used to elevate others. As far as he was concerned the title win might as well have not even happened, as his status in the company hadn't changed.

OTHER THAN the Rumble match itself, the main attraction on the show was WWF Champion Diesel making the first defence on pay-per-view of his new title. The still *green* (inexperienced) giant had been the recipient of one of the most intense pushes in company history, and the title win capped a thunderous twelve-months for Kevin Nash, who went from the cusp of being culled as part of cost-cutting measures in early 1994, to the WWF Champion and the man Vince looked towards to build the promotion around come the end of the year.

Diesel's title win was a unique spectacle. Bob Backlund had beaten Bret Hart to lift the championship at *Survivor Series* on November 23, 1994 following a screwy finish that protected Hart, and theoretically led to a series of rematches around the loop, as was customary. But Hart was taking time off to recharge his batteries and film an episode of television show *Lonesome Dove*, so Diesel was drafted in as his substitute on the house show circuit.

It was expected that Diesel would beat Backlund via count out or disqualification much like Davey Boy Smith had been doing against the new champion for the past few nights. Instead, at Madison Square Garden a mere three days after Backlund's shocking win, Nash was allowed to kick him in the stomach and deliver his trademark jack knife powerbomb for an eight-second title win. If Nash's post match celebration of running around the ring with his arms outstretched by his waist while furiously nodding and roaring like a proud lion was odd, it is only because the reaction was genuine. Nobody had managed a rise as meteoric as Diesel's in such a short time frame.

McMahon had decided to go with Kevin Nash as his top guy because he was tall; there was no deeper explanation. Nash himself knew this, and had been smartened to the probability that it could happen some months earlier by an eagle-eyed Lex Luger, who had stood and observed McMahon's reaction to Diesel back in May, when he had worked a stellar match with buddy Scott Hall at Madison Square Garden. Nash was obviously delighted at being given the opportunity to run with the ball, but now his challenge was retaining fan acceptance having being thrust into such a major league spot so quickly.

His first opponent was former champion Bret Hart, one of the patriarchs of the locker-room and a man respected by most. He had also been one of the first to help show what Kevin Nash was capable of, thanks to a stirring contest at the previous year's *King of the Ring*. Of that match, *The Wrestling Observer* had written:

> Considering Diesel was working much longer than he's ever had to on a major card and was working with a torn groin, he deserves praise for at least being good enough that Hart could carry him. Hart was great in doing the impossible and making this almost a great match except for a few screwed up spots.

With Bret on the opposite side of the ring, the quality of Nash's first title defence was not a concern, but the potential reaction of the fans very much was. Both performers were considered babyfaces and presented as such to the WWF audience, so the pairing was a strange one, with Nash still finding his feet as champion. The prevailing concern was that Nash would be booed coming up against the popular and much smaller Hart. Vince's theory was that giving Diesel an opponent who had beat him before would raise interest and people would suspect they might see a title change. At the same time, Hart could lead Nash through a strong match and help him to bring the fans onto his side with his work.

But no matter much how he justified the booking, Vince was still worried about Diesel getting a heel response, which was the last thing he wanted for his new hero champion. Nash couldn't quite understand the program either and wondered, often aloud, if Vince had any faith in him as champion or if he was purposely being tested and intentionally set up to fail.

Luckily Bret understood what his role was, and made sure to alter his usual game plan so that he wouldn't be cheered more than Nash, because as the much smaller guy the natural instinct for the crowd would be to side with the underdog. He avoided *selling*[18] for long periods and made sure not to educe too much sympathy, whilst upping his aggression levels very subtly so that Nash would be the one to sell. All the while he had to delicately balance things, making sure he didn't go too far and cross a line into getting booed himself. As a self-proclaimed hero and a wholesome character that fans could believe in, he certainly didn't want that to happen. He just about achieved the objective, and while he did still elicit more cheers than Diesel, at least there were no boos for the champion.

The whole dance was executed masterfully by the savvy Hart, and Nash thanked him after the contest for giving him his first good match in months. Bret appreciated the gratitude, but later pointed out, "He didn't seem to understand that all I would have had to do to turn him heel was to have started selling dramatically, but I didn't operate like that."

Even though the body of the work was good and the crowd responded as the WWF had hoped, the match finish which saw both men battle to a draw after outside interference from a number of guys on both sides, left the fans feeling cheated. "It was like they didn't want to put the Bret Hart eggs in the Diesel basket, in case I didn't work out as champion," carped Nash. The match received some praise from critics, but the cheap, unsatisfying finish left most annoyed. Lee Maughan in *The Complete WWF Video Guide, Vol. 3* wrote:

> There's a clear story, it's actually something of a throwback in terms of a slow building bout and layering psychology in. But, it has an utterly *infuriating* resolution to something they were asking you to invest a significant chunk of time into. Just a total slap in the face.

Dave Meltzer in *The Wrestling Observer Newsletter* shared similar frustrations:

---

[18] Reacting to moves as if they had hurt and caused actual physical damage

While the Hart-Diesel match was excellent, not so much from a moves standpoint as from telling a story standpoint, and Hart did a great job of getting Diesel over as a gutsy, credible champion, the booking was also too preposterous. Not calling DQ's for outside interference is fine if they are trying to get across the message that they are eliminating screw-jobs. But instead, they ended without a finish after all that anyway. Three run-ins and one ref bump gets a little silly.

The same thing was happening with Diesel as had happened to all of the other "next Hulk Hogans". Vince had given him the mega-push in 1994 and had him win the title in the hallowed Madison Square Garden by quickly defeating his adversary, just like Hogan had in 1984 when he dethroned The Iron Sheik. But unlike Hogan, Kevin Nash wasn't then strapped to a promotional rocket and allowed to comfortably beat everyone he worked against. Instead he was asked to change his persona and drop some of the character's attitude, smile more when he was on-screen and work competitive matches on the house shows and television. When he was booked to not beat Hart, Nash figured they might as well have just, "Cut my cock and balls off and had done with it." Within the company there was already talk that Diesel wasn't the answer to the post-Hogan conundrum, and it seemed like only a matter of time before Vince would go with Shawn Michaels, or back to Bret.

Hart sat back and watched the Diesel experiment play out, just as he had done with Lex Luger, Yokozuna and Bob Backlund. He wondered to himself what it would take for McMahon to stop wasting his time trying to get everyone else over by force, when he was already over on merit. He knew that Vince saw him as the dependable, solid guy he could rely on when his flavour of the month failed, but couldn't understand why he had no faith in him as the number one guy. Many of the boys felt the same way, with Hart recalling more than one occasion where guys had complained about pay-offs having dropped since Diesel became champion, and that business was in a much better state when he had the belt.

Tom Prichard was one of them. As he told the story, "A lot of guys weren't happy with Diesel as champion, but he was friends with all the right people. And hey, it's not like you could teach someone else to be seven-foot tall. Vince was determined to stick with him because he was desperately trying to replace Hulk Hogan. He went through a number of guys looking for someone to take his spot, and of course he definitely had a preference for big men and larger than life people. Kev was just that, because he was certainly charismatic and had something about him, but once the bell rang people could see through him."

Bret hoped that slowly, in time, Vince would come to see things the same way as the rest of the locker-room. Hart wanted him to realise that he was the right man for the job, not some flash-in-the-pan genetic anomaly like Nash, Luger, or Yokozuna, and that McMahon would finally commit to him for the long haul.

THE CAST of characters in the *Royal Rumble* match was among the most eclectic in memory. The difference compared to previous years was that few who participated were viewed as legitimate potential winners. The feeling inside the company was that it was the weakest field they had ever had, which necessitated a change from the usual two minute intervals between combatants to just one minute, making the match feel much quicker and thus much better than it actually was. Among the names involved:

Native Tongan 'Headshrinker Sione' Vailahi had been a powerful midcard heel for McMahon in the late eighties and early nineties as 'The Barbarian'. But the muscled Vailahi was released as part of Vince's mass talent cull, and wound up treading water in WCW. Having shed sixty pounds of muscle from his lanky six-foot-two frame, he returned to Titan in 1994. Vailahi's day had been and gone and the WWF didn't have much for him to do, so he was paired with Solofa Fatu, Jr. and shunted into the tag ranks. Once an imposing yet agile monster, Sione was reduced to being just another generic tall guy on a roster already full of them.

Ray Liachelli worked under the makeup of Doink the Clown, a character previously played by the underrated Matthew Osborne, who was more commonly known as Matt Borne. The gimmick had started as a sinister manifestation of the darker side of Vince's psyche, with Borne playing the role of evil clown to perfection, turning a ridiculous cartoon gimmick on paper into a genuinely frightening and captivating act. But Borne was blighted by an addiction to prescription drugs that led to his firing in the fall of 1993.[19]

Vince persevered with the Doink persona, deigning that the individual playing the role didn't matter because it was the character who was over. A few men donned the costume but long-time journeyman Liachelli was given the job permanently, and the character underwent a makeover with a babyface turn and the addition of a midget doppelgänger. It damaged Doink beyond repair, and no longer ahead of its time, the character was

---

[19] Osborne's drug habit ultimately led to his untimely death in 2013 from an accidental overdose of morphine and hydrocodone.

now the personification of the often repeated negative barb levelled against the WWF, that it had more in common with a circus than with traditional pro wrestling. Even the kids in the audience hated babyface Doink, and were among the many chanting, "Kill the clown," at him during live shows across the country.

Juan Rivera had Scott Hall's recommendation to thank for his job in the WWF. The two had become friends during Hall's stint working in Rivera's native Puerto Rico, with Rivera taking care of him in the notoriously dangerous territory. McMahon hired him on Hall's word, but as usual set about changing him into something unrecognisable from his previous work. He put Rivera under a hood and renamed him the onomatopoeic Kwang, a typically clichéd interpretation of what the WWF thought a Japanese ninja to be. The name was frequently the butt of jokes amongst wrestling fans, who quipped, "What is the sound of two-hundred-and-fifty pounds of shit hitting the fan? Kwang!"

Rivera did what he could with the alien role, throwing unconvincing and phony looking martial arts kicks and thrusts, and lifting the use of "poisonous mist" (a condom filled with food colouring that he would bite down on mid-match, before spitting the residue into the face of his opponent to "blind" them) directly from Japanese stars The Great Muta and The Great Kabuki. Unimpressed with the hackneyed nature of the character, fans didn't take to Kwang, and Rivera was repackaged later in the year.

There was Rick Martel, a good-looking and well toned veteran, and another in a long line of French-Canadian imports, who had been a consistently solid hand for McMahon on-and-off since the seventies. Previously adept as a babyface tag team specialist, Martel flew solo in 1989 and was repackaged as 'The Model', an arrogant heel who donned bright baby blue, purple or pink trunks and carried a large Acme sized atomiser that he used to spray his own brand of "Arrogance" cologne into the eyes of his opponents.

The Model gimmick was consistent with the prevailing zeitgeist of its time, but by 1995 Martel was approaching forty-years-old and becoming somewhat long in the tooth. Despite having always played a heel as The Model, McMahon was considering using Martel on a semi-regular basis as a babyface, so he could present him as the top local guy during the company's regular visits to French Canadian territories such as Quebec, but plans were ultimately shelved. The *Royal Rumble* appearance turned out to be Martel's last hurrah for the company[20], and he only lasted two minutes in the match.

Tag team Well Dunn (Steve 'Steven Dunn' Doll and Timothy 'Timothy Well' Smith), a pretty boy duo better known elsewhere as The Southern Rockers, were also involved, but they only managed a collective ring time of less than five minutes in the Rumble match. When they arrived in New York they were given a comedic name and combined bow-ties with pink thongs as part of their attire. Booked and treated like a comedy afterthought, the pair failed to get over.

The same couldn't be said for their perennial opponents The Bushwhackers, an enduring WWF act since the eighties who remained popular with the kids. Now used sparingly as a special attraction while fulfilling their primary role as company ambassadors, the New Zealand natives appealed to the pre-teen demographic that Vince was actively targeting. However, many older fans were sick of the duo, considering them to be anachronistic, stale, and not in keeping with the WWF's fresher, younger roster. The Bushwhackers' involvement in the match was merely for the purpose of a nostalgia *pop* (crowd reaction) and to make up the numbers.

Vince's latest attempt to tap into what he perceived as being modern day pop culture were tag team Men on a Mission. Known as Mo (Barry Horne) and Mabel (Nelson Frazier), both were burly, black super-heavyweights from Harlem, who dressed in purple and gold muumuus, and sported bleached white mohawks on their heads. After having a modicum of success in the territories as the Harlem Knights, the pair arrived in New York in 1993 and were given a dancing and rapping gimmick.[21]

The duo were also given a manager known as Oscar, who was hired by McMahon after he had rapped for him in an elevator following *WrestleMania IX* in Las Vegas. Despite having no experience in the wrestling business whatsoever, McMahon figured Oscar was perfect for what he considered to be his new cutting edge tag team, who he wanted to use to capitalise on the infamous and then ongoing East Coast-West Coast hip hop rivalry that he had read about in the papers. Others like Kevin Nash thought the act was derivative, and he pointed out that, "To me it was so fucking white-bread. It

---

[20] Though he did make one more appearance as a one-off surprise for a spot on an untelevised Montreal show a few months later, where he helped fellow French-Canadian Carl Ouellet, preventing a beat down from Shawn Michaels.

[21] According to Horne, the gimmick worked, and years later he would make outlandish claims that the majority of WWE's characters in 2014 were inspired by the group's dancing and rapping, citing the duo as innovators.

was like guys doing the old school black-face. You mean to tell me that the best fucking rapper they could find was Oscar?"

Men on a Mission were not the first to combine rap with wrestling; in the mainstream alone there had been Paul 'P.N. News' Neu years earlier in WCW. Neu was a four-hundred-and-fifty pounds bull of a man with a monstrous gut, who was forced to wrestle in a neon blue and pink singlet and came to the ring donning a backwards baseball cap, an oversized gold medallion and star-shaped sunglasses. It was an ill-fitting persona for the man previously known as Cannonball Grizzly, and he lasted less than a year under the guise before being released in March 1992, a year before Men on a Mission first appeared on WWF television.

Curiously enough, Neu's cousin Mike Halac actually competed in the 1995 Rumble. He had debuted in late 1994, after being given one of the most outlandish and ridiculous gimmicks that McMahon had ever signed off on. The WWF called him Mantaur, a hybrid of Greek mythological demigod The Minotaur, and a play on words of "man tower". The dumpy super-heavyweight was given a large bull's head to wear to the ring (which was eventually dropped because it kept getting caught in the ropes during Halac's entrance) and the directive to act like an animal. Halac was perplexed, and all he could come up with was to charge and moo, which fans naturally responded to with howls of derisive laughter. "It was stupid, he knew it was stupid, but I think he was just happy to be there," observed Halac's occasional tag partner Tom Prichard.

Halac was briefly given veteran manager Jim Cornette to help get him over (something Cornette later claimed was likely a cruel joke that someone on the booking team was playing on him), but that didn't work. Mantaur was gone within five months, after doing some customary jobs on the way out for such luminaries as Duke 'The Dumpster' Droese, Man Mountain Rock and Tekno Team 2000, consigned to the annals of history as another failed career-killing experiment born from the mind of Vince McMahon.

Peter Polaco had worked semi-frequently in the WWF for a couple of years as TV enhancement talent P.J. Walker. Having made friends with the right people he was signed to a permanent contract, but his diminutive stature meant he was yet another performer saddled with a typically goofy gimmick. Due to his Portuguese heritage, he was re-dubbed Aldo Montoya, 'Portuguese Man o' War'. Polaco wasn't playing a military character in the vein of Sgt. Slaughter, but rather wore a yellow mask that very closely resembled a jockstrap, and colourful tights in the maroon, green and yellow of the Portuguese flag.

He was given the role after impressing Vince and Pat Patterson while serving as a bump dummy for Brian Lee, who was honing his facsimile version of The Undertaker. The Aldo Montoya character had been on Vince's drawing board for some time, and his learning of Polaco's Portuguese heritage sealed the deal for him. Despite now having a character, Polaco's fortunes hadn't changed much in the ring, where he was still booked and presented as a jobber.

Vince McMahon was born in North Carolina in the Deep South, and resented what he felt was the redneck stigma attached to his roots. He made every effort to distance himself from them by disparagingly presenting unflattering southern stereotypes on his television shows. Decking out his more burly and unkempt performers in overalls and having them work as "Scufflin" hillbillies was one of his favourite ways to dig at the south. Cartoon hillbillies were always a part of wrestling when Vince grew up watching in the fifties, so he had a soft spot for the gimmick. Mark Canterbury as Henry Orpheus Godwinn was the latest in a long line of cartoon brawlers, following in the footsteps of Hillbilly Jim, Cousin Luke, Uncle Elmer and Haystacks Calhoun.

Godwinn, whose initials whimsically spelled out the word "hog", was cast as a pig farmer from Bitters, Arkansas, and was forced to wear a dirty yellow shirt under his overalls (to differentiate him from Hillbilly Jim), carry a bucket of pig slop to the ring to dump on his opponents, and crawl around on his hands and knees shouting, "sooey."

Another tag team in the bout were a mild-mannered pair of Rexall cowboys called The Smoking Gunns (Monty 'Billy Gunn' Sopp and Mike 'Bart Gunn' Polchlopek), who sported long moustaches straight out of cheap seventies porn, wrestled in jeans and fired blank pistols into the crowd as part of their pre-match ritual. As much as their gimmick was another overblown cartoon, in this case there was at least an element of truth behind it, with Sopp having previously worked full-time as a rodeo clown before hanging up his spurs for a pair of wrestling boots.

The Gunns had been the focal point of the WWF tag team scene for over a year, but they were a one-trick act and had grown stale. Fans who had grown up on stellar tandems such as The Hart Foundation, The Rockers, The British Bulldogs and The Legion of Doom were resentful of a push they didn't feel was fully warranted or justified, but rather necessitated by a lack of other real options.

Then there was Dick Murdoch, a surly, hard-faced veteran from Waxahachie, Texas, who had been wrestling for thirty years, and was used in the match as a one-off attraction. Murdoch was a former WWF Tag

Team Champion having held the titles with Adrian Adonis in 1984, but he was now forty-eight-years-old and with his best days far behind him. He also came with an unsavoury reputation, as would be revealed in testimonies years later from Allen 'Bad News Brown' Coage, Merced 'Tito Santana' Solis, and Eldridge Wayne 'Superstar Billy Graham' Coleman, who all made allegations that Murdoch was a racist affiliated with the Ku Klux Klan.

Others who were close to Murdoch dismissed such claims, "He was just a pretty typical child of his generation," offered former Texas-based referee James Beard. "He was brought up in a segregated world and his views were influenced by that, but I never saw or heard Dick do or say anything that made me think of him as being extreme in his feelings towards other races. He was willing to work with anyone of any colour and judged everyone by the same criteria, be they black or white. Dick was definitely a redneck and he had his prejudices, no doubt, but I never saw him abuse anyone because of race." Murdoch died just eighteen months after his brief *Royal Rumble* appearance from a heart attack, two months short of his fiftieth birthday.

Bryan Clarke appeared to be everything Vince McMahon looked for in a WWF Superstar. He was tall, standing at six-foot-six, with a muscular frame and the ability to move around the ring like someone half his size. But he was hampered from the off when he got saddled with the distasteful gimmick of Adam Bomb, purportedly a survivor of the Three Mile Island nuclear meltdown, which in reality didn't cause any casualties at all.

His name was a not so subtle play on "atom bomb", and he wore acid yellow contact lenses and had his trademark hold wittily renamed "The Meltdown" to complete the absurdity. As both a heel and a babyface he failed to get over, and had no protection in the booking or any sustained push to support him. Like over half of the other participants in the bout, he was no longer with the promotion by the time the 1996 version of the event rolled around.

The Harris twins, Ron and Don, were carved from a similarly imposing, hulking mould as Clarke, but they too were given a gimmick that ensured they would never get over beyond a certain level. In their case they were afro-haired Appalachian mountain men The Blu Brothers, another crude southern stereotype, managed by veteran booker and wrestler Wayne 'Dirty Dutch Mantel' Keown, who was recast as Uncle Zebekiah.

Brian Adams had wrestled for the WWF since 1990 as Crush, and had been repackaged, recycled and re-pushed a number of times. Vince persisted with Adams because he was well built, but also because he was very good friends with Mark Calaway. It didn't matter that Adams was notoriously bad in the ring, where sloppy and unconvincing martial arts moves and strained wooden selling characterised his matches; he was connected.

But even his friendship with Calaway couldn't save him when he was arrested at his home in Kona, Hawaii, a few weeks after the *Royal Rumble* appearance, for illegal possession of firearms, as well as for purchasing steroids. Adams was fired by McMahon immediately and wound up serving time in jail, before being welcomed back into the company in 1996 when the furore had died down.

OF THE remaining field, the only names considered to have a genuine chance of winning the battle royal were Shawn Michaels, Davey Boy Smith, Lex Luger, Owen Hart, and to a lesser extent King Kong Bundy and Bob Backlund, but everyone watching still realised that this was going to be Shawn's match.

Chris 'King Kong Bundy' Pallies, a four-hundred-and-fifty-pounder whose pale complexion and black singlet had led to manager-turned-commentator Bobby Heenan nicknaming him, "Shamu," after the famous SeaWorld killer whale, had previously worked for Vince in the eighties. He had been one of the top heels in the company, given storyline credit for crushing Hulk Hogan's ribs in an angle before putting him over in a poorly-received cage match in the main event of *WrestleMania 2*.

He put Hogan over again on *Saturday Night's Main Event* in 1988 and then left the territory. When he returned in 1994 he had a significantly reduced status, but still had a modicum of star power that was enough for him to be considered among the favourites in the Rumble. But while Bundy was still big, in his years away the big guys had got bigger, and he was only given three minutes in the match before being eliminated by the gargantuan Mabel, Vince's current lardy fascination.

Bob Backlund was another who had been a notable name in a long-forgotten era, having ruled the company as WWF Champion in the seventies and early eighties, playing the role of a clean-cut All-American babyface hero. But fans had grown tired of his act and had began to reject him, so Vince pulled the trigger on a shock title defeat to Iranian former Olympic power-lifter the Iron Sheik, in order to transition the belt to Hulk Hogan and kick-start the biggest boom period in WWF history to that point. Backlund wasn't happy with the changing of the guard and felt he had been disrespected, so left the WWF for nearly a decade.

A return in late 1992 when Vince was repositioning his talent and rebuilding a smaller roster didn't at first herald positive results, with the passé Backlund babyface character seeming completely at odds with the WWF of the time. His act no longer resonated with fans, many of whom had no idea who he was because they weren't even born when he was popular. A heel turn changed everything for Backlund, and he adopted a new wide-eyed, crazy, and delusional persona. It was a perfect fit for the modern WWF, even if his ring-style perhaps wasn't. Backlund got over so quickly as a heel and was so good in the role, that a nostalgic Vince put the WWF Championship on him again in late 1994, having him defeat Bret Hart in a long-winded encounter at *Survivor Series*.

But like the Iron Sheik had been when he beat him all those years ago, Backlund was merely a transitional champion, the guy used to transfer the belt from one babyface to another without having to create a divide in the audience. It was a role many had filled before, including famously Ivan Koloff in 1971 when he stunned Madison Square Garden by dethroning perennial champion Bruno Sammartino. That moment caused first an eerie silence amongst the sold out crowd, and then turned into a wake as women burst into tears as their shocked husbands tried to console them. The great Andre the Giant had played the role too, famously beating Hulk Hogan thanks to an evil referee storyline only to have the title stripped from him and put up in a tournament at *WrestleMania IV* that the increasingly popular Macho Man Randy Savage won. At that point, having the babyface Savage beat the all-conquering and still exceptionally popular Hogan would have been career suicide for him.

Unlike with Bruno's dethronement, there were no tears when Backlund dropped his newly won title to Diesel just three days after winning it. As soon as he was squashed by the seven-footer, Backlund's stock fell dramatically and he was only retained by the company to return favours and put others over. But on-screen he was still the previous champion, and it wasn't unrealistic to predict that he might at least come close to winning the *Royal Rumble* match, especially after having lasted sixty-one minutes in the 1993 version of the event. It wasn't to be, and Backlund's swift fall from grace was acutely highlighted when Lex Luger dumped him out of the match after just sixteen seconds.

Luger himself was on a comedown following his own failed push, but having co-won the bout last year with Bret Hart, there was a belief amongst some fans that he could repeat that success and go on to win it again. There was the possibility that Luger could turn heel and there would have been some mileage in a Diesel-Luger program after they had worked a series of matches the year previous that surpassed most expectations. That scenario never materialised, because as far as Vince was concerned Luger was yesterdays news, and he had no interest in pumping any more money into marketing him, when he had already decisively proven that he couldn't draw as hoped. Luger was given a twenty minute stint in the match and presented as a guy who might win it, but was dumped by Crush and Michaels at the end. Soon afterwards he was shifted into a tag team with Davey Boy Smith, far away from the main events.

The story was similar for Owen Hart, who had enjoyed a stellar 1994 and established himself as one of the company's best heels and one of its superior workers. He had spent the majority of the year contesting classic matches with his brother Bret, including a deceptively simple but wonderfully effective mat classic at *WrestleMania X*, and one of the most heralded cage matches of the era in a return at *SummerSlam*. But the defeats to Bret up and down the circuit had caused Owen to lose some of his steam, and fan perception was that he was a great wrestler who could hang with the stars, but was not able to beat them and be the top star himself.

Even so, Owen was considered one of the top guys in the match and probably the second favourite going in due to his heel status (with Diesel being a babyface, the odds were in favour of a heel victory as to not split the crowd again at *WrestleMania*). But like Backlund, Owen was only given mere seconds in the bout before he was eliminated, which to most seemed like a criminal misuse of a tremendous talent. Like Lex Luger, Owen's next move was into the tag team ranks, once again far away from the top of the card.

That left 'The British Bulldog', Davey Boy Smith, and the charismatic Shawn Michaels. Both had been fixtures in the WWF for some time and were long-established household names that the audience could get behind. The only issue was that either man winning potentially led to problems for Kevin Nash, because both were immensely popular.

Two-and-a-half years earlier Smith had headlined *SummerSlam* at Wembley Stadium in front of a legitimate 80,000 people against brother-in-law Bret Hart. Smith was on top of the world and had looked in good stead to become the first British World Champion since Billy Robinson, until he was fired two months later. The following year was spent working in WCW, and then he returned to the WWF in 1994, less over and relevant than he had ever been in his previous runs with the company, but still a favourite amongst many.

Michaels was positioned on television as a heel, but fan support for him had been swelling for years due to his exciting work, believable over-the-top persona and his immense charisma that shined through in everything he did. He also had previous with Diesel, who was first introduced to the company as his on-screen bodyguard, and later tag team partner, and the smart money was on a confrontation between the two at the biggest show of the year.

It was Shawn who came up with the idea of being in the match before anyone else as the number one entrant. Michaels was booked to go over, and he thought entering first made it look like he had no chance of winning, because no one had ever managed to do so from that spot before. Vince worried that there was a risk it would turn him fully babyface as the match wore on, due to his dogged tenacity and resiliency, but Shawn wore him down and he eventually agreed to do it. It was Pat Patterson, the architect of the match, who made the call for Davey Boy to be number two and for them to both survive until the very end, because that way the fans had a babyface going the distance who they could support, rather than being drawn into cheering for Shawn.

For the finish, Michaels wanted to do a risky stunt that would see Smith seemingly eliminate him with a clothesline and win the match, only for everyone to discover that he had held onto the top rope and prevented his feet from hitting the floor, and thus was still in the bout. Michaels would then pull himself back into the ring and dump Smith out to win the match. Vince was hesitant; he had tried a similar controversial finish the previous year with Lex Luger and Bret Hart, and it hadn't really worked. Rather than it splitting the crowd and making them take sides in support of both as he had hoped, instead they just cheered for Bret loudly and vociferously while passionately booing Luger, signalling the beginning of the end for his push as Vince's "next Hulk Hogan".

Vince didn't want any such confusion this year, but he trusted Pat and Shawn's judgement. If they were sure they could pull it off without making Shawn the babyface, and leaving no doubt as to who the winner was, he would go with it. The chairman was also worried about Michaels' proclivity for histrionics, concerned that if Shawn overdid the dramatics, he wouldn't be able to hold onto the ropes with his sweaty palms after having worked for over thirty minutes, and that the whole match would be ruined by a botched finish.

Michaels assured Vince it would be fine and that he could pull it off, and eventually he relented to Shawn, but warned him, "I know how you are Shawn, just hit with one foot and come right back up, forget about all the melodramatics. You don't have to go all the way with it, because if he hits you too hard and you can't control yourself..." Michaels was determined to steal the show and ignored McMahon's warning. He did the spot as dramatically as he possibly could, clinging to the top rope for dear life and writhing around, seemingly pitched in an intense battle of gravity versus muscle as he teased both feet touching the floor. He enjoyed the thought of Vince's face turning beetroot red with anger at his insolence, but also knew that he had made the moment far more exciting and memorable, and that by the time Vince caught up with him backstage he would have forgiven him for defying his wishes.

On television the finish came off even better than Shawn or Vince could have hoped, and having initially been cautious by only showing the wide shot at first, the director showed a slow-motion replay of the near elimination that captured the spot from a close-up angle, which assuaged any fears that Michaels had not executed it right. Meanwhile Shawn danced around the ring with an unimpressed Pamela Anderson, who was set to accompany the winner of the bout to *WrestleMania*.

Anderson simply rolled her eyes and got out of the way as Michaels gyrated in her direction, looking for all the world like she regretted signing up for the gig. Her demeanour behind the scenes was more accommodating. "She was a pro," remembered Tom Prichard, "She had her own dressing room, but she was happy to take pictures with the boys. I don't know that she knew too much about wrestling though, she was fairly hard to read."

Once the dust had settled on the *Royal Rumble*, the pieces were finally all in place for the charge towards *WrestleMania*, the biggest event on the WWF calendar. But getting to that point had been an ordeal; it had taken Vince months before he decided on the headline attraction for his annual spring-time blowout. When he finally settled on his feature contest he was elated; he felt he had just unlocked the door to the WWF's return to the big time.

FIVE

VINCE MADE SURE THAT IN its first decade *WrestleMania* always featured a hook to draw people in, making the event feel more important than the three-hundred to eight-hundred other live shows ran by the group each year. The first *WrestleMania* in 1985 had celebrities galore and a promotional hype that made it the absolute must-see event amongst the entertainment world's bourgeoisie, even if they had no real idea what the WWF was. Vince McMahon's brand of wrestling had simply become the "in thing" amongst the pop culture-influencing hipster crowd, and everyone clamoured to jump on the bandwagon and be a part of it.

Eager to better the inaugural show's success and maximise live gate revenue from the supershow in a pre-pay-per-view era, Vince made the bold decision to stage *WrestleMania 2* in three different venues. As well as three sets of gate receipts, the WWF was also able to garner publicity in three separate cities, and Vince chose his venues wisely in opting for the strong media markets of New York, Chicago, and Los Angeles. The venture was not without risks for McMahon, especially in an era of primitive technology; a single feed failing to work would have probably bankrupted his company. It was a risk that ultimately paid off and established the WWF as being ahead of its rivals, and at the forefront when it came to delivering incredible cutting edge production values and a big time spectacle.

Feeling invincible, Vince and the WWF were on a role by the time *WrestleMania III* came around in 1987. In order to prolong the unprecedented boom period his company was enjoying, Vince knew he had to go even further for that year's *WrestleMania* show, and so booked the gigantic Silverdome in Pontiac, Michigan. Despite the company's runaway success, many of Vince's closest confidants were privately concerned that the ballsy chairman had made one brash move too many. They worried over the possibility of the venue being only half full at best, and *WrestleMania III* labelled a failure, embarrassing the company on a global platform and thus halting their momentum.

Not only that, but they had the weather to deal with. In order that the majority of fans in attendance could actually see the matches, the WWF installed four giant screens to show the live action on, but weeks before the event the company received bad news: the screens wouldn't be visible until ninety minutes into the show due to the natural lighting in the building caused by the enormous transparent dome above. Officials and executives racked their brains to come up with solutions, from giant tarpaulins to painting the roof, with every possibility dismissed as infeasible.

Someone in the room finally asked the question, "What's the earliest time of day that the screens will be clearly visible?" Vince listened intently to the answer, and then his ears pricked up immediately when he heard the words, "If it's dark and cloudy, we will be fine." That was all McMahon needed to hear. He stood up triumphantly from his seat, slammed the desk with his hand and declared confidently, "Done! It'll rain. End of discussion!". Sure enough, the weather was overcast with rain come show day, leading some to suspect that McMahon may very well be either the luckiest man on earth, or that even Mother Nature was fearful of his legendary temper.

The historic card may not have legitimately had the 93,000 paid attendance that the company routinely claimed[22], but the Silverdome was undeniably jam-packed. In the ring there were a number of iconic moments, two of which remained at the forefront of WWF lore for years to come. The first was the legendary battle for the Intercontinental Championship between Ricky Steamboat and Randy Savage, and the second came in the main event between Hulk Hogan and Andre the Giant, two of the most notable and recognisable names in the business. The specific moment that would be repeated more than almost any other on WWF television was a monumental Hogan body slam on Andre, which generated a crowd response that shook the building. Hogan then delivered his trademark legdrop on the undefeated giant (according to the storyline, at least) and scored the clean pinfall victory, cementing him as the undisputed biggest star in wrestling.

Both *WrestleMania IV* and *WrestleMania V* were held at Donald Trump's distinctive Trump Plaza building. Though the shows looked impressive on television, the crowd consisted mostly of Atlantic City tourists who were there just for the occasion rather than because they were interested in the product, leading to a muted and unresponsive crowd. That in turn hurt the quality of the wrestling presented, with neither card having anything on offer approaching the quality of Steamboat-Savage. Nonetheless, there was still plenty that happened of significance, as *WrestleMania IV* hosted a one

---

[22] While in reality the WWF could have probably sold out the building twice due to the anticipation and hype for the show, the reality was that they sold 76,000 paid tickets. There were actually 78,000 in the building, but the extra 2,000 was papered, with tickets going to sponsors, friends and family, media, local schools, and various others partners that the WWF had.

night tournament for the vacant WWF Championship (won by Macho Man Randy Savage), and the following year saw Hogan regain his status as top dog in the company when he defeated Savage for the same belt in a culmination of a year-long feud, which had set box office records that still stood in 1995.

In 1990, the WWF took the show to Canada for the first time with *WrestleMania VI* at the SkyDome in Toronto, where a lacklustre card was headlined by a better than expected confrontation between the Federation's top two babyfaces, Hulk Hogan and The Ultimate Warrior. The match was supposed to be a passing of the torch to Warrior, with Hogan lying down for a clean defeat to Vince's next great hope, before riding off into the Hollywood sunset to make movies. It didn't quite turn out that way, but the show was still a huge success, drawing in excess of 67,000 people into the building and over 500,000 on pay-per-view.

The first cracks began showing in 1991, when poor ticket sales due to fan backlash against the WWF's distasteful practice of trying to capitalise on the real-life Gulf War with a Sgt. Slaughter Iraqi-sympathiser character, forced a venue change from the 100,000 seat Los Angeles Coliseum to the 16,000 capacity L.A. Sports Arena. Despite the reduced interest, the show delivered one of the most emotional storyline moments in the company's history, when estranged spouses Randy Savage and Miss Elizabeth reunited following Savage's defeat in an epic contest that was billed as a retirement match, to The Ultimate Warrior.

The 1992 event saw the city of Indianapolis host its first *WrestleMania* at the cavernous Hoosier Dome, where Hulk Hogan's swansong against Sid Justice headlined a card that also saw classic battles between Ric Flair and Randy Savage, and babyfaces Roddy Piper and Bret Hart. For many this was not what they expected, as long time fans were hoping for a dream encounter between NWA legend Flair, who had recently jumped ship to Titan, and WWF hero Hogan. A series of poorly received house show matches between the two had convinced Vince to change course, and the match never happened on pay-per-view in a WWF ring. It wasn't until 1994 that fans got their Flair-Hogan confrontation, only it was in Ted Turner's WCW. The match smashed all WCW pay-per-view records and set the company on a course that would eventually see them pull ahead of the WWF as the undisputed number one wrestling promotion in America for two years.

Aesthetically, *WrestleMania IX* was a triumph, with the WWF pulling out all the stops to create a memorable Roman-themed set at outdoor venue Caesar's Palace in Las Vegas, Nevada. But by now the sheen had come off the WWF thanks to the majority of the stars from the eighties having been moved on due to their ages or artificially enhanced physiques. Unable to push or even use inflated monsters anymore, Vince instead turned to guys who were simply big without the bodies. Two of the feature performers on the card were just that; one was the five-hundred pounds Yokozuna. Despite only having debuted on television five months earlier, he was in the main event with reliable technician Bret Hart, the man who had carried the company for the past six months.

The second was the uncoordinated seven-foot-six Jorge Gonzalez, a former basketball player for the Argentine national team who was once on the books for the Atlanta Hawks. Vince clad him in a bodysuit with painted-on abs and fur covering his groin, renaming him Giant Gonzalez. He stumbled around the ring with The Undertaker in something that almost resembled a wrestling match, in a bout heavily criticised by industry writers as among the worst in the history of the annual super-show. The event was panned by critics; *The Wrestling Observer* called it, "A *WrestleMania* that promised little on paper and delivered even less." It had now become apparent to most that the glory days of the Federation were well and truly over.

In 1994, *WrestleMania* finally returned "home" to Madison Square Garden for the tenth anniversary of the event, and at that point was considered by observers to be the best show the WWF had ever produced from an in-ring point of view. Real life brothers Bret Hart and Owen Hart opened the card with a beautifully crafted technical masterpiece, only to be surpassed later in the night by Scott Hall and Shawn Michaels. The Kliq allies stole the show in the WWF's first ever pay-per-view ladder match, which *The Wrestling Observer* described as thus:

> Shawn Michaels put on one of the greatest individual performances in the history of the business at *WrestleMania X* in New York's Madison Square Garden, to highlight what the consensus is the best pay-per-view show in WWF history. Michaels, in one of his last shows with the company before going on a what is planned to be a several month long sabbatical, put on a performance that left just about everyone in wrestling in awe in his ladder match loss to Razor Ramon. The match, probably the best match ever on a WWF pay-per-view show, somehow overshadowed one of the greatest matches in WWF history between Bret Hart and Owen Hart that opened the show, and a WWF title change with Bret's later regaining of the WWF title from Yokozuna in an average match in the evening's finale.

ON THE drawing board, *WrestleMania XI* had nothing like that to distinguish itself, and the 15,000 capacity Hartford Civic Center in Connecticut was hardly befitting the biggest show of the year. The venue had been chosen partly because the Titan offices were located in Connecticut and it was technically the company's base state, even though they were more closely linked with New York. The more cynical observers viewed the decision to go with Connecticut as more a transparent attempt to siphon some of the publicity from the Special Olympics - which would take place in the state over the summer - by linking *WrestleMania* with the event.

Vince thought the tie-in would give the WWF a level of mainstream acceptance they otherwise lacked, and that being associated with the games would go some way towards rebuilding their battered reputation. Many entities, including the games themselves, were still reluctant to get into bed with the WWF after the bad PR the company had endured in the first half of the decade. Mindful of the ill-feeling and residual resentment that still lingered following the steroid trial, the WWF made sure to highlight their new stringent substance abuse policy at the press conference hyping the show.

With the roster the WWF had in 1995 the weakest and most bereft of star power in years, concern grew within the company that *WrestleMania* didn't look like it was going to have the feel of being something special for the first time in the show's history. Vince was not confident that his proposed main event of Diesel against Shawn Michaels had the ability to pull a strong pay-per-view number on its own. It was a blow to their egos but an understandable decision based on recent live event numbers, even to Shawn, who like everyone else, could see that business was down.

Not wanting his biggest show of the year to fail, Vince searched for a solution, then did what he had always done when his talent pool needed a boost in drawing-power; he brought in outsiders. *WrestleMania XI* became the most celebrity-heavy card since the early days of the show, with former Super Bowl winner and NFL great Lawrence Taylor positioned as the main attraction. Taylor was paid in the region of $150,000 (claimed to be $1 million at the time) to not only work a match, but to headline the show opposite burly tattoo-headed veteran Scott 'Bam Bam' Bigelow, following their ringside clash at the *Royal Rumble*. In addition, Pamela Anderson would be there to fulfil her own commitment to the company that had also started at the January pay-per-view, as well as a number of other television stars that Vince perceived as being bigger mainstream names than his depleted roster.

Lawrence Taylor's involvement was set up initially by Lex Luger, who had first pitched the idea of him coming to the WWF during a charity golf game. Taylor took the proposal seriously, and Vince loved the idea because of the potential for mainstream coverage. He also saw it as a chance for the WWF to further rebuild its image nationally after the very public lynching the company had endured for the past four years. According to opponent Bam Bam Bigelow, the real reason that Taylor agreed to participate in the event would not have been in line with the company's new clean image at all. "He was just there for the money. He was all messed up on drugs and needed the million dollars (sic) that Vince was going to pay him," Bigelow claimed.

The show was sold firmly on the involvement of Taylor, and Vince hoped that the media buzz generated by having him wrestle a match for the group would inject the company with a desperately needed awareness boost, much like having Mr. T, Cyndi Lauper, Liberace and Muhammad Ali involved with *WrestleMania* in 1985 had done. The WWF attempted to use Taylor to give champion Diesel the celebrity endorsement, but it didn't work. Wrote Dave Meltzer in *The Wrestling Observer Newsletter* at the time:

> The WWF had Taylor attempt to get Diesel over as an athlete and get the rub as a celebrity, largely the same way they created Hulk Hogan as something more than a top drawing wrestler by getting the rub off Cyndi Lauper and Mr. T in 1984. The difference, of course, being Hogan was an incredible drawing card as a wrestler in the AWA and with New Japan, whereas Diesel isn't one yet despite a WWF mega-push.

Rather than getting on board with the latest champion, the press were far more interested in the fact that Titan had lost Hulk Hogan to WCW the previous year. The WWF responded with overkill, drafting in six more footballers to serve as corner-men for Taylor in his match, with Reggie White, Ricky Jackson, Ken Norton, Jr., Steve 'Mongo' McMichael[23], Carl Banks and Chris Spielman all signed on to appear at the show. Vince theorised that using the mass of football players would help the WWF gain acceptance in the sports community, but that was never likely to happen. Wrestling was still viewed as having an audience primarily filled with idiots,

---

[23] McMichael went on to become a full-time wrestler in WCW, where he captured secondary title belts and was even given a berth in Ric Flair's Four Horsemen stable.

inbreeds and undesirables, and the dedicated sports media had no intention of giving it coverage past criticising Taylor's involvement.

The mainstream press certainly covered L.T.'s role at *WrestleMania XI* though, with heavy hitters such as *Sports Illustrated* and *USA Today* running stories about Taylor's foray into the world of sports entertainment. But WWF officials were distressed and disappointed to see the way his participation was viewed. Dave Anderson of the *New York Times,* one of the country's most renowned sports writers, derided pro wrestling and its performers as being actors rather an athletes, referring to them as con-artists who practiced the art of deception. Of Taylor he wrote:

> Taylor is accepting permanent damage to his dignity, the dignity that dominated his career as a Giants linebacker. For all his sacks, no quarterback ever accused him of a cheap shot. But now he'll be involved in a cheap stunt that evolved from his ringside presence at the *Royal Rumble* wrestling show in Tampa in January.

Even more critical was *Newsday's* Bob Glauber, whose article was later picked up and syndicated nationally by the *Los Angeles Times.* He declared that Taylor's involvement in *WrestleMania* would be, "The most embarrassing moment in his life," and that it would turn him into, "Just another pathetic figure in the world of sports." Long-serving WWF Director of Promotion Basil V. DeVito, Jr. later commented, "The reaction from the press was unduly harsh. It was as if Lawrence had personally disappointed the writers, editors and broadcasters who control the media in this country. They branded him a loser... which was completely unfair."

What the media didn't pick up on was that Taylor had been involved in wrestling before. In 1991, when he was still an active football player, L.T. participated in an angle for WCW thanks to a deal orchestrated by Paul Heyman and Jim Ross. The appearance saw Taylor paid $10,000 to second Lex Luger in what was billed as a "Football Match" against Curtis Hughes, during an event on January 11th at a snowstorm-hit Nassau Coliseum in East Rutherford, New Jersey. Taylor's appearance came just two days before his Giants defeated the Bears in an NFC championship game, and two weeks later he helped his team win the Super Bowl.

No one made any mention of that in the stories about *WrestleMania,* with the WWF not about to acknowledge that their rivals had used Taylor first, and the media just not that interested. Even though Taylor's WCW stint obviously did nothing to cheapen or diminish his subsequent football success, the press had their narrative and they were sticking to it; Taylor was blemishing his legacy and risking his football Hall of Fame status by becoming a wrestler, even for just one night.

Irrespective of the derision he received from the sports media, in the WWF, Taylor was accepted by the wrestlers in the locker-room. Most didn't resent an outsider coming in and taking the lucrative money spot on the biggest show of the year, because they assumed he would make everyone on the card a bigger star simply by association - and more than likely, the increased draw would improve their respective pay-checks. As Jim Cornette noted, "It wasn't like it was Jay Leno, or even Mr. T coming in. Taylor was a legitimate Hall of Fame quality athlete and a worldwide household name. He was huge in pro football, so he brought a lot of publicity and notoriety. When it is someone of that level coming in, the guys usually give athletes like that passes. Most are marks for football anyway!"

THE EVENING before *WrestleMania*, Vince sent a memo around that instructed his entire crew to convene first thing in the morning at the arena. There were predictable grumblings, with the performers unhappy that their night of pre-show decadence would have to be cut short because of the early wake-up call. The unofficial rule amongst many of the boys was that when it came to doing pay-per-view, having a hangover was a prerequisite because it made you sulky and focussed. Of course, the risk was that someone would go too far and be in no condition to perform come show time, but Vince's meeting made sure there would be little chance of that. Sure enough, everyone was accounted for on that dreary Sunday morning, tired, but for the most part sober.

The boys sat with sunglasses covering their heavy eyes, sipping black coffee from the local Starbucks while wondering what was so urgent that Vince had dragged them out of bed at the crack of dawn. Those who had known McMahon for a while had a good inkling; the meeting wasn't about anything at all. It was simply a front to keep everyone in check and make sure there were no major problems caused by someone having a little too much fun the night before the biggest show of the year. "I betcha Vince doesn't even show," whispered Paul Bearer to no one in particular, and sure enough, he didn't. Instead J.J. Dillon wandered into the room, and told the amassed throng that Vince wasn't coming, but he just wanted to tell them all to have a good show. It was classic McMahon; keeping his troops in check and running things from afar under his authoritarian rule.

THE THEME of the show was made abundantly clear by the opening video, which highlighted the celebrities who had appeared on previous

WrestleMania events, but didn't show a second of wrestling. Footage was then shown of the copious celebrities involved in the evening's event, with no mention made at all of the matches taking place.

It wasn't a celebrity as such who fulfilled the annual show-opening tradition of singing *America The Beautiful,* but rather blind Special Olympian Kathy Huey who was given the task. She offered up a warbling and nervous rendition of the emotive song, while the WWF laid it on thick in the background by airing a video highlighting some of the athletes appearing at the games. Hartford was respectful of Huey and applauded her following the performance, but not everyone was impressed with the shameless pandering. As Ryan Dilbert from *The Bleacher Report* put it:

> The WWF selecting a Special Olympian to sing *America The Beautiful* made it feel like they were trying too hard to look good-hearted. It just ended up being awkward.

The in-ring action began with the muscle-bound duo of Lex Luger and Davey Boy Smith teaming up as the Allied Powers. Both used the patriotism card as part of their acts, and due to the well-documented real-life political union between the United States and the United Kingdom, they were a logical pairing. Their opponents were the Harris twins, still doing their dated Blu Brothers gimmick. Luger was looking less motivated than at any other point previously in his WWF run; he was going through the motions and riding out his contract, something which would become significant as the year played out. The result of Luger's apathy, Smith's relatively lowly status, and the lumbering nature of the Harris brothers, was a dreary opening contest that served to aptly set the scene for one of the most disappointing and underwhelming *WrestleMania* shows of all time.

THE LATEST monster heel for The Undertaker character to slay was a nod to the past, with *WrestleMania 2* headliner King Kong Bundy used to put him over. For Mark Calaway it continued an as yet unheralded kayfabe winning streak at *WrestleMania,* which would go on to become one of the supercard's biggest selling points until it was finally snapped by Brock Lesnar at *WrestleMania XXX* nearly twenty years later. Turning over every rock in an effort to revive his ailing brand, Vince had brought back a series of stars from the company's boom years, with Bundy joining the likes of Nikolai Volkoff, Bob Backlund, The Barbarian (now known as Sione) and Bam Bam Bigelow[24] in making a mockery of the WWF's latest marketing slogan: *The New Generation.*

Calaway's Undertaker was very much at the forefront of that movement. His act was pure theatre, an enduring persona that never should have lasted on paper because of how outlandish a premise it was (a wrestling zombie), but had developed into one of the characters most synonymous with Vince's sports entertainment brand. With each passing year the WWF had moved further and further away from the athletic, realistic sporting contests of the past put forth by Messrs. Steamboat, Sammartino and Flair, with the emphasis geared firmly towards pure unadulterated "sports entertainment".

The term was Vince's euphemism to describe the nature of his business, which he had coined in order to avoid paying the excessive fees demanded by perfunctory, superfluous athletic commissions. By dismissing the notion that wrestling was a sport, and instead openly admitting it was pre-determined entertainment, he saved himself millions of dollars per year. It mattered little to him that the shroud of kayfabe was now lost forever and that old-school promoters and performers were up in arms about his flippant disregard for the traditions of the business, and calling for his head. He didn't care; they were a dying breed and the company's bottom line was more important than continuing to pretend what they did was real.

This shift in ideals was acutely encapsulated by The Undertaker character, whose ring entrance was becoming more lavish and dramatic each year. That night he walked to the ring accompanied as always by manager Paul Bearer, swathed in a blanket of darkness. The occasional spark of simulated lightning provided courtesy of the special effects team, intermittently bathed the entire building in a brilliant blue and white glow, providing an intimidating visual of the cloaked leviathan slowly walking to the ring with an unmoveable conviction. Bundy feigned fear when The Undertaker flung his arms into the air and magically caused the lights in the Hartford Civic Center to flicker back on, as his manager Ted DiBiase clung desperately onto the gold urn that he had stolen from the ghoulish duo. It was WWF theatre at its finest, a demonstration of presentation unrivalled in spectacle.

Spectacle is exactly what McMahon had envisioned in pitting the two behemoths against each other, but unfortunately fans had already seen the most captivating portion of the contest by the time the first bell rang. Limited in what they could do due to their collective girth, the pair struggled to sustain audience interest for the duration of their brief six-minute contest. They opted for a simple story of strength and size against speed and agility, before returning to the theatrics when The Undertaker

---

[24] They would be followed in the next twelve months by Dan Spivey, Jake Roberts, The Ultimate Warrior and Marty Jannetty.

retrieved his urn from DiBiase and with it the supposed magical powers that it granted him. Paul Bearer cradled the reclaimed trinket like a precious newborn, removing the lid to reveal a beam of weak white light that emitted from a small torch concealed inside.

This was the cue for the arrival of another of DiBiase's charges, the six-foot-six Charles Wright. A heavily tattooed former bar tender and real-life good friend of Calaway, Wright was in his second spell with the company after a failed run as Baron Samedi-inspired voodoo practitioner Papa Shango. After plans for the Shango character to return were nixed, instead Wright was repackaged as Kama Mustafa, an ultimate fighter based on UFC star Kimo, as the WWF looked to capitalise on the increasing popularity of the fledgling MMA group. Wright's task was to set up a future program with Calaway, and he did so by kicking Paul Bearer in his pudgy gut and making off with the same urn that the manager had just salvaged.

In the ring, Bundy was running out of ideas and threw a series of weak-looking clotheslines, a move used by both repeatedly already. Struggling for breath, he applied a chinlock so he could discreetly lean into Calaway's ear and ask for advice. Calaway knew the bout wasn't going well and was eager to put it out of its misery. "Just take it home," he told Bundy, wrestling terminology for ending the match.

Bundy followed the instruction and allowed Calaway to fight back, then led him to the corner, the starting point for them to begin the pre-planned end sequence that they had discussed earlier in the locker-room. Bundy charged and connected with a splash, but Calaway shook off the effects of the blow as if he had become invulnerable to pain. Bundy feigned shock and charged at him again, but this time was met with a size seventeen boot to the chin that caused him to stumble and stagger, before he allowed Calaway to slam him to the canvas. Unable to do his Tombstone piledriver finishing move due to Bundy's mass, Calaway instead fittingly finished him off with the most popular move of the match; the clothesline. If ever there was a perfect example of match quality not meaning a thing to McMahon compared with razzmatazz, it was this one.

Calaway's initial program at the show was not originally set to be with Bundy at all, as early plans called for an encounter against Scott Hall's Razor Ramon character. McMahon first pitched the idea to Hall in November the night after *Survivor Series*, laying out all the proposed matches on the *WrestleMania* card before giving Scott the big reveal, "I got it! Razor Ramon will go one-on-one with... The Undertaker... at *WrestleMania*!" he said, trying to give the impression that the idea had just come to him there and then in a eureka moment. Hall was pleased; he knew that working against Calaway would mean a heel turn and a rejuvenation of his stale babyface character. As a fan favourite, Hall had taken the gimmick as high up the card as he could, but with Nash as the babyface champion and he as a heel, there was potential for a top level feud against his Kliq buddy, and the chance to make genuine main event money for the first time in his career.

Things got further than the planning stage, with a series of never-aired vignettes filmed during Calaway and Hall's days off that would be used to generate interest in the program on television, one of which saw Razor thrown into an open grave by The Undertaker after arrogantly predicting victory when they clashed. The storyline was supposed to kick off around the *Royal Rumble*, but out of the blue Vince changed his mind - as he had a tendency to do - and dropped the whole thing. "I remember blowing a gasket at Vince, he pissed us both off mightily," recalled Hall, "That could have been a match for the ages; two big, strong, agile guys who could work and bump with the best of them. We even had the match planned out, we were ready."

Instead Hall ended up in yet another encounter against perennial storyline nemesis Jeff Jarrett, in a rerun of a match the two had done hundreds of times already. Hall was apathetic about working with Jarrett again, realising that while he remained in the WWF he was doomed to play the role of the guy who got beat by the top guys, rather than being *the* top guy. He would later describe his performance against Jarrett that night as, "Half-assed and unprofessional," because Vince's change of heart had continued to bother him.

Little did McMahon realise that his decision to change everything on a whim in order to accommodate the mammoth Bundy, would have far greater long-lasting effects that he could have ever imagined.

MIRED IN the middle of the card in an uninspired submission-only clash with forty-five-year-old veteran Bob Backlund, was former two-time WWF Champion Bret Hart. Having lost the title to Backlund back in November, it was Backlund's turn to repay the loss to Hart, but the Hitman would have preferred to not do the match at all. "I was dreading my match with Bob because I knew Vince's idea that the two of us would only use submission holds was guaranteed to stink the building out," he commented.

Also involved in the match was Roddy Piper, headliner at the inaugural *WrestleMania* event. His last appearance for the company had been in an outdated and poorly received match against fellow forty-something Jerry Lawler at *King of the Ring* the previous June, but here he was just playing the role of referee. Hart was close with Piper after Roddy had done the honours for him in a very rare pinfall defeat three years earlier, but that still didn't appease Hart, who complained about his involvement. "The match deteriorated into a farce because Piper kept asking, 'What do ya say?' and it made the match comical. I didn't want anyone making my matches funny except me." The bout was one of Hart's weakest major outings in some years, with Bret going a step further and describing it as, "Without a doubt, my worst pay-per-view match ever."

The contest also marked Backlund's final pay-per-view singles outing for the WWF. Vince realised that Bob was better served as a non-wrestling personality than an active performer, thanks in part to some leaning from The Kliq. The group's problem with Backlund stemmed from a series of matches between he and Kevin Nash. The two worked the circuit shortly after Nash had won the WWF Championship, and as the heel and the veteran, it was down to Backlund to call the matches. Nash soon became frustrated with Bob's erratic calling of inappropriately placed holds that made him look foolish, and with their complete lack of chemistry together.

Nash remembered one such example where Backlund called for him to do a sunset flip, a move more commonly associated with fiery babyfaces six-foot and under, as it involves the person doing the move flipping over the back of his opponent and rolling him into a pin. For a giant like Kevin Nash, it looked phony and ridiculous. When Nash got backstage he was immediately chewed out by a watching Mark Calaway, who warned him to never do the move again. Bob's problem was that he was set in his ways and had a specific match that he liked to wrestle, and was unwilling to change it or vary it even slightly when he worked with different opponents. In the seventies and eighties it wasn't a problem, but in the WWF circus of the nineties where the performers ranged from expert mat wrestling technicians to gimmick-heavy comedy acts, all the way up to five-hundred-pound behemoths, his approach was never going to fly.

Prior to *WrestleMania* The Kliq had already convinced McMahon to stop running Diesel-Backlund bouts on the house shows, with group ally Jeff Jarrett inserted into the matches in his place. Backlund got shifted to bouts with Scott Hall, but The Kliq didn't want to work with him full stop. Hall decreed that it was impossible to get a match out of Backlund and while he didn't refuse to work with him, he did ask for assistance. It was duly provided, with veteran Dick Murdoch drafted in to act as Backlund's second, giving Razor an extra personality to play off.

Having returned the favour and done the honours for Hart at *WrestleMania*, Backlund was used increasingly sparingly from that point onwards. He spent the rest of the year on the non-televised spot shows, exchanging wins with newcomer Man Mountain Rock over the summer and then putting over the 1-2-3 Kid and Savio Vega as the year closed out. By the end of 1995, his career as an active performer was all but finished.

THERE WAS much anticipation amongst fans for the WWF Tag Team Championship match, regarding who challenger Owen Hart's mystery partner would be against champions The Smoking Gunns. Owen was on a storyline quest to top his brother Bret by repeating all of his past feats but doing them better. For his character the starting point was the tag titles, like it had been for Bret way back in 1987, but behind the veil of kayfabe Owen knew what it really was; demotion. He had been a headliner the year before, but his stock had fallen with too many defeats, as Vince never fully believed in him as a top guy due to his average stature. Nevertheless, Owen was fully committed to the reduced role he found himself in, and continued to perform at his remarkably high standard.

Much like The Undertaker-Bundy confrontation, the bout on paper had a very different complexion as the card was originally being formulated. Talk at one point was that Owen would work opposite Davey Boy Smith in a one-on-one encounter, and in keeping with the storyline Owen would be looking to beat Smith on the big stage, because Bret had lost to him famously at Wembley in 1992. The tag title match would have instead seen the incumbent Gunns defend the belts against Men on a Mission, who would have likely lifted the titles after turning heel. Vince changed his mind and decided he didn't want to put the belts on the duo, because he looked at Mabel and saw a bigger picture; he wanted him to have a run as a top singles heel. Things were shuffled and Men on a Mission didn't even make it onto the show, whereas Owen was given the mystery partner stipulation to add intrigue.

There was talk within the industry of the role going to Canadian-born Japanese wrestling standout Chris Benoit, who was tearing up rings in ECW and winning over legions of fans with his tight, smooth and believable ring work. But it was just wishful thinking on the part of many who wanted to see Benoit working at a higher level, and he was never considered for the spot.

A few months later, Bret Hart did actually get Benoit a series of tryout matches with the company, and he put forth impressive showings in his matches with Bob Holly, Adam Bomb and Owen Hart, but Pat Patterson and Jim Ross both turned down the chance to sign him. Bret was shocked, especially with Vince desperate for talent, and couldn't understand why he wouldn't hire Benoit on the spot.[25] The reason was obvious to others;

Benoit wasn't six-foot tall and he wasn't charismatic. While he was well put-together, an exceptional in-ring technician, possessed a steely-eyed stare and a wicked sneer, he wasn't what Vince perceived a WWF Superstar to be.

Instead of Benoit, the role went to the returning Rodney Anoa'i. After a few years on top, his Yokozuna act had worn thin and Anoa'i increasingly struggled with his weight. He was taken off TV in November of 1994, written out of the storylines after The Undertaker had stuffed him in a casket at *Survivor Series*.

Anoa'i was given time off to reduce his ballooning weight, which had seen him go from a big guy who could move around at a decent pace in 1992, to a dangerously obese mass of skin and blubber. Yokozuna's return put to rest any rumours of him being on the verge of signing for WCW, but also caused many to question just what he had really been doing with his five months out, as he returned looking bigger than ever before. But Anoa'i wasn't punished for wasting six months of resources and time, and he and Owen defeated the Gunns in a brief encounter. Like Owen, Anoa'i also considered it something of a demotion, having held the WWF Championship for nine months between June 1993 and March 1994. He assumed it to be the work of The Kliq trying to keep him away from the top spots.

TRADITIONALLY THE WWF title match would close out the show, but this year it was relegated to the middle of the card thanks to the involvement of Taylor. It was the only time other than 1992 that the belt had been on the line at *WrestleMania* but not contested in the main event, and in that instance it was only because of Hulk Hogan's much ballyhooed swansong and The Ultimate Warrior's surprise return to the company after seven months in exile. It was a bitter pill to swallow for Kliq allies Shawn Michaels and Kevin Nash, with Nash in particular irritated that the hype for the show centred around Taylor-Bigelow rather than he and Shawn. "We should have closed the show because we were the title match. It was not like [it was] one of the boys coming back, and no one knew what kind of match they (Bigelow and Taylor) were gonna have," he complained.

---

[25] Benoit eventually signed on with the WWF in 2000 after walking out of WCW alongside Dean Malenko, Eddie Guerrero, and Perry Saturn. By then he was generally regarded as one of the best wrestlers on the planet, and had significantly bulked up in size to the point that he looked far more like a "WWF Superstar" than he had in 1995. Vince remained reluctant to push Benoit, but he got over based on his ring work, despite his charisma deficiency, and was afforded a WWE World Title run in 2004, winning the belt in the main event of *WrestleMania XX*.

From an entertainment standpoint the Michaels-Diesel contest was easily the best wrestling match on the show, but Vince had reservations about even booking the program between the two in the first place. "Vince was concerned about whether I could draw people to watch me," remembered Michaels. As usual with Vince it came down to the issue of size, with McMahon not convinced that fans would buy into Michaels as a heel against the near seven-foot Diesel, and would respond in his favour as the underdog babyface.

Believing he needed help getting the fans to boo Michaels, Vince decided to bring in another monster to act as Shawn's bodyguard, the same thing Nash had been tasked with when he first signed on as Diesel. After racking his brain looking for a suitable person to play the role, Vince was eventually pressured by The Kliq to rehire Sidney Eudy, previously known to WWF fans as Sid Justice. The Kliq wanted Sid for the gig because as Nash pointed out, "I always got along with Sid, I thought he was money."

Money or not, Vince had reservations about working with Eudy again following a fractious business relationship in 1992 that ended with Sid walking out of the WWF, rather than facing suspension for a drug test failure. In some ways Vince was relieved about that. He had grown frustrated with Eudy, having offered him the chance to step into Hulk Hogan's role as the company's number one babyface, only for Sid to decline and cite his preference for being a heel. "It's hard to come back from that. Vince offered Sid the keys to the kingdom and he turned him down," commented Kevin Nash, who believed Vince had given up on Sid at that point.

In the years since, Sid had returned to WCW working under his previous moniker of Sid Vicious, but he was fired after an ugly incident in Blackburn, England involving Martin Lunde, who everyone on the inside and outside of the business knew as Arn Anderson. Eudy and Anderson had gotten into a drunken disagreement that escalated far beyond normal wrestling arguments, and the night ended with Anderson having lost a pint of blood as a result of Sid repeatedly stabbing him in the back, chest and throat with a pair of scissors. It had been headline news in the UK tabloids, and when the word made it back to America, newly appointed WCW Vice President Eric Bischoff had no option but to terminate Eudy's contract. Bischoff immediately cancelled all plans that were in place for Sid to be pushed as the next major star in the company and dethrone Leon 'Vader' White to win the WCW Championship at *Starrcade,* instead turning to the ever reliable Ric Flair. It was another case of Eudy being his own worst enemy, and he had once again cost himself a run as top guy in a company.

The bad press and Sid's unstable reputation worried Vince. He had already been through enough negative media reports to last him a lifetime, and the last thing he wanted was any more headaches in his locker-room. But as was frequently the case, the political power of The Kliq proved too much for him to resist. "We had to lobby to get Sid in," recalled Nash, "He'd had the problem with Arn and he had that loose cannon reputation." Vince eventually agreed to the deal, realising that it solved his *WrestleMania* problem of Michaels coming off as the underdog and potentially getting cheered, but he warned Nash and Michaels, "You guys deal with him. If you want him as part of your program then you guys can deal with him."

Not everyone was happy about Sid being given yet another chance in the business, especially those who were friends with Anderson and had heard about the stabbing incident. Ted DiBiase counted Arn among his closest friends, and was distressed when he learned that Eudy would be rejoining the Federation's ranks. When he was then informed that Vince wanted him to serve as Sid's advisor and mentor both on the road and in the ring, he was aghast. DiBiase protested and flat out told agents that he would have no part of it, but he knew that once Vince's mind was made up, there was little that could be done to change it. Despite his protests DiBiase did go on the road with Eudy, and even ended up managing him on television. He would later take credit for Sid's marked improvement as a performer that eventually saw him reach the level of WWF Champion in late 1996.

Even with Sid in his corner, Michaels realised that it would be a tough sell getting the fans to believe he could dominate Diesel for long periods of their match, and that he would have to adjust the way he worked accordingly. "I couldn't just go out there and beat him up, nobody would buy that," Shawn remarked, "Instead I chopped him down and *then* I beat him up. It worked, and a lot of people say it was one of his best matches. I take that as a huge compliment."

As good as the contest was, there were still problems with it, not least with Vince's insistence on directing the two performers. McMahon asked them to do a spot where Michaels would hit his superkick finisher, but for Nash to kick out strong after a one count, rather than selling the move and building the drama with a late kickout just before three. Shawn and Nash were both against the idea because they thought the fans would see through it for what it was; Vince pushing Diesel down their throats too hard and fast. The duo had seen it happen before when Vince had tried the same tactic with Lex Luger in the role of the company-ordained babyface hero. But Vince was adamant so they had little choice but to run with the spot, and as they had predicted, the fans hated it.

"I knew it," grumbled Nash as boos echoed around the Hartford Civic Center. Michaels had expected the reaction too and without missing a beat he called for Nash to do a laboured kick out on the next pinfall attempt. Nash did as he was told, and the crowd responded favourably to the near fall. Despite the attempted save, the damage had already been done, and when Nash drilled Michaels with his powerbomb finisher and beat him, the crowd booed the result. The two were annoyed and frustrated when they stepped back through the curtain, and complained to Vince about it after the show. "Yep, bad call," conceded McMahon casually when he caught up with them later on.

While the match was generally praised by wrestling critics, many of the other boys were unhappy with the performance of Michaels, believing that he had purposely overshadowed Nash in the match and tried to make him look bad, pulling subtle tricks like intentionally not taking his moves correctly, purposely trying to *blow him up* (wrestling vernacular for tiring him out) and selling to such a degree that he would generate sympathy and get cheered. "Shawn played Kevin, he went out of his way to outshine him," claimed Bret Hart, "All anyone would remember was Shawn Michaels, which was clearly what Shawn [had] intended all along." Nash felt the same way, but was not surprised by his friend's behaviour, "I knew Shawn was gonna try and blow me up and try to outperform me, because he wanted my spot. We were best friends, but I knew what his motivations were," he theorised.

Some also questioned Shawn's uncharacteristically sloppy bump from Nash's powerbomb finisher, with Michaels over-rotating and almost landing on his feet rather than his back, significantly lessening the impact of the move, and making Nash look foolish to the casual fans in the audience who didn't understand the mechanics of the business or its cooperative nature. Nash mused, "Shawn could have stood and took a powerbomb without anyone even giving it to him better than the one he took in that match. There was no animosity though, that's just the shark environment. It was still business and Shawn wanted that spot. Everyone knew that Shawn was lobbying for that spot, but I was still the biggest guy, so Vince didn't care because he still thought it was a big man's sport."

BAM BAM Bigelow had known he was losing to Lawrence Taylor in the much hyped and publicised main event well in advance; he had agreed to it when Vince first pitched the bout to him. He didn't like it one bit because he knew a lot of people were going to see him lose to a football player, but he justified it with the thought of his six-figure pay-off. Rather than being excited at the prospect of his career skyrocketing after a *WrestleMania* main event, Bigelow was in a bad mood in the months leading up to the contest, worried about letting the company and himself down on the biggest stage in wrestling by having a bad match. He needed to live up to the hype and was under a lot of pressure to do so.

It wasn't an entirely unfamiliar pressure though. In 1988 Bigelow was asked to work with Russian freestyle wrestling champion Salman Hashimikov in New Japan Pro Wrestling, and do what amounted to teach him on the job. Hashimikov had never even seen a worked wrestling match prior to agreeing to compete for the Japanese outfit, so Bigelow was cautious when he accepted, realising the strong reputation he had built for himself in Japan could be in jeopardy if they had a poor outing. They didn't, and while short, the bout in fact came off well. Bigelow received a lot of deserved credit for pulling it off, and the experience made him a perfect choice to square off with Taylor seven years later.

In the weeks leading up to the *WrestleMania* showdown, an increasingly concerned Bigelow confided in Taylor that he didn't want to be embarrassed and told him that it would be in his best interests to take his training for the match seriously. Taylor had no intention of looking foolish either and he agreed, spending hours at a time being put through the paces and learning the bare minimum required to put together a semi-decent match. He worked with Bigelow on designing spots, listening intently to the veteran wrestler as he was told what to do and how to do it.

Bigelow was more confident in their ability to have a reasonable match when it came to the day of the showdown, but before the bout he still took Taylor to one side and warned him that if he screwed up or tried to make him look bad, he was going to forcibly *call an audible* (change the finish) while they were in the ring.

Bigelow stomped to the ring with little sign of nerves or apprehension, taking the opportunity to frighten the life out of female pop group Salt n Peppa by taking off his jacket and lunging menacingly towards them as they watched from the aisle-adjacent stage. Taylor too carried himself with an aloof confidence as he walked purposefully to the ring. He was met with a favourable response from the Hartford audience, who showed no signs of resenting a non-wrestler working in the main event at the biggest show of the year.

Both milked a pre-bell stare-down for all it was worth, soaking in the spectacle and the grandeur of the moment as dozens of flashbulbs went off in the background, preserving the image in time and providing the mass of media in attendance with something they could print in the next day's papers.

When the bell eventually rang, Taylor reared back and slapped Bigelow as hard as he could. Backstage before the match various wrestlers had offered him morsels of advice, and one thing he remembered being told was that it was better to connect with Bigelow for real than miss something or make it look hokey and fake, and he took the advice to heart. The crowd loved it, and were equally thrilled with Taylor bouncing Bigelow off the canvas with a hard forearm, a knee to the face and a Biel throw across the ring. Bigelow was there for every step, and shouted out the next move to Taylor while he stood and sold with his head in his hands. The former linebacker heard the call and did as he was told, throwing his arm out to clothesline Bigelow, who then made it look vicious by flinging himself backwards over the top rope.

When they got going again, Taylor proved once more that he had been paying attention during his secret pre-show training sessions in Stamford, hitting a smoothly executed bulldog and some ferocious looking forearms. When it came time to sell, Taylor did a capable job of that too, though he fired up a little too often for Bigelow's liking and had to be told to both calm down and slow things a little. A body slam from Bigelow was Taylor's first real bump of the match, and he passed that test with aplomb as well, landing safely on his back to spread his weight like a veteran.

Bigelow knew the pace needed to slow further in order for Taylor to survive the encounter without losing his wind. Even though Taylor was a world class athlete and had been at the top of his profession, Bigelow was well aware from talking to other ex-footballers turned full-time wrestlers that being in ring shape was very different to any other form of conditioning. "Let's take it easy," he whispered, before turning Taylor over into a double leg hook submission hold known as the Boston crab.

Bigelow expertly made it look like he was wrenching back hard on Taylor's legs, twisting and bending them to breaking point. In reality he had applied the hold even more gently than usual, with the strain on his face and the faux pain etched on Taylor's giving the illusion that the footballer was in agony. Bigelow knew that a lot of the boys, especially those from the old school mode of thinking, would have enjoyed seeing him beat on Taylor a little by cinching back on the hold to give him a taste of respect for the business, but he was too smart for that. The match going well was worth a lot of money to him, and he realised that injuring the guest star would hardly endear him to Vince McMahon and could have a detrimental effect on his pay-off.

With Taylor struggling to make the ropes with the weight of the hefty wrestler to drag along, Bigelow switched to a much simpler leg hold, allowing Taylor to grab the bottom rope and break the move. Bigelow pulled him back to the centre of the ring and applied it again, showing the audience that he was in control. When Bigelow let Taylor get up he was met with an unexpected and unplanned forearm, so grabbed a headlock to keep him in check and told him to, "Lift me and drop." Once again, Taylor followed the command to the letter and Bigelow in return jumped high into the air before slamming himself into the canvas, making it look like Taylor had just drilled him with a huge back suplex.

Bigelow knew that because he was losing he needed an excuse, so when he connected with a headbutt from the top rope that the crowd sensed could be the finish, he purposely rolled off Taylor instead of covering him, acting like he had hurt his knee. Now when fans watched it back later, they would see that Bam Bam had the match won if not for the apparent knee tweak. It was a smart, veteran move from Bigelow and a way to preserve his credibility.

Taylor tired as the match went on. His selling became less pronounced and his comebacks took ostensibly more effort to execute, but he gutted it out and leathered Bigelow with forearm shots as hard as he could muster once they entered the home stretch of the contest. Knowing the bout was about to reach its finale, Taylor dug deep and used his last morsels of energy to tentatively scale the ropes, and with one final push he hurled himself at Bigelow from the middle rope with a diving forearm.

Taylor was supposed to land directly on Bam Bam and act semi-conscious as he sprawled over him for a win that he wouldn't know much about, but he had bounced off Bigelow's stocky frame and landed on the other side of the ring after connecting with the blow. Realising he would look weak if he lay down for too long before being pinned, Bigelow yelled to Taylor, "Roll the fuck over! Cover me!" and then let the exhausted footballer beat him. After the match, Bigelow's manager DiBiase gave him a scripted berating as they were storming up the aisle, telling him he was an embarrassment. It was the seeds for the babyface turn that Bam Bam had been promised.

Fortunately for Taylor he made it through the match without any issues, other than blowing up so severely that he could barely stand by the end of the bout. Roddy Piper recounted how he saw Taylor when he came back through the curtain and he was completely spent, propping himself up on a wall and barely able to stand. Taylor realised he had escaped a potentially reputation-shattering incident by coming through the match unscathed, and he knew that Bigelow had made him look like a star between the ropes. Opting for tact and a charm offensive, Taylor was full of praise for his opponent after the match, calling him, "The greatest athlete I have ever seen."

Once the dust had settled, it was clear that Bigelow needn't have worried about the bout delivering. The main event had exceeded all expectations, with Taylor appearing to have a ring awareness and grasp of wrestling psychology far beyond his experience, thanks to the incredible job Bigelow had done to make the football player look at home in an alien environment. It was a testament to his ability that the match not only went off without a hitch, but that the wrestling audience believed and accepted Taylor winning the bout.

Vince was relieved with how well the match had come off, "It was very risky putting a non-WWF star in the main event, but at the same time his athleticism was world class, and he was competing with Bam Bam Bigelow, who at the time, his athleticism was world class," he gushed, "I have to give credit to Bam Bam Bigelow for helping make that match live up to its expectation." Not everyone liked it though. Bob Holly grumbled, "Bam Bam just about killed himself to get L.T. over and [he] had to lead him through everything. L.T. had no idea what he was doing and Bam Bam was pretty much holding his hand through the whole thing and sacrificing himself."

Bigelow remained troubled about what the defeat would do to his career. He was still worried that losing to the footballer had shattered his credibility, but Vince reassured Bam Bam, reminding him of his forthcoming singles push once he turned babyface, while also lining his pockets with a huge pay-off for the match that exceeded $250,000. That satiated Bigelow, but while the turn did come (saturating the babyface side of the roster even further), the big push never did. Within eight months of having headlined *WrestleMania*, he was gone from the company and never returned.

THE MARKETING strategy for *WrestleMania XI* had clearly been to gear the show towards a non-wrestling audience, with Vince believing that wrestling fans would buy the event regardless simply because it was *WrestleMania*. He predicted that the new eyeballs Taylor drew would be exposed to the likes of Michaels, Diesel, Hart, and the rest of the regular crew, making them all household names in the same way that Hulk Hogan, Randy Savage, Roddy Piper, and The Ultimate Warrior had been in previous years.

Initial reaction internally was that *WrestleMania* had surpassed expectations at the box office, but when the final numbers came in it took the collective wind out of everyone working for Titan. The event was near enough sold out on the night with a gate of around $750,000, but crucially it had only drawn 340,000 pay-per-view buys, the lowest performing *WrestleMania* of all time. Taylor hadn't drawn as expected, that much was clear, and any plans to use him in a return match teaming with Bigelow at *SummerSlam* as had been discussed, were immediately shelved.

The show wasn't even the most successful of the night, as an event in Japan promoted by New Japan Pro Wrestling had drawn in excess of 60,000 people for a gate of $5.6 million, obliterating *WrestleMania* even when pay-per-view revenue was factored in. What was supposed to be the WWF's biggest show of the year, that some within the company were championing as potentially the highest grossing wrestling show of all time, had bombed.

VINCE HAD been listening to the reaction towards Shawn Michaels leading up to and at *WrestleMania*, and realised that keeping him heel wasn't going to work. The fans wanted to cheer Shawn, and Vince was going to let them. The night after *WrestleMania* at a live *Monday Night Raw* taping, Vince asked Shawn into his makeshift office to break the news. He expected Shawn to be delighted, especially with the merchandise possibilities that the Shawn Michaels brand presented. He wanted Shawn to be his babyface underdog hero, someone the fans could rally behind and support.

To Vince's surprise, Shawn didn't take the news well. Instead he was furious. Michaels didn't want to be a good guy, because like Scott Hall, he had surveyed the babyface scene and realised that he would no longer be working with any of his friends. Instead he would be lost in the shuffle of a stacked babyface deck that not only included Scott and Kevin, who would now be his rivals for top spots, but also Bret Hart, Lex Luger, Davey Boy Smith and The Undertaker. There would be no one left for him to work with who he actually wanted and was willing to work with. Shawn blamed the kick out spot from the night before, yelling at Vince, "You made the mistake and it costs me my career!" before storming out of the room.

Despite Michaels' protests, the turn went ahead as planned. Vince had known this was coming long before *WrestleMania*, it had been in the works for months, he was just pulling the trigger a little earlier to strike while the momentum was there. Michaels needn't have worried anyway, because with the exception of perhaps Bret Hart, he was by far the most popular performer in the company and garnered the loudest fan response of anyone.

Even though Michaels was practically a de facto babyface as it was, Vince still felt the need to run an angle to cement his new official status, and instructed Sid to go rogue on his storyline employer and take him out with three spine-crushing powerbombs. The angle left Michaels injured and out of action for a few weeks.

Not that Shawn was even really injured. He later claimed that Vince forced him to take six weeks off on sabbatical to sell the angle, but the truth according to Kevin Nash was somewhat different. "Shawn was a teacher," he remarked admiringly, "He only worked nine months a year and liked to have summer off." For Michaels it was a chance to go home and recharge, forget the pressures of being on the road, the politics, and the endlessly tiring backstage drama. He was frustrated with Vince for turning him, and the three powerbombs from the disreputably clumsy Sid were all the excuses he needed to claim he had been hurt.

When Scott Hall heard that Shawn was turning babyface, he pursed his lips and breathed in through his teeth. He had no intention of complaining to his friend, but was privately very unhappy about it. Not only had his own heel turn been taken away from him, but he was now even further down the babyface food chain. He made a mental note to remember that when his contract came up for negotiation, and then silently carried on as if nothing was any different.

SIX

WCW CHANGED THE LANDSCAPE OF wrestling in 1995 when they confirmed that they would be expanding their pay-per-view output and running ten such events per year. Immediately there was concern expressed by industry commentators about a possible over-saturation of the market, but for WCW it was a gamble worth taking. In their business model, pay-per-view was the lifeblood. Pay-per-view shows in 1994 had generated between $1 million and $2 million per event, one of the few consistent sources of money-making revenue they had, at a time when nearly every other aspect of their business was losing money. The only reason they hadn't gone under already was because they were being propped up by Ted Turner's vast wealth.

Vince McMahon was cautious about following suit, because he had always argued that pay-per-view events should be infrequent special attractions. That, he felt, increased interest in the shows and gave him plenty of time to promote the storylines and angles that would sell them to his punters. Needless to say, when he saw that WCW was increasing their pay-per-view schedule, thus running more of the events than the WWF, it caused him consternation. Vince had been one of the pioneers of the medium in the mid-eighties, and he couldn't stand the thought of his rivals making more money from it than he was. Not only that, but it made WCW look to outsiders like the bigger company. That was something his ego simply couldn't allow.

Within a few weeks of the WCW announcement, Vince returned fire with a revelation of his own: as of May, the WWF would be running monthly pay-per-view shows, two more annually than WCW, adding the newly branded *In Your House*. It went against everything he had previously said, but Vince was smart about it, undercutting WCW by $10 for the new events. In order to differentiate *In Your House* from his already ingrained pay-per-views, McMahon proposed that the new shows would be more akin to his old *Saturday Night's Main Event* broadcasts with a two hour running time and all of the main stars not necessarily featuring at each event.

To offset the cost of promoting monthly shows, the price of his already established pay-per-view cards were increased, based on accumulated market research which revealed that price didn't generally affect buy rates. McMahon was convinced that fans were prepared to pay whatever he charged for his top-tier shows. As the years went on it transpired that this theory was correct, and pay-per-view prices more than doubled without a drop in buys or revenue. Many years would actually see a significant increase on 1995 levels in the number of people who bought the shows, often at record prices.

For the business, the idea to expand the pay-per-view market made fiscal sense on paper. At that point neither the WWF nor WCW had ever promoted a pay-per-view that had lost money. Quite the opposite, the shows were always profitable, in some cases extremely so. Even a badly drawing pay-per-view event was likely to gross well over $1 million, compared to a really strong house show pulling in around $100,000, but those were increasingly a rarity. Of course no one knew just how much the sudden massive increase in the frequency of events would affect the number of buys, but even if a show completely tanked it would still theoretically obliterate a standard house show event with regards to proceeds.

On the flip side, the pay-per-view expansion would mean changes elsewhere in the company, with the number of house shows to be phased down as the year progressed. In 1995 they were money losers anyway, unlike in the eighties where they were still the main source of income. The new business model would see many of the house shows being sold overseas to outside promoters, who would buy the show from the WWF, thus guaranteeing them a strong return regardless of the attendance. This was a major negative for those at the bottom of the card who relied on live event earnings to survive, but for those at the top it was potentially good news. Pay-per-views were always the best pay-offs, especially if working in the main event, and adding seven more to the year could improve their declining income if the gamble succeeded.

Despite that, some within the company were apprehensive, both in the office and the dressing room. Veteran Bret Hart, who had been with the WWF before pay-per-view was even part of the lexicon, worried about the affordability for fans of producing so many paid events, especially with WCW doing the same. He was also concerned about whether an already burned out and morale-bereft crew would cope with the added pressure, and if it would just escalate internal tensions further as competition for prime spots became more intense.

JUST AS the business was changing, so were many of the WWF's time-honoured venues. 1995 saw the group run its final shows at both the Maple Leaf Gardens in Toronto, and the Spectrum in Philadelphia, at least in their traditional forms.

On May 13, 1995, the WWF presented its final card from the historic Boston Garden. Dubbed *A Night To Remember*, the evening was one of celebration. Many past performers who had lit up the building in years gone by, the majority of them now working as road agents, turned up for one last swansong. The veterans were treated with respect, and incorporated into the show throughout alongside the regular roster. Some of the matches set for the following evening's inaugural *In Your House* pay-per-view were given dry runs, in slightly different forms, but for the most part the "new generation" was unable to live up to the standards that the venue had grown to expect.

As Vince stood in the ring that night surrounded by headliners from the past, he gave thought to his current crop of performers, many of whom simply went through the motions and barely gave a thought for the prestige of the venue and the WWF's rich history there. It made him pine for the eighties when the WWF would sell out the arena nearly every month. Here they could only attract 10,000 people for the last ever show in the building, and that was after having given away thousands of tickets for free. It was a sobering notion, but he was confident that things would change the next night with the WWF's first monthly pay-per-view. That, he felt, could be the dawning of a new boom era.

TAKING PLACE on Mother's Day 1995, Vince had just the gimmick to generate interest in the debut edition of his new *In Your House* concept; he would give away an actual house to a random fan watching on pay-per-view. Midway through the event, the WWF's resident hype machine Todd Pettengill, an overbearingly chirpy former radio presenter with a penchant for telling bad jokes, called up the winner. It turned out to be an eleven-year-old kid, Matthew Pomposelli, who quickly sold the house on six months later for a cool $175,000. It was more than the majority of Vince's undercard made in a year.

The wrestling on the show started well, with a match between Bret Hart and high-flying Japanese star Jinsei 'Hakushi' Shinzaki ushering in the new era of monthly pay-per-views. Hart had been treading water since his title reign had ended in November, but he tried to make the most of a bad situation by putting in a typically reliable performance. On-screen, Bret had been typecast as a racist by commentator Jerry Lawler, which was a move from the WWF to reboot a stale feud the pair had contested two years earlier. Lawler claimed that Hart, "Wasn't a fan of the Jap people," leading to the bout between Bret and the Oriental import.

Shinzaki introduced WWF audiences to hitherto unseen aerial manoeuvres which left show announcers Vince McMahon and Michael 'Dok Hendrix' Seitz (better known in wrestling as Michael 'P.S.' Hayes) struggling to keep up. Cast as a heel in keeping with Vince's usual handling of ethnic minorities in his company, Shinzaki was so exciting compared to many of the slow-moving members of the roster, that fans had a hard time booing him. Luckily he was against Hart, who was still the most popular performer in the WWF despite having been shunted down into the midcard, and the Canadian did everything he could to make Shinzaki appear to be a legitimate threat. The two crafted a bout that set an early high standard for what the *In Your House* shows could be, with Hart succeeding in making the newcomer look like his equal, before he eventually out-wrestled and defeated him.

Hart would wrestle again later, competing against Lawler in the evening's penultimate match. Vowing revenge for his earlier defeat, Shinzaki interjected himself in the contest and caused Hart to lose. After the show, Hart wondered just what was going on in the WWF when he was putting over an announcer in a throwaway match. He felt like he was being wasted and could be far more productive higher up the card. His current lowly position didn't sit right with him one bit.

The second match on the card was an unusual handicap bout, pitting Scott Hall's Razor Ramon character against the team of Jeff Jarrett and The Roadie. Initially the match was to feature Sean Waltman on his Kliq buddy's team as a follow up to *WrestleMania*, but he had injured his neck and was forced to pull out[26]. Bob Holly had recently worked a program with Jeff Jarrett on television that saw him briefly win the Intercontinental Championship - only for it to be overturned - and he fully expected that he would be put into the match as Waltman's replacement. He was a logical choice, as not only had he been working with Jarrett but he had also been Waltman's tag partner earlier in the year. Instead the WWF went with the two-on-one handicap match, something Holly blamed on The Kliq. "God forbid anyone else got a chance to get over or collect a payday," he grumbled. As it turned out, Hall didn't need any help, and was booked to beat both Jarrett and James on his own.

Also on the card, the hulking frame of the freshly-turned heel Mabel made short work of Adam Bomb in under two minutes, reaffirming Vince's unquenchable determination to push big men regardless of talent.

---

[26] Waltman injured his neck during a match with Jinsei Shinzaki in Germany, and the initial diagnosis from doctors called for him to retire, so severe was the damage. Waltman sought other opinions and returned to the ring a few months later.

Following that, Owen Hart and another giant, Yokozuna, quickly defeated The Smoking Gunns in a *WrestleMania* rematch. The brevity of the contest, with the champions allowed to defeat their top challengers in just six-minutes, only served to highlight the weakened state of the tag team division.

THE MAIN event of *In Your House* saw Kevin Nash defend the WWF Championship against Sid Eudy, in a piece of matchmaking that further highlighted Vince's prevailing booking mentality. Both were approaching seven-feet tall and turned heads in airports, which to McMahon was the definition of what a top guy should be. But while the visual of seeing the two titans collide may have been impressive, the action which they put forth was not.

As the screeching opening tones of a *Psycho*-inspired musical score echoed throughout the arena, the visage of the wild-eyed, ultra-intense Sid filled up the screens at home. He unblinkingly marched to the ring, intermittently turning his head from side to side like a paranoid schizophrenic before standing on the apron, closing his eyes and breathing in the atmosphere. He absorbed the boos from the crowd, before dismissing them with a simple sneer. As his similarly huge opponent made his way down the aisle, Sid didn't even look up and acknowledge him, instead standing at ringside and boring a hole through the side of Vince McMahon's head with a piercing and unwavering stare.

Once both combatants entered the ring and prepared to do battle, they stood nose-to-nose and jawed at each other, with Sid blinking rapidly and snarling through gritted teeth. Nash tried to take Sid seriously before playfully mocking him by pulling a goofy face, causing both men to struggle not to break character and burst into laughter.

The pre-match posturing had been handled well, but the action in the ring couldn't live up to the hype that McMahon and his television crew had been lavishly swathing the bout with over the weeks. Michael Hayes recognised that, warning viewers, "This won't be a mat wrestling classic." Kevin Nash knew that much too, "Trying to do a match with Sid was hard," he complained, "I had four moves and I couldn't do any of them to him. Where's the excitement? Why would you book that?" he added.

The result was a plodding start, as the two titans tried to find a way to work around their collective limitations. Both Nash and Sid were mountains of men, comparable in build and stature. It irked Nash no end; he didn't understand why he was constantly booked to work with opponents of a similar height, as it only served to make him look less physically imposing and impressive and the matches were usually poor.

Because Sid was the heel and the veteran, he was called upon to lead the match, but was soon out of ideas. He began wildly pounding away at Nash, locking his hands together and dropping double hammer fists across the back of the champion in order to give the impression that he was weakening it to set up his powerbomb finishing move. Seeing the opportunity to eat up some time and weave a further strand of the tale he had decided to tell, Sid arched over Nash's back and reached forward, grabbed him under the chin with both hands and pulled backwards in a move known as the camel clutch.

At first the use of the hold was reasonable enough, it made logical sense for Sid to do it. But as the minutes ticked slowly by, Sid kept hold of the move and the interest levels in the match quickly waned. The pair waited out the crowd's ennui, knowing that if they lingered in the move long enough the audience would come back around. They did, and Nash timed his fight out and comeback with the crescendo of the noise levels, before Sid abruptly silenced them again - this time intentionally - with an awkward chokeslam.

When Sid followed that up with his usually-match-ending powerbomb, many watching suspected that this was it for the Diesel experiment. He hadn't been drawing at live shows or on pay-per-view, so it was a reasonable thing to assume that he could be done as a headliner following the match. After all, Sid was everything that McMahon looked for in a main event performer; that was as true in 1995 as it had been when he first tried pushing him as such in 1992.

But Vince was stubborn and steadfast, determined not to fail again in creating a top, marketable babyface. After Nash was given a visual win following a powerbomb of his own, the bout ended with an unsatisfying disqualification following interference from Tatanka, who was being given one last push as a top guy. It was a finish the WWF would never have dreamed of presenting on a full-priced pay-per-view, and set an unfortunate early precedent for main events on the cut-price shows. *The Wrestling Observer Newsletter* would later describe the main event performance as, "Clumsy and predictable," adding that, "The two guys couldn't work together at all."

THE *IN Your House* venture had started off flat, with the screwy finish in the main event leaving fans less inclined to buy the next show than wanting to see the inevitable rematch. The card had also struggled to draw locally, with only 3,500 fans paying for tickets, with the same again given away for free. People didn't believe the event was special, the very issue Vince had worried over before embarking on the show.

Subsequently, there was very little optimism within the company for the buy rate, especially after the embarrassment of *WrestleMania* flopping. It was soon revealed that *In Your House* had pulled a 0.83 buy rate for around 180,000 buys and a $1.2 million company gross, which WWF officials were publicly championing as a success (and also massaging the figure, claiming it as a 1.0). In reality, the number was not a total disaster, but certainly wasn't anywhere near as high as Titan had hoped. Before the show, some had predicted that the price cut would boost the buy rate to approximately double what the show ended up doing. Instead it turned out to be one of their worst to date, and the price slash rendered it easily the lowest grossing WWF pay-per-view ever to that point. Dave Meltzer in *The Wrestling Observer Newsletter* summarised:

> Let's not kid anybody; when cutting the price in half results in less people buying the product, you can spin things all you want. It's still not a success and it's certainly not a sign of a popularity turnaround.

JUST FOUR days after the show, Vince assembled his tired, aching and increasingly gloomy roster for a "State of the WWF" team meeting at Titan Tower, with the purpose being to break down the barriers separating the boys from the office. He hoped a tour of the building and showing the assembled throng a series of videos that detailed the roles of the various departments within the company would engender unity, but instead it turned into an ugly all-day mud-slinging contest amongst the boys.

For many it was a rare moment of direct public access to Vince, and Scott Bigelow took it as a chance to vent his feelings on The Kliq. Seizing the opportunity, Bigelow stood up and looked around the room, then turned to Vince and declared, "I gotta problem; on the last European trip, Scott Hall was working against Kevin and Shawn, but he was on their bus every night after the show and the marks were following them to the next town." He was trying to appeal to Vince's sense of pride in the old-school traditions of kayfabe, but as one of his colleagues in the room that day pointed out, "It was entirely the wrong approach to take; Vince didn't care about any of that. He was the one who told the world it was all scripted in the first place!"

As soon as the words had left Bigelow's mouth, Shawn Michaels immediately popped out of his seat and angrily snarled at him, "Hey motherfucker, I'm on the road three-hundred-and-fifty days a fucking year! Don't you dare try and tell me who I'm gonna spend my fucking life with, you dumb motherfucker." With Michaels on the verge of launching himself across the room at Bigelow, Scott Hall stepped in and summed the situation up in his usual no-frills way, "Hey, Bam Bam, think about it; they're going to each town watching the *exact* same match for fourteen nights, I think they get it!" Vince just sat back in his chair and let the scenario play out. If these guys had things to get off their chest, he felt it was better to let them do it now than blow up at each other in a locker-room somewhere down the road.

As well as being allowed to air their grievances, the boys were also given two important pieces of information from Vince regarding the company. Business, he claimed, was picking up. He cited the *In Your House* buy rate as an example of that, championing the higher 1.0 rating than the number it had actually drawn, and noting that the group last year had grossed nearly $84 million. That caused some instant furrowed brows, with guys who were living hand-to-mouth wondering why the hell their pay-offs were so low if the company was apparently thriving. Vince immediately sensed the bewilderment, and was quick to add that despite the gross figure, the group had actually spent in excess of that on hiring venues, splitting revenue with pay-per-view providers, advertising, paying the talent, upkeep of the offices, transport and numerous other expenses, such that Titan had lost $3.8 million in 1994.

Vince added that he had lost even more than that in years previous, but the company had survived the ordeal and was about to come through the other side stronger. The monthly pay-per-view events, he told them, were just the beginning of that. He hoped to imbue optimism in his talent, and to make them more focused on working with him to improve the company, but many were sceptical and viewed it as just another tactic from McMahon to keep his crew in check.

The far bigger news as far as the boys were concerned pertained to the announcement of a new drug policy, which would be the most stringent the company had ever enforced. J.J. Dillon outlined the parameters to the growingly dejected crew, who were warned that they faced suspension or even termination for violating any of the terms of the policy. Those terms ranged from recreational drug use (including, to the horror of the majority, marijuana users facing a six week suspension) to anabolic steroids and prescription drugs.

There were instant grumblings, with complaints that everyone would become an alcoholic as drinking was the only thing left that they were permitted to do, and that the people who came up with the policy didn't understand the lifestyle of being a wrestler. Even if Vince had wanted to listen to his livid roster and modify the policy, he couldn't; his hands were tied. After the close call of last year's trial, he had no choice but to implement it and stick with it. He couldn't risk the reputation of the company any further after having survived the ordeal, and saw it as the only way of restraining his oft-roisterous crew. Simply asking them to toe the line just wasn't enough anymore.

That had been proven in January with Brian Adams' arrest, which fortunately for Titan didn't receive significant media attention. A recent Sports Illustrated *Wide World of Sports* special aired by ABC on April 29th called *Requiem For The Heavyweights* had also caused consternation, as it tried to link the recent deaths of Art Barr, Eddie Gilbert and 'Big' John Studd to steroid use. Another scandal relating to drug abuse like the one that broke in 1990 would have killed the group.

But for the boys it had a doubly negative effect. Not only were their "gimmicks"[27] being taken away from them, but the cost to the company of the testing was reflected in their pay-checks. There was no way for them to cheat the tests either, or tamper with them in any way, because the Federal Government were keeping a very close eye on everything. There was no guarantee that the boys were safe for a few weeks, days, or even hours if they had been tested already on a given day, as sometimes guys would be tested on both legs of a *double shot*.[28]

Tom Prichard recounted the story of when he failed one of the tests, "The WWF worked with a third party to administer the tests, and we all thought they wouldn't test us outside of the US! Subsequently, I got popped in Germany after I had been riding with Razor, and we may or may not have smoked a joint or two. I got fined six weeks pay, but I could still work the shows and get a $200 *draw* (advance) each night. I couldn't say for certain why I was tested and failed when other guys blatantly got away with smoking pot and using pills, but put it this way; if you were "in" and a top guy, it wouldn't help anyone for them to suspend you. I did see some crazy things as guys tried to avoid the tests. Kid used to come to the back and pretend to pass out, making out like he was hurt so they couldn't test him. I remember Sid once had a squirt bottle filled with someone else's piss, but

---

[27] Ordinarily a wrestling term for a performer's on-screen persona, but when used by the boys it referred to whatever happened to be their vice of choice, be it pills, pot or any host of other exotic drugs.

[28] Two shows in one day.

he got caught. Someone, and I can't remember who it was, even tried using a fake dick!"

The Titan Tower assembly ultimately had the opposite to the desired effect. Prior to it, everyone was already on board and behind the company. Subsequently, instead of the meeting boosting morale and creating a harmony amongst the troupe, they were now at odds with each other even further, more concerned than ever about their pay, and no longer able to fall back on the various vices which they relied upon to cope. Morale was at the all-time lowest it had ever been.

IT PLUMMETED even further within the company due to a fiasco involving network television station *NBC*. Vince was boisterous and gloating in late May when the WWF announced they were returning to the channel for a one-off special on June 4th that would air the two main events from *WrestleMania*, with fresh, current audio. It would be their first linkup with the station since *The Main Event V* in February 1991 had done such a poor rating that the *NBC*/WWF partnership disintegrated. The near $250,000 that Titan would pocket from the deal would help edge the company towards black ink on the balance sheets, and if it performed well in the ratings, the potential was there for the return of *Saturday Night's Main Event* and *The Main Event* further down the road.

Only a few days later, euphoria turned to despondency when *NBC* abruptly pulled the plug on the deal. The official story coming out of Titan was that the NBA play-offs were the cause of the show dropping from the schedule, with uncertainty over the timeslot of an upcoming game. Most saw through this, because even when the WWF show was announced, that uncertainty was already there.

The reality of the situation was that the *NBC* Director of Programming was away on vacation when the deal was made, and when finding out about it upon his return, he immediately nixed it. He thought wrestling was a fad from the eighties and that its day had been and gone. In 1995, *NBC* wanted to do nineties programming, not rehash something from a decade ago. Vince was furious, but the deal was dead and there was little chance of it being exhumed. It would be a further decade before the two would work together again, with the then-WWE presenting the revival of *Saturday Night's Main Event* in 2006.

On the same evening that McMahon found out the *NBC* deal was off, things got even worse for Titan when WCW performers Hulk Hogan and Jimmy Hart were shown in the crowd during a Magic-Pacers basketball game aired on *NBC*, and received plenty of airtime and shout outs.

Petulantly, on *Monday Night Raw* the next night, Vince had his video editing department splice in some footage of Yokozuna pinning Hogan at *King of the Ring* back in 1993.

The special was eventually revived, but not on *NBC*. Instead rival network *Fox* stepped in and signed off on the show, airing it in late September. The program pulled an impressive 3.9 rating in an 11pm Saturday evening timeslot, which led to Vince trying to convince *Fox* to run more similar specials, only for the network to infuriatingly reject the proposal.

1995 MIGHT have been a struggle for the WWF, but over in Atlanta things weren't much better for WCW. The company had been operating in the red for years, and even though renegade president Eric Bischoff had moved heaven and earth to sign Hulk Hogan, Randy Savage and a slew of other stars from the eighties boom period away from the WWF, WCW was still not able to turn a profit. Hogan had improved the ratings and pay-per-view buy rates initially but things had levelled off, and although live attendances had increased since his arrival in mid-1994, WCW was still the distant number two promotion in the eyes of both the wrestling audience and the mainstream.

Bischoff was running out of ideas, and he realised that while his boss Ted Turner's pockets might run almost endlessly deep, he would be unable to keep holding out his hand for money without showing proof that he was investing it wisely. Bischoff sat in his office and reclined in his leather seat as he pondered the situation. Then in a flash of inspiration it hit him: international distribution. The WWF had always done well overseas where their product was many times more visible than WCW's, and it generated them significant revenue each year.

With big markets in England, Germany and India tied up by Titan, Bischoff had limited options. One thing he did have on his side though was Hogan, and to a lesser extent Savage, because both were enduring household names that he could use to sell his product to non-wrestling executives. He hoped that whoever he pitched to would be enough of a mark for Hogan or at the very least his name value, that a deal could be struck to make WCW profitable and so justify Hulk's astronomical annual salary. It was a win-win situation for Bischoff if he could get a deal done, because the footage was already shot and paid for, and thus anything WCW made from selling it on would be pure profit.

Having explored the options and weighed up the figures, Bischoff was finally able to strike up a provisional deal with *Star TV* in China for the rights to then-flagship show *WCW Saturday Night*. *Star TV* was not his first choice by any means, but with very few gaps in the market, that didn't matter to him. Their six-figure offer meant WCW would stop losing money, and he would be the first president of the company in years to actually put something back in to the Turner coffers.

Bischoff was feeling confident as he contemplated how Turner would respond, but the slight smugness and self-satisfaction he had allowed himself soon turned to concern when he was told a galling fact; *Star TV* was owned by Rupert Murdoch, the international media mogul with whom Turner had a long-running and ill-tempered public feud. The two despised each other. The revelation changed everything for Eric, and he realised that getting Turner to sign off on the deal was going to be a tough sell to say the least.

Bischoff was granted a personal audience with the chairman on June 5th so he could make his pitch, after having enlisted the help of Turner executive Scott Sassa. Sassa was the overseer of all Turner networks and heir apparent within the company to Ted himself, and he joined Eric at the meeting along with Dr. Harvey Schiller, a former Air Force colonel and chairman of the U.S. Olympic committee, and current head of *TBS* Sports.

Prior to the meeting Eric wondered what job he might be forced to take after Turner inevitably fired him on the spot for even suggesting becoming bedfellows with Murdoch. Perhaps Titan had a spot for him, or maybe he could move into broadcasting away from wrestling. Bischoff didn't allow his apprehension to betray his confident front, and launched into his pitch with a self-assurance and charm that would have captivated most. But less than two minutes in, Turner stood up and interrupted him, then dropped a bombshell question, "Eric, what do we need to do to become competitive with Vince?" It was the last thing Bischoff was expecting and he wasn't remotely prepared. He had the answers to every question possible regarding the *Star TV* deal, but competing with Vince? He had no idea what to say.

Responding to the question like a ring veteran would respond between the ropes to a mistake in a match, Bischoff thought on his feet and called one on the fly, "I think we need prime time!" he blurted out, barely believing that the words had just come out of his mouth. While the answer may have been off the top of his head, when Bischoff allowed himself to hear what he had just said, he realised he might actually be right. Prime time was the one significant thing Vince had that he didn't. Still, he waited with trepidation for Turner's answer, worried that he would laugh him out of his office. To his and the rest of the room's surprise, Turner agreed with Eric. He turned to Sassa, "Scott, give Eric Monday nights on *TNT*."

It wasn't just an off-the-cuff response from Turner, and the timeslot was no coincidence either; he had actually been thinking about how to get back at Vince for a few months. The latest heat between the two stemmed from a series of faxes which McMahon had sent to Turner earlier in the year that derided the content WCW was offering. The first concerned the gratuitous violence advertised for WCW's *Uncensored* pay-per-view and the second was regarding the unsavoury nature of a crude promotional trick on Gene Okerlund's premium rate hotline number. The controversial hotline had promised to dish the dirt on the death of a forty-seven-year-old former "World Champion", and was sold as if it were Ric Flair, but was actually referring to 'Big' John Studd, who was a WWWF World Tag Team Champion in 1976 alongside Killer Kowalski.

Vince added that WCW was an embarrassment to Turner's company and that he should consider folding it before it shamed him further. Turner saw through the missives for what they were; Vince was worried about the competition and wanted him out of the wrestling business the easy way. The notes bothered Turner, and from then on he became more driven about hurting Vince's product and putting him out of business.

Bischoff worried that Sassa would think he had intentionally screwed him by asking for prime time, but the executive was savvy to Turner's whims and erratic behaviour, and had seen it all before. While he viewed professional wrestling as entertainment designed for rednecks and not something for his slick, hip network, he realised that once Turner had made up this mind there was little chance of him changing it. He told Eric to at least call *TNT* president Brad Siegel and talk to him directly about the new show that would be appearing on his station, rather than have him find out about it via an impersonal company memo. Bischoff expected understandable resentment from Siegel, but he too was used to this sort of thing from Turner. He simply set about working with Bischoff closely in order that WCW's new prime time show would be as good as possible to justify its place on *TNT*.

Bischoff worked on coming up with a name for the show, and at first was set on *Head to Head*, which was the working title for a couple of weeks, but was shelved because it was considered too inflammatory and adversarial. Instead he went with *Monday Nitro*, which both captured the explosive nature of the show that Bischoff envisioned and fit in with the name of the network they were on. Not to mention that if it was said fast enough, it sounded suspiciously like "Monday Night Raw". That was not unintentional, as Bischoff hoped to trick WWF fans into thinking the show had changed station and then hook them with what he believed to be a superior product.

When Schiller had first taken his position, he had declared, "Companies that spend time worrying about their competition aren't spending enough time worrying about their own product," but he had a complete shift in attitude when Turner green-lighted the *TNT* show. He now openly talked about putting the WWF down and making WCW the only game in town. Company officials were told one simple directive: prepare for war.

SEVEN

JIM ROSS, A SMOOTH TONGUED Oklahoma native who plied his trade on-screen as a commentator, was given the position of Vince McMahon's assistant in January due to Pat Patterson's desire to reduce his workload. McMahon was uncomfortable with Ross' distinctive regional accent being heard on air, but respected his knowledge of the business enough that he was happy to grant him powers behind the scenes.

Given his ability to influence additions to the WWF's talent pool, Ross looked to make a number of quasi-nepotistic hires, while also engendering changes that he felt would be positive for the company. One major play he attempted was to try and employ no-nonsense fellow Oklahoma native 'Dr. Death' Steve Williams. A rugged and burly brawler with a tough guy reputation and a collegiate football background, Williams had been making waves in the booming Japanese wrestling scene for years. Ross felt he was the perfect candidate to headline as a top heel in the WWF.

Ross believed it was an area the company was desperately short in, especially since the babyface turn of Shawn Michaels and the shifting of Yokozuna and Owen Hart into the tag team division. Bob Backlund had been quickly phased down too, and like Michaels, Bam Bam Bigelow had turned babyface since *WrestleMania*. It left only Sid as a genuine headline-calibre heel. Ross wanted to bring Williams in to win the *King of the Ring* tournament on his debut, then immediately challenge Kevin Nash for the WWF Championship over the summer.

Jim Cornette salivated over the prospect, "I would have loved, loved, *loved* to have seen Dr. Death work with Kevin Nash. I would have loved even more for Nash and his crew to have tried to tell Doc what he was doing wrong. That would have ended very badly for them!" Unfortunately for Ross and Cornette, Williams was committed to All Japan Pro Wrestling, both because of his status as a well-paid main eventer, and because of the much lighter road schedule, so he turned down the chance to work for the WWF.

Instead, Vince McMahon had to turn star maker and create a monster heel from within. He looked around the locker-room and saw a generally much leaner and less impressive-looking crop of talent than had ever worked for him. Then he saw Mabel. Nelson Frazier, the five-hundred-pound giant behind the purple shell suit, was a confident kid and always tried hard for him, even if he was limited in the ring. With size coming at an artificially enhanced premium that Vince could scarcely afford anymore, he saw the massive Frazier as the next best thing.

ON JUNE 25th in front of a very healthy crowd of 16,590 (with 14,181 paid) at frequent boom-era venue the Spectrum in Philadelphia, Pennsylvania, the third annual pay-per-view edition of the *King of the Ring* was an event that became part of wrestling folklore, but for all the wrong reasons.

The crowd was raucous, with a number of fans who regularly graced local Extreme Championship Wrestling (ECW) shows in the area in attendance. As the night went on, they would become so disgusted with the action being presented that they loudly and vociferously turned on the product.

The principal resentment was directed towards the man that Vince had deemed worthy of winning the night's round robin tournament; Mabel. Having shockingly dispatched of The Undertaker in the quarter finals, Mabel then received a bye to the final by virtue of Kama and Shawn Michaels working a fifteen-minute time limit draw in their own quarter final, giving him a clear route to the showpiece match.

On the other side of the bracket, Juan Rivera was being given the promotional push of his life. Having abandoned the shoddy ninja impression gimmick of Kwang, Rivera was asked to portray a character a little closer to home with fiery Hispanic Savio Vega, a role Vince hoped would be 1995's answer to Pedro Morales. Rivera was entered into the tournament as a late substitute due to Scott Hall having to pull out with a rib injury, and the pieces aligned for him to be given the same surprise one-night mega push that Steve Williams would have had, only with a different final result. With Hall originally booked to reach the final for the second year running, creative decided that Rivera could just take his place, and he was asked to work an exhausting four times that evening.

First he disposed of IRS in a tacked-on qualifier aired on the pre-show before the main pay-per-view had even began, with the WWF trying to sell any undecided potential last minute buyers on the fairytale story of underdog Savio Vega potentially winning the tournament. Further wins over Yokozuna (via count out) and The Roadie meant the dream was within touching distance for the character, with only the massive Mabel standing between him and glory.

No one in the audience could quite believe that Mabel and Savio Vega were going to be contesting the *King of the Ring* final. Not because they had bought into the rags to riches story of Vega, but because they were so appalled at what they considered to be abysmal booking. Surely Shawn Michaels, freshly turned babyface and the undoubted outstanding performer in the tournament, was the man who should be going over, they thought. If not him, then The Undertaker would have made sense; it had been years since he was last involved in a genuine main event program. It didn't matter to Vince what they or anyone else thought. He had deigned Mabel as his chosen one, and he was running with him.

Bob Holly didn't understand it either, and put it down to politics. Rivera and Frazier were friendly with Mark Calaway he figured, and even though they weren't good workers in his estimation, they were still getting pushed regardless. Holly didn't like it because once again he felt he was being shunned, used merely as a stepping stone who could illuminate his opponents, but never allowed to shine himself. He recalled a conversation with Jerry Brisco, who told him that the WWF needed selfless guys like him to make other lesser talents look good.

That night, Holly was asked to put over Brian James, who at that point was known more for being Jeff Jarrett's roadie than as an in-ring performer. Losing to him, Holly thought, was seriously damaging to his credibility. He understood how Bam Bam had felt putting over Lawrence Taylor at *WrestleMania*, because The Roadie character was considered a manager by fans, a non-wrestler, but Holly didn't have a six-figure pay-off to soften the blow to his pride like Bigelow did. Holly would grouse, "How the hell was I supposed to have any credibility if I couldn't beat a roadie?! That was the night I really started to question company politics and began to think that it didn't matter how good somebody was."

BY THE time the *King of the Ring* final was due to begin, the crowd were at boiling point as a result of sitting through an extremely bad show. "There we see, yes, the *King of the Ring* final; Mabel against Savio," said Vince from behind the announce desk, almost as if trying to convince himself that his idea to run with the match was a good one.

Vega came to the ring tired from his three earlier matches, and even though he was being presented as an ethnic underdog with no chance of winning, just like fictional Philadelphia hero Rocky Balboa, by now the crowd were thoroughly sick of him. They didn't even provide him with the customary polite reaction that nearly all babyfaces generally received, choosing instead to sit on their hands. As the match got underway Vega tried to get their interest by hitting Mabel hard with big chops that echoed throughout the silent building, but it didn't work. Neither did a clothesline that sent Mabel upside down and out of the ring.

The spectators were sapped of their remaining interest when a fatigued Mabel locked on a bearhug. They grew increasingly restless, starting to boo the match when Savio fought out of the hold only to be immediately caught in another. Out of gas, Mabel had to keep resting and his next move was a chinlock, which caused McMahon to gush about the enormous wrestler's arm being the size of a regular persons' leg.

At ringside, Scott Hall, who had accompanied Savio in the bout, was bored too. He started furiously banging on the mat to try and drum up at least some interest in the contest, but the response he got wasn't quite what he had envisioned. At the end of their collective tether, the Philadelphia crowd turned on the match and burst into a spontaneous roar of, "ECW, ECW, ECW." It was so loud that McMahon even acknowledged it, "Listen to this!" he said, but he had no idea what his audience were saying or that they were vehemently rejecting what was in front of them.

The two performers in the ring didn't know what was going on either, and carried on sleepwalking at a snail's pace through their pre-rehearsed routine. Savio rallied, but his evening's exertions were to prove too much, and he succumbed to a Mabel splash before he allowed himself to be counted down for the three. As Mabel grinned while sitting on a tacky golden throne that made up part of the set, his tag partner, Mo, stumbled through a longwinded promo declaring Mabel as the WWF's new king. Revolted, the crowd resorted to pelting the pair with garbage to show their disapproval. This wasn't heel heat; the audience were just disgusted that Mabel had won what had previously been a well-regarded tournament.

Dave Meltzer of *The Wrestling Observer Newsletter* was equally galled, but not wholly surprised. He simply saw it as Vince reverting to type by casting the largest member of his roster in a role at the top of the card. He wrote:

> What took place at this show was no surprise. In almost every business when things get tough, those in charge usually go to their instinctive upbringing. McMahon's father ran a big man's territory. McMahon, Jr. ran a big man's territory. Big isn't necessarily bad by any means, but big is bad in this case when big is being pushed regardless of quality and when the interest of the crowds have changed. The best crowd responses on this show came from the smaller and more talented men.

OF THE other non-tournament matches on the card, the one with the biggest storyline issue going in was the third and final pay-per-view meeting between veterans Bret Hart and Jerry 'the King' Lawler. The pair were first programmed together back in 1993, when Lawler jumped Hart following his own *King of the Ring* win. Lawler got a little too boisterous during that segment, hurting Hart for real with a vicious shot from a prop sceptre. When they met later in the year at *SummerSlam*, Hart made sure to cinch back on his sharpshooter submission hold extra tight to make Lawler suffer and make them even for the sceptre blow (*a receipt*). Lawler was an unpopular figure in the locker-room at the time due to the notoriously low pay-offs he dished out while running the Memphis territory. It was a place many of the boys in the back had competed in, and most nearly starved there due to Lawler's thriftiness, so they enjoyed seeing the King suffer.

The feud was shelved in November 1993 when Lawler endured legal troubles stemming from accusations that he had raped and sodomised a fifteen-year-old girl[29]. Lawler was immediately taken off television, and a proposed Team Bret Hart vs. Team Jerry Lawler *Survivor Series* match saw Shawn Michaels step in to take 'the King's' place. The pair were kept apart until their feud was rekindled in 1995 following *WrestleMania*, which was a way to keep Hart in a hot program, but nowhere near babyface champion Diesel in the main event. As had been the case throughout the year, it was a source of irritation for 'the Hitman', who still felt like he was wasting his time.

The *King of the Ring* encounter was billed as a "Kiss My Foot Match", with the stipulation that the loser would be forced to kiss the foot of the winner. They had done the match once before on a house show in Providence and it had garnered a strong response, so the decision was made to try it on pay-per-view, with the aim of providing a fresh feel to an already well-worn encounter.

Building to the match on television, Lawler donned a dirty, discoloured sock that was full of holes, threatening not to wash it until Hart had been forced to kiss it. He tried to make the garment appear so disgusting to the viewers that even the thought of it being in anyone's mouth would be enough to induce vomiting.

In Philadelphia, Hart generated a bigger response than anyone else on the card, but the resultant match was a flat, insipid affair. The two had shown surprisingly little chemistry for the duration of their program, remarkable given their collective forty-two years experience in the business. But both were also becoming long in the tooth, with Hart thirty-seven-years-old and Lawler forty-five, and for both it could be argued that their best days were behind them.

---

[29] The charges were eventually dropped when the girl, a resident of Louisville, Kentucky, admitted to having made the whole thing up in order to make her boyfriend jealous.

Lawler, once a major regional and national star in the seventies and eighties, was now left with a repertoire consisting of shortcuts, cheap tricks and exaggerated over-selling. The serious Hart was not the right opponent for Lawler's comedy-based working style, as he preferred to be in the ring with hard-hitters, technical masters and realistic brawlers.

While anything but a classic, the fans at least were able to lose themselves in the bout's cartoonish silliness for the nine-minute duration. After finishing Lawler off with his sharpshooter, Bret forced his foot into 'the King's' mouth, who grimaced, protested and dry-heaved for the benefit of the cameras. Not finished, Hart then removed Lawler's boot and twisted his mangy foot into his own mouth, causing him to act like he was about to throw up. When the cameras caught up with Lawler backstage later on, he took things a step further. Before they started rolling he secretly took a swig of cola and then shoved gram crackers into his mouth, spitting it all over a bathroom mirror as if it were vomit.

TO THE surprise of no one, *King of the Ring* was panned mercilessly by fans and critics alike. Most concurred that it was the worst pay-per-view that the group had ever presented. "It was so bad, one can only speculate on how those booking the show in the first place thought they'd be able to pull it off," snarled *The Wrestling Observer*. Others classified it as rock bottom for the once thriving company. It was a combination of factors, they said, from the bad wrestling to the complete failure to comprehend what the fans of the era wanted.

Within the WWF there was the feeling that the show had been bad and hadn't captured the imagination of the public, but the strong house generated a modicum of positivity that it may have drawn well on pay-per-view too. When the buy rate came in, company executives were blindsided. *King of the Ring* had only managed a 0.65 buy rate, which translated to approximately 150,000 buys. It was the lowest in company history by a significant distance.

Mixed martial arts group UFC presented their *UFC VI* pay-per-view three weeks later and demolished the *King of the Ring* number, doing so without the aid of a national cable television show to hype the event. The card was sold around Ken Shamrock against Dan Severn, and pulled 240,000 buys, far more than everything else in wrestling that year other than *WrestleMania*.

The growing success of UFC, which many in wrestling felt was just an evolution of their own sport, combined with the loud ECW chants at *King of the Ring*, made it clear to a bewildered Vince McMahon that the business had evolved and the WWF was far behind. The numbers served as a major wake-up call that things needed to change.

EVEN WITH the locker-room policing of the BSKs, tensions had continued to escalate amongst the boys for a multitude of reasons. Chief amongst those; many still had substantial problems with The Kliq. More often than not it was performers who were new to the company whom the group had perceived as potential threats to their spots, or who simply rubbed them up the wrong way upon their arrival.

One newcomer in particular caused quite a stir within The Kliq and the rest of the locker-room. Tamara Lynn Sytch was a salty, obnoxious blonde with girl-next-door good looks and a *Baywatch* body, brought into the WWF alongside real-life boyfriend Chris Candido after a stint working for Jim Cornette's Smoky Mountain Wrestling. Candido was a gifted talent, a solid mechanic with a smooth ring style, but his upside was diminished by his five-foot-eight frame. Despite possessing deceptive strength for his size, he never would have been hired by the group a decade prior. Even though the business was changing, he was still a small man in a giant's world and wasn't ever taken seriously by Vince and his booking team.

Tammy on the other hand, was a perfect fit. Showing an aptitude for the business that many girlfriends of workers shoehorned into the industry rarely did, Tammy appeared for Titan a few months earlier than Chris, and originally settled into the role of live event commentator on the group's syndicated shows, under the name Tamara Murphy Fytch. When Candido hit the screen as Skip, he was paired with Sytch, now branded Sunny, with the two collectively known as the Body Donnas - fitness gurus. Sunny was scantily clad, overbearing and flirtatious, which was new ground for the WWF.

The company's portrayal of its ladies in the past had been anything but sexual. With the product then geared towards a pre-pubescent crowd, the role of women had to match the wholesome family image that the WWF were presenting. There were still "good" women and "bad" women, with the likes of Elizabeth Hulette portraying the former as the virtuous Miss Elizabeth, while Sherri Martel became known as Sensational Sherri, a conniving, backstabbing witch with gigantic breasts and a dress sense straight out of the *Rocky Horror Picture Show*.

Historically in wrestling, business struggling had usually led to a foregoing of moral righteousness and a willingness to push the envelope, resulting in what was known in the business as *hotshotting*. The portrayal of Sunny fit into that category, because she was from a new mould: her appeal *was* strictly sexual. Fans were allowed to see tantalising glimpses of her and were encouraged to fantasise. It was a far cry from the pure athleticism presented in previous years by The Fabulous Moolah, Judy Grable, Mildred Burke and their contemporaries.

AMIDST THE raging horde of testosterone behind the curtain, Tammy became an easy target for some of the boys looking to engage in "afternoon delights". Chris's problem was that Tammy was all too eager to accept their advances, leading to serious tension brewing beneath the surface. For some the main issue was not so much that Tammy was unfaithful to Chris right under his nose, but rather that she was doing it with the eternally unpopular Shawn Michaels, The Kliq head honcho. And she was brazen about it too - they both were. "Sometimes we would use Vince's office," Sytch casually recalled about one of their many transgressions.

In later years when Tammy had outgrown Chris on-screen and they were split as a television duo, she would get frisky with Shawn in the showers or a storage closet while an oblivious Candido worked his match. Kevin Nash recalled numerous times where he went from playing a bodyguard for Shawn in the storylines to actually being one for him backstage, and on occasion he would act as a bouncer too, guarding the door to prevent Chris from catching Shawn and Tammy in the act.

Many nights it was close. Sean Waltman told the story that one evening Michaels and Sytch had holed themselves in a room while Candido was wrestling, but they had lost track of time. Candido had finished his match and was coming down the corridor, approaching the room that the two were in. Nash gave a code red knock on the door to let Shawn know, and he quickly evacuated the room, his face a picture of innocence. What Michaels didn't realise was that he had fuzz from Tammy's distinctive mohair sweater stuck in the stubble on his chin. It didn't take much imagination to realise what was going on.

Shawn enjoyed the thrill of his steamy encounters with Sytch while Candido was in the next room, especially because he wasn't too keen on him anyway. He wasn't fond of anyone in particular outside of his band of buddies, but he found Chris particularly irksome. Candido himself credited that to an incident on a house show on March 3, 1996 in Springfield[30], during a Shawn Michaels and Bret Hart lumberjack match. It was a typically pro wrestling issue where a mountain was made out of a molehill, but he believed it had caused their heat.

---

[30] Though Chris publicly credited this date for the origin of the heat between the pair, Michaels and Sytch were having an affair many months prior to that.

It stemmed from a spot that went wrong in the bout after a Michaels spill to the outside. Owen Hart and Davey Boy Smith were out of position and thus no one was there to lay the boots in to Shawn and make him sell, as per the plan. Candido realised someone needed to throw a few blows in so that Shawn wouldn't look stupid lying there selling nothing, so took it upon himself to do just that. Backstage, a petulant and ungrateful Michaels chewed him out for trying to take his heat and get over at his expense, so Chris lost his cool and argued back with Michaels. Things escalated to the point that the two were going to fight in the parking lot, but they were held back by members of the roster. It was the first nail in the coffin of Candido's WWF career.

IN THE locker-room, opinions regarding Sytch were especially polarised. There was a prevailing belief amongst some that Candido was punching far above his weight with Tammy, thus she was fair game for Michaels' advances. "It's only Skip," appeared to be the attitude adopted by Michaels apologists, apparently happy to judge a man's perceived worth based on his push rather than the person beneath it.

Sean Waltman would state that he was convinced Candido knew what was going on, but he didn't bring it up with Sytch because he just wanted her to be happy. Others thought the way Sytch treated Candido was unacceptable, and they didn't think he had any idea what she was up to while he was in the ring. Feeling it was none of their business to intervene, they wouldn't tell him to his face what was taking place, but were happy to extol their own brands of justice on Sytch.

The Godwinns in particular didn't care for Tammy's hypocrisy in keeping Chris on a leash while fulfilling her own hedonism, so when an angle arose that called for them to pour a bucket of their trademark pig slop over her head, they used it as an opportunity to exact some revenge. As Dennis Knight, who played hillbilly pig handler Phineas Godwinn recalled, "I left the bucket in the locker-room and said to no one in particular, 'So, I am slopping Sunny tonight. Don't anybody be touching this bucket...' and sure enough the bucket was full when I got back. She got a mixture of a little bit of everyone that night."

Sytch was an easy target for ribbing, and even her sexual relationship with Shawn Michaels couldn't save her from the rest of The Kliq and their unique brand of hazing. One night, she found to her revulsion that human excrement had been placed inside her duffel bag. Within the industry the golden rule was that you never sold a rib, no matter how mean-spirited or vile, because it made you a prime target for further abuse. Sytch did the opposite, running from the locker-room in tears. Sean Waltman pointed to Alundra Blayze as an example of how to correctly react to a rib of that nature, "She didn't sell it one fucking bit," he noted when remembering a similar incident involving the women's champion.

Waltman took things even further during a tour of Germany. Irritated by Sytch's whining about how long The Kliq were taking to get on the tour bus after shows, which she had complained to the agents was cutting into her workout schedule, Waltman vowed revenge. "At the time, that seemed like a big enough offence to do what I did," he declared. What he did, was scale a locked fence behind which Sytch's gear was hidden (after the incident with the duffel bag, she had decided to start taking precautions) and delicately placed pre-prepared faeces under a chicken breast that she had set aside for lunch. Sytch didn't find it until hours later when the crew arrived back at the hotel.

As Tom Prichard remembers, "Because I was teaming with Chris and Tammy at the time, Sean had came up to me earlier in the night and asked me, 'Are you gonna get any heat if something happens to these guys?' I said, 'Man, I am my own guy. I don't wanna be connected with anyone.' Chris and Tammy had told me to put my bags with theirs away from everyone else, but I said no, because I could just sense something was going to go down that night."

The scene at the hotel was chaos. "Chris Candido was hotter than a sum-bitch," remembered Steve Austin, who witnessed the fallout from the hotel bar. Sytch was so distraught by the ordeal that she demanded to be flown home to the States on the next flight available. "There's gonna be a lot of heat for this," said Davey Boy Smith pensively to Austin, "Chris is as mad as a motherfucker."

"I will never forget agents Gerald Brisco and George Steele in the bar that night," said Prichard, "Brisco grabbed me and asked me who had messed with Tammy's food, but I knew full well that he already knew, and he knew full well that I knew. I just said to him, 'No sir, Jerry, you know I would tell you if I knew.' I wasn't about to say anything, because I didn't want shit to start happening to me. I later explained to Tammy and Chris that they needed to calm their shit down to stop things like this happening, but Tammy wouldn't listen."

Candido for his part would later downplay that kind of behaviour as boys simply being boys. It was just the result of long road trips and boredom, he argued. He claimed it was sophomoric, guys entertaining themselves with pranks to see who they could crack, just like high school.

112 | P a g e

The Kliq had the tenure so they were the seniors, whereas he and Tammy were new to the company and were the freshmen.

Sytch wound up others too, but none more so than William Moody, the former real-life mortician who was now playing the role on television as Paul Bearer, manager of The Undertaker. Moody admitted that he very rarely hated anyone, but he *detested* Tammy. The two exchanged vicious barbs with each other on an almost daily basis, to the point that Jim Cornette - mutual friend of both - was drafted in by McMahon to serve as a mediator in their rapidly escalating war.

Moody liked Chris, as most of the boys who weren't in The Kliq did, but he couldn't understand why he would let himself be emasculated by Sytch in the way that he was. "I called him out in front of all the boys at Madison Square Garden and flat out told him what was going on with her, that she was a two-timing whore and that he was following her around everywhere like a puppy dog," Moody remembered. Chris's response was simple, "Percy, I love her."[31] Moody begrudgingly accepted that, but still sniped to his friend, "Well, I just wanted you to know that I *don't* love her."

Even those who worked closely with Sytch recounted tales of having problems with her. In Tom Prichard's case, he had rode with Chris and Tammy to try and create a bond between the three of them in light of their newly established on-screen union, but he could barely endure it. "She just berated Chris the whole time," remembered Tom, "When we got to the arena, I asked 'Taker if I could ride with him so I could get away from her."

For Prichard it got to the point that he didn't even want to be seen near Sytch, lest he acquire her intense heat via osmosis. As Prichard told it, he was walking several paces behind Candido and Sytch one day when fans were around, clearly intentionally trying to distance himself from the pair. Road agent George Steele spotted that and later pulled Prichard to one side, cryptically advising, "Let's not everyone know of our problems." Prichard knew exactly what he meant, and simply shrugged and told him, "Got it," but it was obvious to all onlookers that he didn't get on with Sytch.

THE BELIEF in the locker-room was that Candido was clearly very adept at denial or genuinely had no idea what was going on right beneath his nose, and in several interviews conducted years later, he dismissed the stories of Shawn and Tammy. "His girlfriend was sleeping with everyone in the

---

[31] Candido, like many of the boys, referred to Moody as "Percy" due to his time spent managing under the guise of Percy Pringle III in the territories, prior to becoming Paul Bearer.

territory and he was acting like he didn't know what was going on. He was walking around like a dumb stooge," observed Kevin Nash.

"I don't think he wanted to know what she was doing, even though backstage *everyone* knew," added Prichard. "Myself, Chris, and Louie Spicolli did a shot in L.A. one time, and Spicolli implied that Tammy, how can I put it... wasn't the most honourable person. Chris got really pissed about that and kicked a bag on the floor in anger, then stormed off. The thing is, Tammy didn't even try and hide that she was a bitch, so it did make Chris look bad to everyone when he acted like nothing was going on. He wasn't stupid, he just didn't want to make any waves. He loved wrestling and he did love Tammy, but she made it very difficult for him."

Jim Cornette was responsible for first breaking Sytch into the business, utilising the then twenty-year old in SMW as heel manager Tammy Fytch. He was more tolerant of Sytch than most, but he too recognised how much she had changed since her Knoxville days. "Tammy was thrilled at suddenly being a big star and getting all this attention from the fans, the boys, everyone. Chris never had that attitude, he was always the same guy and he never changed a bit, but Tammy went fucking nuts."

Another name linked with Tammy was Davey Boy Smith. Sytch later claimed to have had an affair with him and cited it as a source of resentment between Smith and Shawn Michaels when the pair fell out in 1997. The situation eventually escalated to the point that Michaels became so jealous of the relationship that he flat out refused to put Smith over in any situation or even work with him.[32]

Publicly however, Candido remained steadfast in his belief that these were nothing but rumours, once quipping that, "Davey never ratted around because Diana (his wife) could legitimately kick his ass," before pointing out that Diana was trained by her father Stu Hart like her brothers in the business, and she knew how to stretch people. Searching for an example to back up his theory, Candido recalled one night in particular where Diana had told him about a new move Stu had showed her, proceeding to make both he and Dustin Runnels instantly plead for mercy when she applied it on them. He pointed to that as proof that Smith wouldn't have dared cheat on her.

---

[32] In their final meeting on UK-only pay-per-view show *One Night Only* in September 1997, Michaels beat Smith in his home country in front of his dying sister, after Smith had promised he would win the match for her. The original booking called for Smith to win, but Michaels politicked for it to be changed. As Bret Hart would later recall, "The fire in Davey's eyes went out that day; he was never the same."

"He probably was the most un-jealous or most forgiving person in the world," said the Honky Tonk Man of Candido, but testimonies from others suggest that Chris knew exactly what was going on with Tammy behind his back and he didn't approve, and that it bothered him far more than he showed. Scott Bigelow recounted that one evening he and a few others found what appeared to be a suicide note in Candido's bag, with the indication being that the Tammy situation combined with The Kliq treating him like dirt, had driven him to the edge. "They were trying to kill the poor guy," Bigelow said, "And they thought it was all a big joke."

DESPITE THE initial underwhelming performance at the box office, the WWF had made a commitment to the *In Your House* series for at least the remainder of the year, and on July 23rd in front of over 6,000 fans in Nashville, they tried it again. This time Vince learned from his mistakes in promoting the event, and offered half-price tickets to children, as well as promising that the only way to see Bret Hart and The Undertaker wrestle was to be there live, as they were not on the pay-per-view broadcast. While the show didn't sell out, and actually drew nearly 2,000 people less than WCW's *Starrcade* had done the previous December, the quality of the in-ring action on the show left most fans satisfied. *The Wrestling Observer Newsletter* too praised the card, but wondered if a spate of recent poor events were skewing people's views. Dave Meltzer wrote of the show:

I'm not sure if it's an indication of decreasing expectations and thus one outstanding match, three better than average and two bad matches constitutes an excellent show nowadays, or simply that people vary their responses based on the price tag, and since this show was $14.95, less is expected than for other shows.

The majority of the action on the card ranged from good to great, with only the main event that once again saw Diesel against Sid, this time in a lumberjack match, failing to deliver. Stealing the show was the inimitable Shawn Michaels, who produced a classic encounter contested for the Intercontinental Championship with Nashville native Jeff Jarrett.

Jarrett was determined to deliver the best performance he could for his hometown crowd, but because he was playing heel, he sauntered to the ring with an air of conceited arrogance. Ever the showman, he made his entrance clad in a white pleather jacket adorned with large flashing red letters of his initials, lighting him up like a cheap motel sign. Michaels danced to the ring with his usual swagger, decked out in white and gold with a heart motif emblazoned directly over his crotch. He was undoubtedly the man the Nashville fans were rooting for, and the booming response to him was vindication to Vince that he had been right to turn Shawn babyface after *WrestleMania*. "Listen to this crowd," he bellowed satisfied from behind his announce desk, "He is hot tonight!"

The two seasoned performers, with twenty years of experience between them, spent the first stage of the bout hamming it up to the max. They did little and barely touched, instead using their collective charisma and strong personalities to keep the crowd on the edge of their seats. After they had taken turns mocking each other's trademark poses, Jarrett acted like he was fed up and threatened to walk out. It was to prove a curious shadow of an incident that occurred directly after the match was over.

Being the son of successful promoter Jerry Jarrett and having worked for his father in his Memphis territory for a number of years, Jeff was well versed in the art of stalling and eating up time in order to generate heat with a crowd. He employed those tricks adroitly, building to the moment where Michaels would finally get his hands on him. When he did, the building erupted.

Michaels, like Jarrett, was determined to have a great match. Not because of the crowd or to impress anyone in particular, but rather to stick it to the boys in the back who resented him. They could say what they wanted, he thought, but one thing they could never take away from him was that he was better than all of them. With that in mind, he launched himself over the top rope onto both Jarrett and his manager The Roadie (Brian James 'Armstrong', another second generation performer) with a daredevil move rarely seen in the US in 1995 called a slingshot plancha.

Michaels followed up that athletic feat with another even more impressive one, allowing Jarrett to backdrop him straight over the top rope and down to the ringside floor some ten-feet below. He landed with a hard thud on his already notoriously wonky back, leaving Vince at a loss for words. Literally, it turned out, as suddenly his microphone stopped working and the television audience could no longer hear him. Seeing his boss's face turning bright red with rage, co-commentator Jerry Lawler played it off as part of the broadcast, taking over announcing duties himself while technicians scrambled to fix the problem with McMahon's headset.

Meanwhile the two combatants quickened the pace, and as the sweat began to pour and their chests began to heave, little by little the excitement of the contest increased. They went back-and-forth, vying for position with neither man taking a clear advantage, until Jarrett decided it was time for a breather and locked on a sleeper hold. "We got 'em brother, we got 'em," whispered a satisfied Jarrett to Michaels as the volume of the crowd continued to rise.

As the two went into the final stage of their epic dance, Michaels began throwing himself at Jarrett from every conceivable angle. It intensified the drama, making the audience question if Shawn possessed the fortitude to beat the champion, especially as he seemed to become increasingly desperate in his attempts to win the match. Michaels allowed the crowd to believe he would be willing to go to any lengths to win the title, showing his darker side as he pulled Jarrett crotch-first into the steel ring post. Jarrett played it to the hilt, first begging for mercy and imploring Shawn not to go through with it, then wincing when he did.

A further layer of intrigue was added to an already gripping contest when the referee was knocked down, allowing Roadie to sneak into the ring and take out Shawn's leg. The fans had seen this kind of interference before and knew it usually spelled defeat for the babyface hero, but not tonight. Michaels defied the odds and kicked out, waiting to fling his shoulder from the mat until the very last second so that the tension was palpable. The heel duo attempted to cheat again, with Roadie turning his back and covertly tripping who he thought was Michaels, only to discover he had actually tripped Jarrett. By the time he realised what he had done it was too late; a Michaels superkick had connected and Jarrett had been pinned for the three count, giving Shawn his third reign with the Intercontinental belt.

Michaels later commented that he felt the bout was among the best of his career and that he was immensely proud of it. He let himself get lost in the moment and smiled as he danced around the ring with the gold, while fireworks went off in the rafters heralding his victory. Realising that Michaels' stock was as hot as ever, Vince took it as an opportunity to shift some of his merchandise, and had on-screen shill Barry Didinsky shout into the camera, imploring the viewers at home to call up and buy some replica Shawn Michaels sunglasses to celebrate.

As good as the match was, what happened next was the bigger story. Following the bout, Jarrett and James were supposed to do an angle cementing their breakup following the miscommunication that led to the finish, resulting in a *SummerSlam* confrontation between the two. But instead the pair walked out of the building and seemingly quit the promotion on the spot.

From his commentary position Vince was only hearing snippets of the situation and didn't know if one of them had been injured, had a family emergency, or a similarly urgent situation. He needed to make a decision quickly and got the message to a highly-caffeinated Michael Hayes to improvise and make up a story about a fight between the two backstage.

The reality was that Jarrett had become fed up with the way he was being used. He was frustrated at rarely winning on pay-per-view and television, despite being the Intercontinental Champion, he was sick of the low pay-offs and he was unhappy with the planned storyline that was in the works between he and James. Jarrett felt the proposed breakup and feud were being rushed, and he didn't like the angle that the WWF were planning to run that would expose him as a lip-synching fraud, which would see Roadie revealed as the real singer of his much-hyped song *With My Baby Tonight*.

According to his father Jerry, Jeff was concerned that the angle would damage his credibility and prevent him from having any longevity, and that he had expressed to McMahon a number of times that he didn't like the direction his character was going in. The final affront was that he was asked to lose the title and be exposed as a phony both in the same night, and in his hometown no less. Jeff felt it would cause too much damage to his persona, to the point where once the Roadie feud was done he would have nowhere to go.

Brian James made the decision to follow Jarrett out of the promotion partly through loyalty. He too felt the angle was being rushed, but he also had concerns about a drug test that he had been asked to take. While James didn't use steroids, he did have a tendency towards marijuana and pills, and he knew he would fail the test. Rather than face the consequences of that, he chose to walk with Jarrett in a display of unity. He would later talk about regretting the decision, claiming future plans called for a three-way match between he, Jarrett and Michaels and that long-term plans were for him to become the Intercontinental Champion.

Unable to go and work for WCW due to his contract with Titan, Jarrett instead sat around for a few months before working some shots for Jerry Lawler's USWA (debuting on November 11th in an angle where he attacked, ironically enough, Brian James), while James pitched up in Jim Cornette's SMW right away. Both Lawler and Cornette were also employed by Vince, who allowed them to use the estranged talent to keep them in ring shape, so they would be prepared if and when a compromise was reached for their returns. Jarrett eventually did come to an agreement with Titan, briefly returning at the end of the year for a program with Ahmed Johnson, before suffering an injury and leaving the promotion, resurfacing in WCW in October 1996.

James didn't appear again until 1996, after Jarrett's departure, coming back as 'The Real Double J' Jesse Jammes. McMahon had made the decision to get closure on the angle of James having sang *With My Baby Tonight*, even without Jarrett in the company anymore. Feuding with someone no longer associated with the WWF proved to be as difficult as it sounded, and Jesse Jammes struggled to get over. His time eventually came in late 1997 when he was paired with fellow struggler Billy Gunn. The two formed the New Age Outlaws, and went onto become one of the most successful tag teams in company history.

FOLLOWING THE pattern of the previous three shows, the slight optimism within the WWF coming out of *In Your House 2* was soon quelled when the buy rate for the event was revealed. It had performed worse than the original, with only 150,000 homes willing to part with their $14.95, generating a revenue of $1.08 million. By contrast WCW's *Bash at the Beach* event, which Eric Bischoff had frustrated Turner executives with by holding it on an actual beach and not charging a penny for tickets, had performed well at the box office. *Bash* pulled 25,000 viewers more than *In Your House 2*, and at a higher price, raking in almost $2.4 million for the company.

Behind the scenes there was increasing concern amongst office employees and the boys in the locker-room that the WWF was in financial trouble. The warning signs were clear for all to see, and eventually Vince was forced to act. To counter the company's falling revenue, he underwent a spot of housecleaning. Business in the first half of the year had been concerning: the *In Your House* series had not started with the bang McMahon had hoped for, *King of the Ring* had been a commercial and creative disaster, and *WrestleMania* had bombed. The projections stated that the WWF was on course to lose more money in 1995 than in any other year in its history, and that was without a series of large legal settlements to pay out as had been the case in 1994.

One of the biggest casualties was John Tunney, Jr. who everyone knew as Jack. Historically the Tunney family had controlled wrestling in Toronto since the 1930s, with Jack's father John, Sr. promoting the Queensbury Athletic Club in the city alongside his brother Frank. The duo were the principle promoters of the newly opened Maple Leaf Gardens, and due to their connections they had the final say on which other groups could run in the town.

When John, Sr. died in 1940, Frank was left in sole charge for the next decade until the seventeen-year-old Jack was brought into the business in 1952. Frank was well respected in the industry, with some historians considering him among the finest promoters in the history of the business. Unfortunately, the Maple Leaf Garden shows were starting to struggle by the time he died in 1983. The Tunneys had started working with George Scott and Jim Crockett and were aligned with the NWA, but crowds had dropped from 15,000 to around 3,000, with no sign of improvement.

For Jack, the timing of Vince McMahon stepping in and making him an offer to take over the territory couldn't have been better. He was eager to work with the audacious promoter, who he recognised as the future of the industry and the perfect man to bring the crowds back to Toronto. Plus their fathers had been friends and frequently vacationed together with their wives, so Tunney had an affinity towards him. He struck an agreement with McMahon at Vince, Sr.'s funeral, forcing Crockett out and turning his back on the NWA, in return for a lucrative deal that would give him a percentage of every house show that the company ran in Canada. Tunney in turn helped McMahon squash the other local territories in the country, playing a large role in helping him dominate the wrestling scene north of the border.

As a token gesture to thank Tunney for the doors he had opened in Canada and for aligning with the WWF ahead of the NWA, McMahon made him the on-screen figurehead president of the company. Tunney was an expensive cognac, thousand-dollar-suit, Rolex watch and Cadillac type of guy, so he was an ideal fit for the gig. He also played a key role in bringing *WrestleMania VI* to Toronto, though his cousin Eddie (Frank's son) nearly scuppered the whole deal. Jack and Eddie didn't get on, and Eddie felt pushed out when Jack started working with Vince, so sued both Jack and Titan Sports. In an attempt to torpedo the supershow, Eddie even trademarked the name *WrestleMania* in Canada, which Vince had to then buy from him at an inflated price, much to his chagrin.

McMahon blamed Jack for the mess, but the two third-generation promoters mostly worked symbiotically for over a decade. Fractures in the relationship started to appear in the early nineties, after Tunney declared he would testify against Terry Garvin in relation to sexual abuse charges levelled by Toronto based referee Mike Clark. Tunney, who was said to have witnessed Garvin's alleged proposition of Clark, was eventually talked out of going public. Nevertheless, McMahon remained annoyed that Tunney was willing to potentially plunge the company into further turmoil at a time when he needed all the internal support he could muster.

Come 1995, Vince decided that he no longer needed Tunney's connections to do business in Canada. He had been paying close attention - as he always did with anything he was involved in - and now Tunney's contacts and connections were *his* contacts and connections. On July 12,

1995, McMahon ended the union for good, parting ways with his enduring ally on somewhat frosty terms.[33] He replaced Tunney as President of WWF Canada with Carl DeMarco, the former business manager of Bret Hart. Long-time WWF veteran wrestler, announcer, and backstage controller Gorilla Monsoon, was given the role of on-screen president.

Few were sad to see Tunney go. "He was a fucking crook!" griped Kevin Nash, "Every time we went up to Toronto, that motherfucker had a new car, and yet the pay-offs up there were always the shits."

There were other victims of Vince's thriftiness. On-camera interviewer Stephanie Wiand was one of them. The Z-list actress had been imported from Hollywood, as Vince attempted to go in a different direction with his non-wrestling personalities in the hope of giving a fresh feel to his product. For Wiand, it didn't work. She was not a wrestling fan and was clearly out of her depth in the role. As she remembered, "Honestly, it was all very odd. I was literally just starting out in the entertainment industry and it was an opportunity that I felt I had to take for a variety of reasons at the time. They pushed me to be this kind of high-energy spaz on-camera, but I am actually pretty low-key in real life." Wiand had no hard feelings about the release; if anything she had long seen it coming, because she knew she didn't fit in. "It was a long time ago, and to me, it was just a job that I did. But I am grateful for my time there, because it was the first in a series of jobs that led me to where I am now,"[34] she added.

Next, a number of high paid executives were released without warning, many of whom had been with the company for years and assumed their jobs were safe. The in-ring talent knew it was only a matter of time before there would be cuts amongst them too, and many were nervous about the security of their own jobs. Vince continued to be ruthless, saving money wherever he felt he could. He even forced 'Lord' Alfred Hayes - a staple of WWF programming since 1982 - into early retirement, when the well-spoken Brit refused to take a 40% pay cut on his salary. The departures of

---

[33] So bitter was the split that when Tunney died at his home from a heart attack in 2004, nobody from the McMahon family or what was now the WWE attended his funeral or offered any on-screen condolences or tributes.

[34] After leaving the WWF, Wiand returned to the lower reaches of Hollywood. Her first job was as an ADR artist on Baz Luhrman's *Romeo + Juliet*, which led to a minor role as an actress in the long-running television series *The Bold and the Beautiful* in 1998. After a few years away from movies, she scored some voice parts in sci-fi web series *Afterworld*. As well working as both a writer and producer, Wiand also starred in the tongue-in-cheek comedy sci-fi flick *Revenge of the Bimbot Zombie Killers* in a leading role.

both Alfred Hayes and Jack Tunney marked something of an end of an era, with the only person still employed who appeared on television at the original *WrestleMania* a decade prior, being ring announcer Howard 'The Fink' Finkel.

A short time later, the day the roster had dreaded finally came, as Titan severed ties with no less than a dozen members of the crew. Amongst them were many of the stars that Vince had brought back from the past, none of whom had made much of an impact in the new-look WWF (including Sione Vailahi, Nikolai Volkoff, King Kong Bundy, Lou Albano and Afa). Others were heavily gimmicked characters that weren't over (Mantaur, Irwin R. Schyster, Doink and Dink) or road agents (Tony Garea). The talent cull combined with the AWOL status of Jeff Jarrett and Brian James resulted in a thinner roster than ever.

Tom Prichard and Jimmy Del Ray, collectively known as the Heavenly Bodies, were also let go. On July 24th in Louisville, Kentucky, the pair were called into the dressing room by Vince McMahon and J.J. Dillon, and told that they would be spending the next few months working in Jim Cornette's Smoky Mountain Wrestling. "Jim really needs you guys down there," the team were informed, but Prichard saw right through that comment for what it was. "I just looked at J.J. and Vince and thought, 'You bullshitting sons of bitches!' We knew that SMW wasn't going to last. Basically they were firing us, but in a nice, bullshit way."

At the time Vince used to hire and fire his talent face-to-face, so he would often look for a way to soften the blow to make it easier for them to take, and also to assuage his conscience. It wasn't a part of the job he enjoyed, but he preferred the personal touch when dealing with his employees. It wasn't necessarily a good thing for the talent to be dealing directly with Vince. Sometimes it could lead to awkward moments if they said or did something inappropriate or stupid.

Prichard told the following anecdote of his own first encounter with McMahon. "Vince told me that when he first met me, I came across like, 'A flaming fucking asshole.' It was 1987 and I was with Ted DiBiase at the gym in Titan Tower, and Vince was there working out. I had never met him, and as it happened I had just heard *Stand Back*[35] the night before and thought it was great. I decided to tell him that as an ice breaker and have a joke with

---

[35] Vince McMahon's musical middle finger to the rest of the industry. Vince performed *Stand Back* at the 1987 Slammy Awards and with lyrics such as "I'm a man running wild, heading for the top, never slowing down, never gonna stop, and along the way you'll see a lot of men drop", it was a very obvious way to stick it to his rivals in typical McMahon fashion.

him about it. He just grunted, 'Great,' and walked away looking annoyed. I didn't realise he had just been in a meeting with Houston promoter Paul Boesch and his partners to discuss Boesch's retirement show, and I later found out that it was a particularly bad meeting because they had wanted to change their agreement with Vince, and had decided they wanted the whole house. He wasn't in the mood to play around."

The cuts continued throughout the year, with the WWF going from having employed over fifty active full-time performers in January, to under thirty-five by December. The way Titan was producing television was changing too, with *Wrestling Challenge,* a show that had endured since 1986, dumped unceremoniously in order to reduce production costs. Not only that, but instead of filming television at fifty different live events per year, the company was scaling back to half of that, and simply increasing their taping blocks to four hours from three as another frugal measure. Those who remembered Vince's bold claims in May that the company was coming through the other side of a perilous financial tunnel, now strongly suspected that this had merely been bluster from the chairman to disguise just how much trouble the WWF was really in.

EIGHT

TROY MARTIN CAME FROM THE independent scene with a lofty reputation. As 'The Franchise' Shane Douglas, Martin had established himself as the top guy in Philadelphia-based renegade outlet ECW thanks to a series of scathing promos, many of which viciously ripped into veterans and industry legends. On August 27, 1994, he was also involved in one of the most infamous and shocking stunts to ever take place on the independent scene, during a tournament to crown a new NWA Champion.

The then Eastern Championship Wrestling was still a member of the NWA, though was establishing itself in its own right as a vibrant, progressive entity. The relationship came to an explosive end on that fateful night in Philadelphia. Shane Douglas, the reigning ECW Heavyweight Champion, beat Peter 'The Tazmaniac' Senerchia and second generation star Dean Malenko in the earlier rounds of the tournament, before downing Charles 'Too Cold Scorpio' Scaggs in the final to become the new NWA World Heavyweight Champion. Following the victory, Martin cut an impassioned speech, acting like he was overcome with emotion. Then in a moment never to be forgotten or forgiven by old-timers, he threw the belt to the ground and began to speak:

> I am not the man who accepts a torch to be handed down to me from an organization that died, R.I.P, seven years ago. The Franchise, Shane Douglas, is the man who ignites the new flame of the sport of professional wrestling. [Shane picks up the ECW Heavyweight title belt] Tonight, before God and my father as witness, I declare myself, The Franchise, as the new ECW Heavyweight Champion of the World! We have set out to change the face of professional wrestling. So tonight, let the new era begin; the era of the sport of professional wrestling, the era of The Franchise, the era of ECW.

It was a bold move, one orchestrated by ECW's perennial puppet master promoter Paul Heyman, and designed to put ECW on the wrestling map. It worked a charm and achieved exactly that, but it left a lot of people upset with Martin for denigrating the legacy of the once-great NWA. In truth, the belt and the waning Alliance were long-since irrelevant. The national expansion and explosion in popularity of the WWF in the Hogan years, followed by the departure of WCW from the NWA some years later, had all but killed them off as a viable entity. If the belt was so prestigious and notable, some commented, then it wouldn't have been contested for in a bingo hall deep in the Philly slums.

The Shane Douglas persona had become a hot commodity in wrestling. So hot, in fact, that Vince McMahon wanted to sign Martin for the WWF before Eric Bischoff inevitably snapped him up for his WCW revolution. Martin was not especially interested in working for the WWF again (he had previously spent an uneventful year there at the start of the decade); he was happy with his role as the top guy in ECW, not to mention the free time that working for them afforded him to pursue his outside-ring career as a teacher.

When McMahon invited him for a meeting at Titan Tower, Martin decided to hear him out in case he was given an offer he couldn't refuse. But he didn't particularly endear himself to the WWF chairman, turning up for negotiations with his wife Carla, who demanded a series of clauses and promises in order for her husband to sign on with the company.

Carla flat out told McMahon that she was concerned with her husband leaving a comfortable teaching position and a wrestling job that meant he was only away on the weekends, for a full-time job on the road. Vince assured her, "I understand that concern, but let me tell you from the bottom of my heart that this will be very lucrative for your husband. I am going to make him a very wealthy man, you have my word on that."

Unlike many others, Martin was not besotted with the lustre of the WWF, and agonised over the decision for several months. He harvested advice from friends in the business who had worked for Vince, all of whom assured him that the WWF boss was a man of his word. He eventually agreed to sign, but only because he figured the WWF was the place to go in order to earn real money in the industry, something he hoped would put him through the $30,000 per year medical school he was hoping to attend. Martin was given the impression from McMahon that the company was in a good state thanks to his words and actions, which had included picking he and Carla up in limousines and putting them up in $1,000 hotels as he tried to woo 'The Franchise' into signing.

Martin had fallen for the pitch, with no idea that the group was actually haemorrhaging money. The company downsizing from an international powerhouse back to being a North East regional territory was a genuine possibility. "I was very wrong," Martin later commented, "The money I made in four months in the WWF turned out to be equal to what I made in one month with ECW. I mistakenly believed the grass was greener on the other side. After leaving, I realised that the grass was actually greener in ECW." Martin later claimed that after tax and expenses, he only made a paltry $1,400 from his WWF tenure, the same as he usually made in a single weekend wrestling for ECW.

It was little surprise to most that Martin became the latest talented performer to be saddled with a no-hope gimmick that seemed almost designed to mock the portrayer. Observers had seen it all before, with numerous guys having arrived in the Federation with impressive backgrounds elsewhere, only to be changed on Vince's whim into just another cartoonified component of the WWF circus. In Martin's case he was cast as a school teacher and rechristened as the alliterative Dean Douglas, which played off his previous real-life profession. Just a year earlier he was considered one of the cutting edge talents in the business, but the Shane Douglas character had been swallowed up by the WWF machine and remoulded to their liking. "Vince is such an egotist he wants to say, 'I created you.' It was pretty ridiculous to try and pretend that I was not somebody that I had been for thirteen years," complained Martin.

The name Dean Douglas itself was another example of a practice Vince was fond of when naming his characters. He liked alliteration as a general rule anyway, but if there was an opportunity to give a performer a moniker that also had dual meaning, such as with Paul Bearer, then he would jump at the chance. Though in this case it was actually Martin himself who came up with the name, because the original creative called for him to be known simply as 'The Dean'. He had pushed for the Douglas surname to be added in a futile attempt at retaining a semblance of his former self, but conceded, "Vince went along with it, but not because I was urging him to. He just thought it sounded better and would be more marketable."

The twist for Martin was that he was asked to portray an *evil* school teacher, one who derogatorily graded matches and dragged his nails down a chalkboard to punctuate his critiques. He did all of that while wearing a garish blue graduation gown, a mortarboard, and a baby blue singlet that made him look like a shapeless rookie rather than a top star. No explanation was given as to why the supposed professor was wearing attire that suggested he had just graduated from high school, but as was soon evident once Dean Douglas debuted in the summer; not a whole lot of thought was put into the character anyway.

Martin was far from the only one to suffer though, with Vince going through a phase of giving everyone on his roster day jobs which they supposedly did alongside wrestling. What McMahon failed to see, or never had pointed out to him, was that giving guys real-life job stripped the aura of them being larger-than-life personas and made them into regular people, the exact opposite of what Vince wanted his WWF Superstars to be. Quipped one member of the roster saddled with such a gimmick, "The money was so bad that in many cases we almost needed those bullshit second jobs in real life in order to balance the bills. We probably would have been better off being garbage men, teachers, or whatever else Vince thought would be amusing that week."

The cast of characters in 1995 read like an occupation guide. There were acts such as an evil dentist portrayed by Glenn Jacobs, known as Isaac Yankem D.D.S., another amusing pun name which came about after Vince endured a particularly unpleasant trip to the dentist one afternoon and wanted to vent his frustrations about it via a visceral personification; NASCAR driver Bob Holly; and a camp magician with a painted face called Phantasio, whose special moves included removing his opponent's pants.

Vince even had a garbage man, Duke 'the Dumpster' Droese, played by Mike Droese, though the reason behind McMahon doing the gimmick was down to his bravado and arrogance more than anything else. He was so confident that he could make literally anyone a star, that he boasted about being able to turn the worst wrestler in the world into a mainstream success with the power of his creative genius. Calling his bluff, one quick-thinking staffer showed Vince a copy of *Pro Wrestling Illustrated*'s brand new *PWI 500*, a list of the supposed top five-hundred performers in the industry. It was pointed out to Vince that a wrestler called 'Garbage Man' was listed at number five-hundred. "Hire him!" Vince barked, "I'll prove it; we will make him a WWF Superstar." Thus, Mike Droese was hired, given the alliteration treatment, a pair of fresh overalls from the company seamstress and the prerequisite object to carry to the ring (a garbage can, of course), then let loose. He lasted just over two years with the company before asking for and being granted his release in 1996, citing an inability to adjust to the intense WWF road schedule.

While Vince was getting a kick out of turning the WWF into a touring *Yellow Pages*, the talent were not impressed with the direction the company was taking. Shawn Michaels was as outspoken as ever, "There were no stories," he complained, "The company were giving guys jobs as gimmicks. They weren't gimmicks, they were occupations. I knew that we needed to be better, much better, and move with the times."

Martin for his part tried to make the best out of the rough hand he had been dealt, and attempted to bring his opinions to the table. Vince told Martin that he could talk to him at any time with problems relating to the character, so Martin took him up on it and called in the middle of the night to share his thoughts on the Dean Douglas look and persona. He wasn't happy with his outfit for one thing, which he believed too closely resembled Lanny Poffo's character 'The Genius' from the late eighties and early nineties. Vince told him that he respected his opinion, but he liked Dean Douglas the way he was, so he was staying that way.

For Martin this was a blow, because he realised that the gimmick was death creatively. "I wouldn't have watched that, it was boring," he said of the character, so he set about trying to make subtle changes that he thought would help. The first pertained to the grading system that he was using on-screen to evaluate performer's matches. Martin wanted it to be legitimate and use standard grading, but Vince opted for the cartoon-esque approach (with mock grades such as, "I.U; for inanely unprepared.") and stubbornly refused to budge. For Vince, the Dean Douglas persona was a typically overblown WWF version of one of his own college professors. Martin recalled that Vince didn't much care for the man who inspired the character because he was stuffy and boring, and thus his directive was that Dean Douglas should be that way too.

At one endless promo shooting session with Vince and the crew, Martin asked if he could try something outside of the monotone norm that he was being asked to deliver. He would give the same verbiage, but with added inflections and passion, something more closely resembling 'The Franchise' character that he had left behind. Vince permitted him to try, and Martin proceeded to cut an interview much more akin to his work as Shane Douglas, which he believed would have gotten him over with the WWF audience.

It just so happened that McMahon had to go and take a call as soon as Martin was finished, leaving him an open floor to canvas opinion from Vince's aides and right-hand men without his imposing spectre looming over them. They all agreed that the more realistic version of the promo was by far the superior one, but as soon as Vince returned and expressed his preference for the original effort, those same supporters regressed to sycophants, agreeing with McMahon that his way was unquestionably the right way. Martin was dejected, and realised that the writing was already on the wall for him.

IN EARLY August, Pat Patterson stepped down from his role as Vince McMahon's right-hand man to take a break and recharge, leaving the position open. Rather than promoting internally, Vince was instead convinced by Jim Ross to hire his former boss and mentor 'Cowboy' Bill Watts. The 'Cowboy' had last been involved in mainstream wrestling as the booker for WCW. He left the post amidst controversy, fired by nervy Turner brass because they got wind of a 1991 interview conducted with him by *The Pro-Wrestling Torch Newsletter*, in which he openly displayed discriminatory views. Prior to that, Watts had promoted both Mid-South and the once-successful UWF promotion in the eighties, but sold up to Jim Crocket when he found himself cash-strapped and losing money. Ironically the failure of the UWF came as a direct result of the WWF's national expansion, which had stripped him of his best talent.

It was a shocking appointment by McMahon, who had been in direct competition with Watts many times over the years. Like Vince, Watts had a long history in wrestling and a mighty reputation, but he could divide a locker-room like few others. Some of the boys detested him for his no-nonsense approach to business. In WCW, he had caused unrest by removing the protective mats from the ringside area as they were too "WWF-like", banning card playing in the dressing room because he wanted the boys focused on their matches, enforcing kayfabe by preventing babyfaces and heels from travelling together, forcing everyone to stay at the arena until the show was finished, and dishing out fines for tardiness.

Others considered him a visionary, someone who presented wrestling "the right way" with his preference for hard-hitting, realistic looking matches. Bret Hart was one of those, and he was pleased when he learned of Watts' hiring. Hart was a fan of his hard-nosed, in-your-face style and tough guy reputation, something that reminded him a lot of his own father.

McMahon had made the call to hire Watts so that he could concentrate on turning around the numerous off-screen problems with the company's business, allowing him to focus his energies into keeping the group afloat. There was also the added bonus that Watts could deal with all the petty bickering, squabbling and complaining that was rife amongst the boys. The 'Cowboy' was a strict disciplinarian who was more than happy to be unpopular within the locker-room in order to get things done his way, so McMahon saw him as the perfect candidate to control the inmate-ran asylum.

Watts was surprised when he first received the call from Vince, and cautious that the intention was for him to be set up to fail. He suspected McMahon may have only wanted to hire him in order to toy with him as a receipt for perceived past wrong-doings against the WWF. He also knew they were worlds apart philosophically regarding how they felt pro wrestling should be presented. But the offer came at the right time for Watts, who was feeling despondent following a failed marriage, and was looking for a project to channel his own energies into. Wrestling was his safety net, something he had been doing, and doing well, for years. Out of curiosity more than anything else, he accepted the offer.

Even though the boys and many in the office weren't fully aware of it at first, Watts was told he would have full autonomy over the creative direction of the product. It didn't take long for 'the Cowboy' to suspect that the union was going to be a brief one, because he realised immediately that McMahon may have promised him complete control, but he had a hard time delegating authority to anyone else. Not having the twenty-four-seven hands-on involvement that he had always possessed was something he struggled to adapt to.

As Watts had expected, he was tested at first, with Vince playing games with him to gauge his commitment and attitude towards the rest of the office. One thing he forced Watts to do was speak directly to all of the Titan executives and listen to their candid opinions of him. Watts saw it for what it was and remained tactful in response, but he struggled to refrain from tearing into Bruce Prichard when the two spoke. Watts had no respect for Prichard, stemming from him having brokered a deal in the eighties that saw Paul Boesch's popular *Houston Wrestling* partner up exclusively with the WWF instead of Watts' UWF. Watts saw Prichard as untrustworthy, and only loyal to whoever was paying him at the time. But Prichard was going to be one of his team, so he had little choice but to agree to work cordially with him.

Watts set about making changes in the WWF and quickly imposed his wrestling philosophy on the television shows. The first thing he noted was that the company was severely short on heel threats to the top babyfaces. He championed Sid Eudy, Mabel and Yokozuna as three guys who should be booked to look strong, and suggested turning Davey Boy Smith heel for the first time in his career to bolster the quality on the villain side.

One of his favourite booking techniques had always been to have babyfaces get pummelled in vicious on-screen assaults by the heels, so they could later avenge the attacks in matches that people would willingly pay to see. He ran that play over the next few months, with Shawn Michaels, Diesel and The Undertaker all booked in compromising situations in some memorable and well-received angles.

Other Watts' hallmarks were implemented also, such as having clean finishes in matches (including for the heels, something McMahon had always been reluctant to do previously), bouts that told a story with their ring-work alone, and logical, long-term booking. Watts, to his surprise, found that he had far more in common with McMahon than he thought he would. For the first few weeks he held the position, Watts found that the chairman agreed with him on nearly everything, especially pertaining to booking with a long-term direction and a definite end goal.

Watts also noticed that because McMahon was present at television tapings, disgruntled members of the roster would frequently take them as an opportunity to air their grievances. That grated with Watts, because it meant production would grind to a halt as Vince stopped what he was supposed to be doing and instead dealt with the talent. Jim Cornette described having similar issues when he was on the creative team, which became a growing source of frustration for him as he sat waiting for Vince so they could ride to the next town together.

As he recalled, "Vince liked having issues because it meant he could deal with them, but because of that it was hard to get him to apply himself to what he needed to do. There was always a massive line of the boys waiting to talk to him until 1am at every TV [taping], because Vince would see *everyone*. When we did finally get out of there we were starving, but he would never use a drive-thru. We always had to go to a local restaurant and he would order ten egg whites, only healthy shit."

When Watts saw how distracting Vince's open door policy was, he took him to one side and suggested that he should put an end to it. "Let's put you off limits to these cry-babies," he told him, "If they want to talk to you, let them schedule a time in the office another day. We are here to produce television."

To his surprise, McMahon agreed, and the policy was implemented immediately. It worked; Vince had never seen a production run so smoothly and was impressed with the way Watts had everything planned out in detail, with everyone knowing exactly what their role was. Following one taping, McMahon pulled over the car the pair were riding in together and gave Watts a warm hug. "I have never seen television run so well. That was fantastic!" beamed the chairman.

THE TRADITIONAL second biggest card on the WWF calendar was *SummerSlam*. It was an institution that had began in 1988, acting as a mid-way buffer point between the yearly *WrestleMania* shows, used to conclude interim storylines which had been developed after the annual extravaganza that the WWF didn't want to continue through to the following year.

The initially announced card for 1995's edition of *SummerSlam* didn't look to have anything that would justify it as being the number two event of the year. The main event had long been set in stone, with Diesel defending his WWF Championship against *King of the Ring* winner Mabel. It was a match-up which many industry analysts commented could be among the worst WWF pay-per-view main events ever presented.

Shawn Michaels was originally set to work with Sid Eudy to blow off their on-screen issue from earlier in the year. However, when Vince evaluated the card he realised there were no matches that could be potential show-stealers, and mindful of the negative response to *King of the Ring*, he decided to make some changes. Creatively, that was easy, because with Gorilla Monsoon newly established as the on-screen "fan-friendly" WWF President, everything Vince did in response to fan negativity could now be attributed to Monsoon's new persona.

In order to placate Shawn - who didn't particularly want to work with Sid - and to get a match of guaranteed quality that he hoped his audience would pay to see, McMahon decided to present a rematch of *WrestleMania X's* iconic ladder match between Michaels and Scott Hall. The first was widely regarded as one of, if not *the* best match his promotion had ever presented, so it was an obvious if not slightly desperate direction to go in.

Vince also added a bout to the card pitting Sean Waltman against Jinsei Shinzaki, as the two worked well together and could deliver a high-flying contest the likes of which were rarely seen in the WWF. It was something different, but as had been demonstrated by the Watts hire, Vince was willing to try almost anything to get people watching again.

The final card change was to the tag team match on the show, which was originally scheduled to see Owen Hart and Yokozuna defend their tag titles against Lex Luger and Davey Boy Smith. Instead, Vince dropped the match from the card and replaced it with The Smoking Gunns vs. The Blu Brothers. It was a reward for their hard work on house shows and a way for Vince to placate some of his undercard, giving them a chance to earn pay-per-view money to boost their income after a year of weak financial returns. *SummerSlam* wasn't going to gain any more orders based on which tag match was presented, so there was little harm in reconfiguring it. Unfortunately, the two replacement tandems didn't take advantage of the six or so minutes with which they had been afforded to impress, and put forth a lacklustre encounter. The four in the original match, who between them had all been involved in the main event at the past three *SummerSlam* shows,[36] were dropped from the event completely. Having appeared on most pay-per-views so far that year, they could afford to miss the event.

---

[36] Smith headlined in 1992 against Bret Hart at Wembley Stadium; Yokozuna and Lex Luger worked with each other in the top match on 1993's show; and Owen fought brother Bret in a cage match for the WWF Championship in 1994, which though it did not go on last, was the show's real main event in the eyes of most.

Another man pleased to be given an opportunity to work on pay-per-view was Bob Holly. He was tasked with being the opponent for Paul Levesque, making his pay-per-view debut for the WWF under the Hunter Hearst Helmsley guise. To make sure the character came across well on the big stage, Levesque had been honing his act on house shows, where he worked against his friend Sean Waltman, and a number of others who were directed to make him look good.

Levesque had also worked with Holly on a couple of dates back in June, and the two got along reasonably well. Holly appreciated Levesque's obvious talent, noting that his timing was excellent, especially for a relative rookie, and that the spots he called always made sense. The two assembled a spirited bout that made the Helmsley character look strong as required, but also saw Holly appear competitive. Holly was pleased with the match, and had no problem with losing to the newcomer. As he recalled, "I didn't mind, I figured one of these days, it would come back to me. I'd started proving that I could hang with these guys and wrestle just as well as them."

ONE OF the most well-received feel-good stories that Vince presented his public with in 1995 was the plight of Barry Horowitz.

Florida-born Horowitz, who had been trained by Boris Malenko and was once forced by David Crockett to wrestle under the moniker 'Brett Hart' in the NWA, had been with the WWF on and off for nearly a decade by 1995. He was small by the standards of any era, but because of his ability to take a convincing beating, he was retained as enhancement talent and used almost exclusively to put over upcoming performers. Horowitz wasn't considered a WWF Superstar or a member of the active roster, but he was allowed to add a little flavour to his persona with customised tights and a less generic look, which few of the other job guys were afforded.

In the WWF, Horowitz stared at the lights without complaint on a nightly basis and barely registered an offensive move. He didn't mind, "There's always got to be a winner and there's always got to be a loser," he reflected, "Everybody's done a job, the guys who didn't wanna do one were marks. I could have said, 'No, I don't wanna do this,' but it didn't hurt *my* career. This is how I look at it: I put people over."

After a career of doing just that, Vince decided to reward Horowitz for his years of uncomplaining service by finally giving him a real program to work in, and a minor push to go with it. During what seemed like a routine victory for Chris Candido's overbearing Skip character on a July episode of *Action Zone*, Horowitz did the unthinkable and caught a fluke win with an inside cradle while Skip was preoccupied showboating. The result prompted a huge response from the crowd at the Wilkes University Marts Centre in Wilkes-Barre, Pennsylvania, who had previously been quiet after having sat through three hours' worth of tapings (with two more to come), featuring endless throwaway matches where the star would inevitably go over the enhancement wrestler.

Announcer Jim Ross was called upon to provide a sense of gravitas to the moment, and he allowed himself to get lost in the underdog story as he bellowed, "Horowitz wins! Horowitz wins! Horowitz wins!" while the crowd stood and applauded. Horowitz, who had in fact won more than his fair share of matches before his WWF tenure, knew that he needed to celebrate like he didn't know what to do with himself, because winning was so unfamiliar and alien to his character. He jumped around like he had just won the lottery, while Candido and Tammy Sytch threw a faux tantrum in the ring.

People latched onto the Horowitz victory, much like they had when Sean Waltman had been introduced in a similar manner in 1993 when he was allowed to beat Scott Hall. The difference was that Waltman was always going to be used as a star, and was simply being presented as an enhancement performer in order to introduce him with the desired impact - plus Hall was a much bigger star than Candido. Despite that, if anything Horowitz winning was still seen as more of a surprise, purely because his streak of losses had lasted so long. The story of the underdog scoring an unlikely victory was one of the most enduring in wrestling lore, and Horowitz briefly became an improbable hero.

Vince being Vince, he couldn't leave Horowitz's newfound popularity alone to develop organically. He forced the issue by giving him a gimmick, almost as if winning that one match had suddenly changed him overnight into somebody else entirely. Vince looked for something about Horowitz's personality that he could use as a hook, and settled on his Jewish heritage. He had Horowitz overplay it to the max, presenting him as the standard American Jewish stereotype of being a "nice Jewish boy", and going so far as to give him a variation of traditional Jewish folk song *Hava Nagila* ("Let's rejoice") as his entrance music. At least, some joked, he stopped short of portraying Horowitz as a money-grabbing scam merchant or giving him a guilt-inducing mother.

Come *SummerSlam* a month after his famous first win, Horowitz was still over enough to be given a spot on the card, and he squared off with Candido again. Horowitz was determined to prove his worth in this elevated position, and Candido was happy to accommodate him. Selflessly, he allowed Horowitz to hurl him around the ring for the first few minutes of their contest, including taking a hard fall on the outside from a ring-to-floor suplex. The crowd at the Civic Arena in Pittsburgh, Pennsylvania were receptive, fully supporting Horowitz in his quest to beat the braggart Skip character.

They cheered for him even louder when Candido continued to arrogantly showboat after each successful move, the very thing that had caused him to lose their first encounter the prior month. After surviving the early flurry, Candido settled into a position of dominance, and Horowitz his more familiar role of getting beaten up. Candido continued to rile the crowd, pulling Horowitz up after connecting with a flying headbutt from the top rope rather than pinning him. It was an intentionally classless move from the character, but also served as a way to give Candido an excuse for losing again.

Another came in the form of Jinsei Shinzaki, who wandered to ringside to serve as a distraction for Candido, allowing Horowitz to cradle the preoccupied Body Donna for another well-received fluke victory. Vince from behind his announce desk couldn't resist taking a stab at Jim Ross's now famous call, roaring his own rendition of, "Horowitz wins!" in his trademark rasping growl.[37]

THE REST of the undercard ranged from excellent (Waltman versus Shinzaki) to mediocre (Bret Hart against the debuting "evil dentist" Glenn 'Isaac Yankem D.D.S.' Jacobs) to outright dismal (Mark Calaway working with his close friend Charles 'Kama' Wright in a casket match), but the overall vibe of the show going into the final two bouts was positive. In truth, the rest of the card hardly mattered, because there was only one match that people were there to see: Shawn vs. Razor II.

As excited as the fans were to see the rematch, Michaels was far from happy to be retreading over old ground. He felt the original was so good that it left he and Scott Hall in a no-win situation, as he didn't see how they could possibly top it. Michaels and Hall spent weeks discussing what they could do to live up to the hype, and about which spots they could recycle from the first encounter and then mirror in the second one. The boys who were on friendly terms with the pair offered ideas and possible sequences

---

[37] For Horowitz, this was as good as it got. He continued to be pushed as a "superstar" rather than an enhancement talent for the next few months, but it was soon clear that his push was just a passing fad, and it faded as quickly as it had emerged. The *Royal Rumble* at the start of 1996 was his final pay-per-view appearance for the group, and he was demoted back to enhancement talent from that point forth, before being released in 1997 and turning up in WCW.

that they might try, with everyone chipping in to help them piece the bout together.

During television tapings a week before the match in Portland, Maine, Vince called Hall and Michaels into his makeshift office and gave them some disquieting news: they couldn't use the ladder as a weapon. "Some people are starting to come down on us," he told them, before explaining that the reason was down to a new violence code which the WWF had being forced to adopt in order to placate censors. The very people that Vince would usually dismiss as ne'er-do-wells were now influencing the output of his product, thanks to their efforts to police the entire entertainment industry. Worried about losing time slots and sponsors if he didn't comply, Vince had no choice but to listen.

The explanation didn't appease the two annoyed wrestlers. "It's a *ladder* match," complained Shawn, "I have to hit him with it!" But Vince wouldn't budge and reinforced his directive, "No. You can't do it," he told them curtly. Already feeling mentally fried from straining to devise fresh ideas for the much-hyped encounter, the pair felt they were back to square one. They sat up until the early hours of the morning the night before the pay-per-view, unsure of what they could do to make the match memorable with the new restrictions imposed.

Eventually Paul Levesque took charge and helped his much more experienced friends to lay the contest out. He reminded them that while using the ladder as a weapon was illegal, using it to launch off of was fine, as was any collision with the object that wasn't intended as an attack, such as running into it. Finally, thanks to some considerable help from their friends, Hall and Michaels were able to assemble the pieces into a coherent contest, and for the first time felt confident about what they were about to present.

Any reservations Shawn might have had about the quality of the bout were not reflected in his pre-match entrance routine. Shawn had always believed his own hype. To him it was not just a hollow boast when he crowed about being the best wrestler in the world; he genuinely believed it. During his elaborate introduction, he was the very picture of confidence as always, dancing, stripping and posing in time with his music. Scott Hall, who was much less understated as a performer, simply stood in the corner of the ring and watched the show, marvelling at how Shawn had the crowd in the palm of his hand. He felt a slight pang of jealousy, because he could see his friend's stock on the rise, whereas he was yet again competing for the Intercontinental title in the same upper midcard spot that he had been in for two years. He glanced up at his buddy and flashed a pensive half-smile, while running through the sequence of planned spots they had discussed in the locker-room one last time in his head.

Referee Jack Doan struggled to place the title belt in the metal loop used to hang it above the ring, positioning it unevenly and prompting Michaels to yell, "You're gonna have to bring it back down." Shawn's infamous insolence once again came to the fore, as he stroppily grabbed the belt and repositioned it in the hanging apparatus himself. "Up!" he bellowed as he motioned for the title to be raised. He hated it when things went wrong in his matches and he was annoyed that there had been a mistake before they had even got going. Luckily, Hall was used to Shawn's temper and tolerant of his friend's erratic bouts of anger. "Hey, Shawn, don't worry about it man," Hall advised him, before they launched into their opening exchanges at speed.

To counter the limitations placed on them by the violence code, the pair decided to delay the introduction of the ladder and utilise the bigger moves in their arsenals early. That way they would have an excuse to sell and move slowly when the ladder was eventually brought into play, thus increasing the drama of the contest. Michaels set up a feigned leg injury by taking a suplex from the ring to the outside - the same spot Barry Horowitz had drilled Chris Candido with earlier - letting his foot expertly graze the guardrail as he fell. Announcer Michael Hayes, who as a former wrestler knew a painful fall when he saw one, winced at the bump and declared, "I think that's it." Looking to add an extra dose of realism, Michaels played it up like he was legitimately hurt, banging his hand on the ringside mats in apparent pain. Vince McMahon had no idea that Shawn was just performing a typically expert sell job, and declared worriedly, "That *is* it."

It wasn't of course, and once Michaels had recovered and returned to the ring, he decided to push his luck with the violence code. He picked up the ladder and swung around while holding it in his hands, seemingly inadvertently smacking Hall with it. His facial expression was a combination of apologetic and nonchalant; he played it like he didn't know Hall was there and that it was simply an accident.

Hall returned the favour with an "accident" of his own, smashing the steel ladder into Shawn's damaged leg as he picked it up. The two collisions between Shawn's leg and the solid inanimate objects elicited sympathy for him and permitted the crowd to fully get behind Michaels as the babyface in the match. Hall had expected the crowd to support Shawn ahead of him and happily played subtle heel, upping his aggression as he mercilessly pounded Shawn's now well-established injured leg. Despite that, the crowd weren't all in favour of Michaels. Hall heard his fair share of cheers too, because the crowd appreciated the self sacrifice of both and the impressive effort levels being displayed.

Always eager to show off his superior athletic skills, Michaels utilised two big moves from the ladder; a moonsault from close to the top which connected, and then a flying splash from the very top, the same move he executed at *WrestleMania X* that became such an iconic and enduring image, repeated for decades on WWF programming. This time, Michaels told his friend to move out of the way, with the story being that Hall knew the move from the previous encounter and he had it scouted.

Little details like that set Michaels apart from the rest, and he provided another example a few minutes later. Hall had regained control of the contest and was about to drive him into the canvas with his Razor's Edge finishing move from the ladder, but before he did, Michaels kicked the ladder away to buy himself some time. He knew it would take an extra few moments for Hall to reposition it, which further added to the illusion of the bout being a legitimate sporting contest, and that Michaels was desperately clinging on to his title.

One obvious difference between the second bout and the *WrestleMania* confrontation was the introduction of a second ladder, a unique first for the match type. Both men feigned exhaustion as they climbed parallel ladders, with Shawn knocking Hall off of his with his superkick finishing move before he made a dive for the belt and missed. It was supposed to be the finish and Shawn was again visibly frustrated by the error. Even though it was an unplanned mistake, it added to the realism and drama of the contest, as to viewers it simply looked like Shawn was too exhausted to make it.

Forced to improvise, Hall shouted across the ring at Shawn, "Razor's Edge," and then set for the move by the ropes, but allowed Michaels to back drop him to the outside so that he could climb the ladder once more and this time claim the belt as planned. No one would know any different. Unfortunately for Shawn, he misjudged the placement of the ladder due to his tired state, and it was off-centre as he began his ascent. It wasn't until he arrived at the top that he noticed he wouldn't be able to reach the belt. He tried grabbing the top of the ladder with both hands and bunny hopping it closer to the belt, then decided to launch himself at the dangling strap and hold on in the hope that his weight would release it. It didn't, and Shawn tumbled to the canvas without the belt in his grasp.

"He can't do it!" exclaimed McMahon, trying to cover the second bungled finish. Shawn's growing frustration had now turned to outright anger. He stopped selling and threw a temper tantrum for the world to see, then grabbed the second ladder and hurled it across the ring before placing the first ladder directly beneath the title. Michaels climbed again, turned around and mouthed an expression of his displeasure to a beleaguered Hall, then finally grabbed the title to win the match.

Despite the mistakes that for some blighted the contest and made it inferior to the near-perfect original, many noted that the drama on offer was still a significant improvement on the celebrated first outing. Even though their hands were tied by the violence code, the pair had pulled the match off so well that the limitations they were forced to work within were barely noticeable. Michaels had rarely looked better, his star shining ever brighter as the match progressed. His sheer presence and unmatched ability had made it clear to all who watched that he was destined to be the top dog in the company.

One man watching who felt exactly that way was Dave Meltzer, who wrote:

There should be no more doubt as to who the star performer is in American pro wrestling. Whatever doubt should have been erased by Shawn Michaels at *SummerSlam*, stealing the show for the third time at a PPV event in 1995. You can call him the Ric Flair of the nineties or the most talented American worker of all-time. You *should* call him WWF Champion. Michaels, in comparison with Flair, is far superior athletically, and as charismatic as Flair was at his peak, Michaels has the potential to far surpass him there. Michaels is not Flair's equal on interviews and Flair's one advantage when it comes to in-ring performance is that in his prime he did it three-hundred nights a year with a level of consistency that Michaels and nobody else in WWF can come close to. But I don't think on Flair's best day he could have put on a show like Michaels did at *SummerSlam*.

WHILE MOST predicted that the ladder match would steal the show, expectations for the match between Kevin 'Diesel' Nash and Nelson 'Mabel' Frazier were at an unprecedented low. Getting fans to accept Mabel as a headline attraction on a major pay-per-view was hard enough, but the pair couldn't hope to follow the ladder match that Michaels and Hall had just delivered. Frazier had realised as much weeks earlier, "We were lobbying for the ladder match to go on last because we knew they were going to outshine us," he remembered. Vince wouldn't budge, he firmly believed that the WWF title match had to go on last no matter what else was on the card. He rarely made an exception unless celebrities were involved, like at *WrestleMania*.

The contest was a difficult one for viewers to stomach. Much like many of Nash's programs as champion, he was once again booked against someone larger than him. Vince loved seeing two big guys go at it, but for Nash it merely restricted his already limited move set, leaving him with little he could actually do. He had been forced to deal with the same issues when he worked with Sid, King Kong Bundy and Yokozuna over the course of his title reign, and his patience with the booking had long since ran out. "I might as well just set myself on fire," he moaned when he first learned of the Mabel program.

Others could see his point of view. "There's no doubt that Kev wasn't helped by the guys he was programmed with," noted Tom Prichard, "Bundy didn't know what to do with him, Backlund wasn't going to let him go out there and hurt him. He didn't have the people to work with who could protect him properly and have a good match with him."

Nash found himself in a quandary during his entire run as WWF Champion. If he wasn't working with oversized monsters in sluggish and unrewarding contests, then he was struggling to remain babyface against the smaller, more talented performers. It seemed that no matter what he did, Nash couldn't find a balance. If he had been a heel then it would have been far easier for him, but Vince was so obsessed with replicating the success of Hogan and having a babyface hero on top, that he wouldn't even consider a long-term heel champion at that point. Meanwhile, the much more popular and talented Bret Hart was once again lost in the shuffle, still wasting away in an exhausted feud with Jerry Lawler, which had now grown to include his "evil dentist", 'Isaac Yankem D.D.S.'

Nash was coming into the *SummerSlam* contest banged up from a hard few months on the road, and his back in particular was bothering him. His opponent meanwhile had developed an unfortunate reputation for accidentally injuring opponents, specifically with a dangerous sit out splash that would see him stand over his prone opponent and then throw his legs out and land hard on their lower back with his considerable backside. Nash was well aware of the danger and knew that Frazier had injured Fatu doing it earlier in the year, as well as others, so warned him not to do it to him under any circumstances.

The combination of Nash's height and Frazier's girth meant that the two struggled to find moves they could perform within their respective comfort zones, so they resorted to clubbing each other with little refinement. Neither man took a clear advantage, with Nash reluctant to sell too much for a man who just a few months earlier had been a midcard tag wrestler, and was perceived by no one other than Vince and his booking team as a bona fide headliner.

Halfway through the bout, Frazier caught Nash with a sloppy one-armed side slam that looked particularly awkward due to Nash's considerable height. With Nash lying on his front, Frazier stood over him and despite the earlier warning, dropped onto the champion's lower back with all of his weight. Nash stopped selling and let out a long, deep scream, with his immediate thought being that Frazier had snapped his back in half because he could barely feel his legs. He was furious, and as Frazier sat on him and attempted to apply a camel clutch hold, Nash audibly yelled at him, "*Motherfucker*! What the fuck are you doing? Fuck!"

Frazier realised he had made a huge error, and was briefly lost for what to do next. Eventually Nash was able to regain some feeling and go back to the planned spots, but he still struggled to move around properly. As had been ironically scripted, Frazier's clumsiness was worked into the match when he knocked down the referee while hitting the ropes, which allowed his tag partner Mo to enter the ring and the duo to lay a double-team beating on Nash.

The next part of the drama to unfold called for Lex Luger to make his way to the ring and even the odds for Nash, but he jumped his cue and came out too early. Nash was already wound up enough as it was because of Frazier's recklessness, and had to improvise. He deviated from the script and belted Luger with a *mostly* worked right hand, then sent him out of the ring and told him, "Wait for the fucking spot." Men on a Mission continued their beating, with Frazier hitting a legdrop on Nash outside of the ring. Only then did Luger realise that this was his moment to get involved, and he ran Mo off to the back as planned. Back in the ring, Frazier went for a splash but Nash moved, but unable to hit his powerbomb finisher because of Frazier's size, he instead settled for a clothesline from the middle rope to win the bout.

It was a different finish to what Frazier had been expecting when the match was first booked, because according to him his *King of the Ring* victory was supposed to be the catalyst for a push that would result in him being WWF Champion. "Vince was leaning towards me winning the belt," Frazier claimed, "But The Kliq got involved and had the finish changed." There is little evidence to support this claim, because while Vince had realised that Diesel was not the answer to the post-Hogan conundrum, Mabel was not proven as a draw. If anything, the reaction to him two months prior when he won the *King of the Ring* tournament had been so negative, that Vince simply wanted to get the Mabel push out of the way and use him as a monster for Diesel to slay.

Mabel was waiting for Nash when he got backstage, full of apologies about the injury he had caused, but Nash didn't want to hear it. Launching into a tirade, he yelled, "Motherfucker, what the fuck dude? I told you not to fucking do that move!" All Frazier could do was apologise, and with the injury not as bad as Nash had first feared, he was somewhat appeased. Vince McMahon wasn't. He was furious and stormed into the locker-room with release papers for Frazier to sign. He wanted him out of the company because he was a liability.

To his credit, Nash wasn't willing to let Frazier get fired over an incident involving him, and used thinly veiled threats to talk McMahon out of it. He told the chairman that if he fired Frazier, he could fire him too, because all he had done was make a mistake. "Let's just make sure it doesn't happen again," Nash said to them both, and Vince for the time being relented.

IN THE ring, *SummerSlam* had been one of the WWF's strongest shows of the year, but the numbers were frustratingly familiar for Vince when they came in. The event had done exceptionally well at the live gate with a near sell-out paid crowd of over 17,000 (with another thousand or so given away as comps), a new attendance record in the Civic Center[38] and the largest crowd of the year in North America for the WWF or anyone else in wrestling.

But on pay-per-view the promise of the Michaels and Hall rematch hadn't been enough for fans, who had clearly been far from eager to see the main event that they were presented with. The show pulled a 0.9 buy rate equating to just over 200,000 buys, a third less than the 1994 version of the show. The number was worse than it seemed on the surface, as the WWF had quietly reduced the price of the show from the standard $27.50 of the previous year to $24.95, meaning their total pay-per-view revenue from the event was nearly $1.5 million less than *SummerSlam* in 1994. The numbers firmly cemented to McMahon that Kevin Nash as his champion wasn't and never would be the draw for him that he had hoped he would be.

---

[38] The company returned to the building for five more pay-per-view events, *King of the Ring* in 1998, *Unforgiven* in 2001, *No Way Out* in 2005, *Armageddon* in 2007 and *Bragging Rights* in 2009, but none of them drew as well as *SummerSlam*. *King of the Ring* featured one of the most famous matches of all time, a Hell in a Cell encounter pitting The Undertaker against Mankind, and was the only event that came close with just over 17,000 in attendance.

THE WWF announced at *SummerSlam* that *WrestleMania* the following year would take place in Anaheim, California, and three days following the August pay-per-view a woman from the city came forward with allegations levelled against a number of WWF performers, claiming sexual and physical abuse. The incident in question was said to have taken place following a live event in Anaheim on December 29, 1994, and among the accused were Chris Chavis (Tatanka) and David Ferrier, who performed as Jimmy Del Ray.

As one member of the locker-room remembered, "Kevin Nash's mom had just died and we all went to a bar. Chris and Del Ray, they knew this girl. The group of us walked back to the hotel, where Chris, Del Ray, and the girl veered towards the bar. The rest of us just kept on walking towards the elevator with the attitude of, 'We don't want any of this,' because we knew something was going to go down. Sure enough, she was in the lobby crying the next morning, but I didn't know anything. Davey told me what he saw.

There was halcyon and a lot of GHB too. It wasn't real nice, and it wasn't real good. I remember getting a call in Evansville a few weeks later to call a lawyer, I was thinking, 'What did I do?' I just had a paranoid feeling. Sure enough, it was about that incident in L.A., because I was a witness. It wasn't the first time it had happened with Del Ray either. It was one of the reasons I stopped hanging out with him."

The unnamed woman threatened criminal charges against the pair, claiming that the announcement of *WrestleMania* coming to the city had reminded her of the incident and brought back the memories of what had allegedly happened to her. In the opinion of Kevin Nash the main perpetrator was Ferrier, with Chavis merely an innocent bystander. "I know for a fact that Chris didn't do anything besides be at the wrong place at the wrong time," said Nash in his defence.

Innocent or not, Vince wasn't taking any chances and suspended Chavis for six months. He was fearful of another sex scandal leading to a media frenzy that might destroy the company, and couldn't risk having any of his active performers involved in something of that nature.

Ferrier was already gone anyway, a victim of budget cuts, but suspending Chavis would prove that the WWF weren't shy about administering internal discipline, something they could point to if the threats of a lawsuit went any further.[39] For the time-being at least, it seemed that Vince was taking the company's new clean-cut image seriously.

---

[39] The threats were dropped and Chavis returned to the WWF in early 1996. He was released later that year and rejected an offer from WCW, deciding to instead work on

NINE

WCW'S NEW *NITRO* SHOW WAS originally earmarked for an August launch but was pushed back to the first Monday of September. Strategic timing was key. That night, the WWF's *Monday Night Raw* show was pre-empted on *The USA Network* due to the U.S. Open, an annual source of irritation for Vince. Every year, WWF programming would go on a brief hiatus in order to accommodate both the tennis tournament and also the Westminster Dog Show. Neither pulled particularly high ratings, certainly nothing comparable to *Raw*, but the advertising during those broadcasts came at a premium as they were considered to be "prestige" events. The hundred-thousand viewers who watched were worth more than the millions of wrestling fans, to both advertisers and the network, due to their perceived higher incomes and social statuses.

Eric Bischoff wanted to take advantage of *Raw*'s pre-emption, realising that with the competition off the air, all eyes would be on his new show. He knew he needed to start with a bang in order to snare jaded WWF viewers looking for their weekly Monday night wrestling fix, and keep them by presenting a superior product.

If Vince was worried about the impending competition, as usual he didn't show it to those around him. Rather than making plans to counter *Nitro*, McMahon bullishly carried on as if nothing was going to change, arrogantly ignoring WCW's forthcoming foray into prime time as a non-factor. The WWF had dominated the wrestling landscape for over a decade, and *Raw* on *USA* every Monday was a firmly ingrained viewing habit for wrestling fans. Vince couldn't foresee how *Nitro* could even dent *Raw*, never mind permanently damage it. It was an attitude adopted by his staff, with one member of the office later commenting, "We were stunned that [WCW] could be so stupid."

"At the time we all thought, 'You fucking idiots, you have to be out of your minds'," remembered Jim Cornette, adding, "Vince probably felt the same way. Why wouldn't he? Ted Turner had owned that company since 1988 and hadn't done a damn thing with it, and yet now they were coming

---

the independent scene so he could spend more time with his family. He was eventually rehired by the WWE in 2005 and had another two year run with the company.

out and saying they were going to compete with the WWF. It seemed comical at the time."

Reaction within the wrestling media was similarly derisory, a mixture of shock and stupefaction. Most believed Bischoff was overplaying his hand by running directly against the all-powerful McMahon. Wrote *The Wrestling Observer Newsletter* in June:

Within the industry, the general consensus is this move is almost suicidal; going head-up with the highest rated wrestling show in the country.

In August, just a few days before the launch of the show, they added:

Everyone in the company will be thrilled if they can come close or beat the WWF in the ratings game. And even if the company's financial fortune improves, it'll be a major downer internally if WWF blitzes them on Mondays, which is still the most predicted scenario.

Bischoff too realised that WCW would be killed in the ratings if he merely presented an alternative reality version of the WWF show. To prevent that, he set about making a number of changes both to the way his product was presented and to the talent at his disposal. He embarked upon an aggressive recruitment drive, the likes of which hadn't been seen since Vince McMahon's national expansion in the mid-eighties. He scoured the industry for the finest talent available in an effort to boost the quality of the matches on his undercard, and unlike Vince he was even willing to go outside of his comfort zone and foray overseas to do so.

The result was the arrival of stars from New Japan Pro Wrestling such as aerial sensation Jushin Liger, and in 1996 a host of talented high flyers from Mexico. Bischoff also raided ECW, stealing away technical masters Chris Benoit, Eddie Guerrero and Dean Malenko, quickly assembling one of the strongest and deepest talent rosters seen in North America since the WWF in its heyday.

The influx of exciting, new talent helped WCW to establish a completely different style and feel to that of its rival, making it the fresher option for fans who were fed-up with the WWF's product. Bischoff's willingness to think outside the box and utilise a different type of performer to what had been in the mainstream before, left McMahon in the same position as the regional promoters had been when he crushed them in the eighties. Now it was he who was in danger of his own archaic business practices and preferences bringing him to ruin.

BISCHOFF'S MOST important acquisition was a man who had worked in WCW before, and more notably worked with the WWF still; Lex Luger. The idea of bringing Lex back to WCW had first been proposed to Bischoff by Luger's close friend Steve Borden, who had performed for the better part of a decade as Sting. Borden had passed on his knowledge that Luger was deeply unhappy in the WWF, and was working in New York without a contract. Bischoff though, wasn't a fan, "I thought he was an arrogant ass. He treated people badly and had too high an opinion of himself. I never really thought much of his talent. Between that and his piss poor attitude I had no interest in him whatsoever, and I told Steve that."

Nevertheless, Borden continued to lobby hard for his friend, perhaps looking for another ally in the Hogan-infested political waters of the locker-room. Finally relenting, in a show of respect for Borden more than anything else, Bischoff agreed to a covert meeting with Luger. Due to the need for the conversation to be completely secret, it took place in Borden's garage, and Bischoff imposed the condition that Luger couldn't utter a word about it to anyone. "I thought that asking him to keep it a secret would act as a test to see how serious Lex was about being a team player. If word got out, I'd know he had leaked it," stated Bischoff.

After meeting with Luger a couple of times, Bischoff was still not fully convinced about the merits of rehiring him, but timing was once again key. Eric realised that Lex would make a great surprise for the debut episode of *Nitro* and would set the unpredictable tone he wanted his new show to have. If Vince McMahon only learned of Luger's departure when he appeared on live television for WCW, that was simply an added bonus.

Despite the possible opportunity to make a statement on the first *Nitro*, Bischoff still considered using Luger to be a gamble. He also wasn't willing to pay him anything near the $500,000 per annum that he had earned the last time he worked for the company, so low-balled him with a $150,000 per year contract that he promised to raise if things worked out. For Bischoff it was another test of character and a chance for Luger to prove he was committed to returning to WCW. Bischoff suspected that Lex would spurn the offer and return to work with Vince, but was surprised yet relatively satisfied when he agreed to the terms of the deal.

Even though the money was less than what Luger had received previously, it was still higher than what a WWF midcarder would generally earn, and any new contract Lex received from the WWF would be sure to take his current lowly status on the roster into account. Not only that, but it was guaranteed money for Lex, which gave him security that Titan was unable to offer.

Before the deal could be finalised, Luger had to pass one more test with Bischoff; he couldn't tell anyone that he was coming in, especially not Vince. It was a take it or leave it offer from Bischoff, and a deal-breaker if Luger said no. For Lex it was a decision he didn't take lightly, because it meant leaving without even giving his final two weeks' notice. Vince had been good to him, both professionally and personally, and he was uncomfortable about doing as Eric had asked. He was already well aware of his unfavourable reputation in the business, and he was loathe to further tarnish it.

Lex thought about things for a while, then dwelled on the fact that for the last few months he had been working without a contract, with Vince in no hurry to work out a new deal with him. He had actually given his customary three months notice some time ago in order to avoid his contract rolling over for another year at the same rate, but he and Vince had been unable to hammer out a new deal and were locked in a standoff. On August 31st, he made a decision and put pen to paper on the WCW offer, and then worked his scheduled house show loop in Canada without breathing a word about it to anyone.

With Luger working on a month-to-month basis at the time of his departure, he later defended his decision to leave in such a manner, pointing out that he didn't walk out on the company because he didn't have a contract, and that he had tried for six months to get Vince to sort a new deal with him. Lex felt the contract offer was never coming, and with a wife and kids to feed at home, ultimately it was the only decision he could make for his family.

When *Nitro* finally hit the screens live from the Mall of America, its presentation and the quality of the action impressed observers, and Vince realised he had real competition for the first time in recent memory. WCW felt fresh, vibrant and exciting, and things were about to get a lot more interesting.

Less than halfway through the broadcast Luger made his surprise return, wandering to the ring during a match between two of his former rivals Sting and Ric Flair, and then later on confronting WCW Champion Hulk Hogan and challenging him to a match the following week. Vince was stunned when he saw Luger on the show; as far as he knew, Lex was under contract with him. He was about to get on the phone to his lawyer Jerry McDevitt, but then he remembered the letter that Luger had sent to him giving his three month notice. It had completely slipped his mind. He realised that, legally at least, Lex was in the right. The first shot in the Monday Night Wars had been fired, and it was WCW that had done the damage.

"I just had to watch that fiasco to see what was going on over there," pointed out Jim Cornette, "And then out walked Lex Luger. I can remember thinking, 'Oh... I bet they didn't know that *this* was taking place.'"

"No one realised what was going on," crowed Bischoff, "The WWF thought Lex was still working for them. It was really, really effective. It set the tone for what I wanted *Nitro* to be." Bob Holly was another member of the WWF locker-room caught by surprise. He recalled having sat with Luger on a plane ride back from *SummerSlam* just days before the first *Nitro*, and Lex not having breathed a word of his impending departure. In fact, Luger had given him his phone number and asked Holly to call him up so they could work out together. Having seen Luger turn up on *Nitro*, Holly called him anyway, but wasn't surprised to find his number had changed. Even though he understood the reason behind Luger walking out, he still viewed him as a traitor. A lot of the boys did. They had seen Vince pump a lot of resources into getting Luger over, and he had been paid well despite never having achieved anything like the success expected of him, so for him to show such a lack of loyalty soured many on him.

"Everyone thought that Lex was a no good bastard, everyone was shocked," remembers Tom Prichard, but at the same time he conceded, "Things were really starting to happen and WCW was starting to look a lot more appealing than before when *Nitro* debuted. We were all shocked that they were going against us head-to-head, but then they really started kicking and doing well. With everything in the business down in 1995, I think a lot of the boys were starting to think about jumping a little more once *Nitro* was a success."

As effective as his shocking appearance on *Nitro* had been, Luger did still feel a sense of guilt about the way he had left Titan, so tried to rebuild bridges with McMahon in case the WCW deal didn't work out. He sent an apologetic letter to Vince after he had left and tried to contact him, but McMahon didn't return his calls. "I felt bad, but at the same time I really tried to come to an agreement with him," Lex claimed. "WCW were an up-and-coming company and I felt it was the right move. The wrong way to do it, but I felt it was the right move. It was a choice I had to make at the time for my family," he added.

WHEN THE ratings for the first *Nitro* came in, Bischoff smiled, though he almost felt like jumping for joy; the show had pulled a 2.9 rating, far surpassing anything the numerous naysayers had predicted. 2.9 was a rating on par with, and occasionally better than, what the already established *Monday Night Raw* was doing. Within the WWF there was a feeling of shock, "There was definitely a little bit of concern," said Kevin Nash, who as the WWF Champion had to shoulder the pressure more than most. The only person who didn't seem flustered was McMahon, at least not outwardly to his employees. "He didn't sell it at all," Nash remembered, with Vince instead adopting a stoic aloofness about the whole thing. He was still confident that *Raw* would cream *Nitro* when it returned to screens the following week.

As good as his initial number was, Bischoff also knew that the real test came the following week when the rival shows ran head-to-head for the first time. Insiders and industry commentators were still convinced that *Raw* would blow *Nitro* away in the weekly Nielsen ratings, but Bischoff had an ace up his sleeve; his show was live whereas McMahon's was taped. Many within the WWF felt that Vince should also have gone live in order to combat *Nitro*, but his show was already in the can, and McMahon was so unconcerned about WCW that he didn't feel any action was necessary. It was a decision he later regretted.

Because *Raw* was taped in August, Bischoff had been able to learn the results of the show, and in an underhanded attempt both to hurt the WWF's rating and reinforce the anything-can-happen nature of his show, he gave them away live on *Nitro*:

> In case you're tempted to grab the remote control and check out the competition, don't bother. It's two or three weeks old. Shawn Michaels beats the big guy with a superkick that couldn't earn a green belt at a YMCA. Stay right here, it's live.

Bischoff had violated one of the unwritten rules of wrestling by not only acknowledging his competition, but by actively trying to damage it. Even when WCW was taping its television in three month blocks and Vince could have easily used the same trick, he never stooped to that level. The boys in Atlanta who had worked for Vince and knew him well, expected that there would be repercussions. No one had ever come at McMahon quite like this before, and his former employees were well aware that when his back was against the wall, he came out swinging like a street fighter. If the United States government couldn't take the guy down what chance did Bischoff have, they thought. Many believed Bischoff was walking a very fine line and fully expected McMahon to go all-out to squash WCW once things had been made personal.

But during the broadcast there was nothing anyone in the WWF could do. They just had to sit and watch as Bischoff's "prophecy" came true, making the WWF's façade of presenting the show as being live come across as hokey and deceitful. The suits at Titan were prepared for their rating to be damaged by Bischoff's unethical stunt, but no one expected them to actually lose that night. The shock of the previous week turned to outright concern when the news filtered through; *Nitro* had done the unthinkable, scoring a 2.5 to *Raw*'s 2.2, and the first head-to-head result in the Monday Night War was unmistakable: WCW had won.

"What we hadn't counted on was that Eric Bischoff did possess one solitary talent," said Cornette, "It wasn't earth-shattering; the talent he had was simply the ability to get *TBS* to spend money." Attitudes towards WCW within the WWF immediately changed once Bischoff had given away the results of *Raw*. Previously they were considered more an annoyance than a worry due to how well-established the WWF brand was, but the stunt lit a fire in some, Vince included, and now it really *was* war. When the office instructed the talent to convene on the roof of Titan Tower just weeks later to film an explosive new opening for *Raw* - a direct response to the threat posed by *Nitro* - those reading between the lines could see the truth: McMahon knew he was in a fight, and for the first time in his life, he was losing.

THE NEW threat posed to the WWF by *Nitro* caused tensions to increase backstage, as Vince's paranoid grapplers fervently tried to protect their spots on the card. Most knew that drastic action was imminent, so wanted to make sure that they were in as advantageous a position as possible. Naturally, The Kliq were at the front of the line in that respect, and issues between the group and other wrestlers started to increase in frequency.

One man of many who had well-publicised run-ins with The Kliq was French-Canadian Carl Ouellet. Ouellet had been with the WWF since 1993, previously as part of The Quebecers tag team with Jacques Rougeau, but in mid-1995 he was being repackaged as a pirate character called Jean-Pierre Lafitte. The previous October, Lafitte had headlined a house show in Montreal against former partner Rougeau (in what was billed as Rougeau's retirement match), which drew a sell-out crowd of over 16,000 people. It was an astonishing number for the WWF at the time, far beyond anything the rest of their live events were pulling.

The WWF did a follow up at the venue in February that was set to host a rare meeting between Shawn Michaels and The Undertaker, but the latter had to withdraw due to a knee injury, and Ouellet (who was currently on the sidelines "cooling off" before he debuted his new persona) was drafted in as his replacement. The show drew another 12,000 people, once again a number far above every other house show the group was running, including more than doubling their January shot at Madison Square Garden.

Meanwhile Jacques Rougeau had been pulling strings to try and get Vince to run a stadium show in the city of Quebec, but McMahon had turned down the idea because he felt the WWF no longer had the roster, infrastructure or capability to pull in the numbers that Rougeau was suggesting.[40] It caused bad blood between the pair, so Rougeau decided that he would run independent cards of his own in the city. With that in mind, he warned his friend Ouellet not to do any jobs in Montreal, because it would kill him in the territory if he ever wanted to work for him there in the future.

No one in the WWF had any idea that Rougeau had been in Ouellet's ear, so officials were stunned when he then refused to put Michaels over in Montreal. Shawn, perhaps understandably, was livid about it. He pointed out to Carl that the entire roster had just put him over at the *Royal Rumble*, yet he was unwilling to do the same. Taking stock of the delicate political situation he found himself in, Ouellet eventually agreed to compromise and lost the bout via a tainted finish, with Michaels cheating to win by putting his foot on the ropes. Post match, Michaels lay a beating on Ouellet that was vindictively designed to undermine him as a babyface draw in the city. The belittlement occurred partly because Ouellet was coming back into the company as a heel character, but primarily to send him a message that he was not the top level star he believed he was.

Despite the fact that Ouellet was only a late stand-in for the February Montreal show, and the previous September event had all been built around

---

[40] Rougeau's plan was for the WWF to promote the Olympic Stadium in Montreal, which for pro wrestling would have been able to house around 80,000 people. At that point it was a number the WWF had only ever come close to achieving twice, at *WrestleMania III* in Pontiac, Michigan (78,000) and *SummerSlam 1992* in London, England (80,000). Both of those cards had strong hooks to draw the numbers and very different circumstances surrounding them. *WrestleMania III* came at the peak of the WWF's popularity in North America, and *SummerSlam* took place just as the boom period was over, but at the height of its popularity in Europe. Not to mention national hero Davey Boy Smith was wrestling in the main event at one of the company's premier pay-per-views.

Rougeau's "retirement", he was under the delusion that his being on the cards was the reason for the strong houses in the city. He was convinced that the next time the WWF went there, he would be beating Kevin Nash for the WWF title, only to drop it back a few days later - something he claimed was backed up by people in the office. To many this was far-fetched. The Jean-Pierre Lafitte character that Ouellet portrayed was a midcard heel, and having Nash drop and then regain the title in such a manner would have weakened him as the company's top babyface. If it was the Intercontinental Championship then the story would have seemed plausible, but Vince McMahon didn't have a habit of changing the WWF Championship on a whim, because he knew it would ruin its prestige. As Jim Cornette would later state, "That was just never, ever, *ever* going to happen."

A month out from the Montreal show scheduled to take place on September 15, 1995, Nash walked up to Ouellet in the locker-room and confirmed that they were indeed booked to work with each other for the belt. Ouellet was pleased, but his mood quickly changed when Nash then informed him that he would be going over clean with the same big boot and powerbomb finish that he always won with. Confused as to why he was finding out a match finish a month before the bout took place - something completely unheard of - Ouellet consulted his friends in the locker-room. They too thought it was strange, and concurred that the only reason Nash had said that to him was because of his reluctance to lose against Michaels back in February, and that Nash was trying to make a statement and put Carl in his place.

Jim Cornette agreed with that assessment, and noted, "Being told the finish a month in advance was all about Pierre not wanting to lose to Shawn last time out. Shawn bitched about it as he delineated the tale to Nash afterwards, who obviously then told Pierre the finish as a "fuck you" to show his authority. That, combined with Jacques being in Pierre's ear the whole time, made for a pretty fucking messy situation."

Despite the purported local hero working in the main event, September's Montreal date drew much worse than expected. Only a third of the crowd that the Rougeau match six-months earlier had pulled turned up to see the now-heel Ouellet get his title shot. "The crowd seems split in favour of me," defiantly claimed Ouellet to Nash, just as agent Tony Garea wandered in to tell them the finish: Nash was going over clean with his big boot and powerbomb. Thanks to a directive from Jim Ross, the WWF had been making an attempt to keep finishes on the road as clean as possible, to avoid alienating their already reduced audience any further with subpar shows and cheap match endings, so that in itself was nothing unusual.

What bothered Carl was that the outcome was the same as the one Nash had told him a month ago. Feeling like he had been played by The Kliq, Ouellet told Garea that he wasn't going to do it and that he wanted the match to go to a non-finish. He also insisted on playing the babyface role, based on his belief that he would be the most popular star on the show. Ouellet suggested they go with a count out finish instead, saying that it made no sense to beat him in what was essentially his hometown, and that it could set up a return match for the next time they were in the city.

Cornette believed that Ouellet's refusal to lose was primarily down to the political manoeuvrings of Rougeau. "Jacques was a manipulator, Carl wasn't real smart and Nash was a prick," he stated, "French Canadians don't like losing in French Canadian cities as it is, but Jacques got into Carl's head and built him up, probably because he wasn't real fond of Nash and wanted to see a *shoot*[41] for his own amusement."

When Shawn Michaels overheard Ouellet refusing to put the WWF champion over, he lost his temper. This was not unusual for Shawn - who was notorious for flying off the handle at the slightest provocation - only this time he wanted to fight. He shouted and raved at Ouellet for believing his own hype, ranting that given his current lowly status on the roster compared to Nash as champion, he should be grateful to even be in such an elevated spot. Furthermore, he should willingly, and cleanly, do the job for Nash. Getting increasingly worked up, Shawn then threatened to hit Ouellet with the closest weapon he could find, his Intercontinental title belt. Unsurprisingly, Ouellet was unfazed, warning him to make it a good shot, because if he missed he was going to break his jaw. Michaels was dragged away from the scene before any damage to either man was caused.

Even with perennial pot-stirrer Michaels out of the way, the locker-room remained in turmoil. Steaming over Michaels' comments, Ouellet threatened to walk out and quit the company if the finish wasn't changed, thus leaving the show without its advertised main event. Ouellet felt The Kliq had no respect for him or the business, so he wouldn't budge from his stance. With the agents fearing a riot if the bout was cancelled, phone calls were frantically exchanged between they and Vince. Eventually they had little choice but to acquiesce to Ouellet. He had fought The Kliq and it seemed he had won.

---

[41] Something in wrestling that is legitimate, be it a promo, angle or fight.

Worried that fans would feel short-changed by a non-finish in the main event, the match was relegated to the semi-final position on the card, with Michaels and Sid Eudy picking up the slack in the top bout. The Ouellet-Nash match went ahead with the two performers exchanging the occasional stiff shot, but for the most part acting professionally. Nash was amused when he heard the crowd reaction, which he later described as, "About ninety-nine percent in favour of me." He said the same thing to Ouellet as he subtly played heel and grabbed him in a chinlock, asking him if he wanted to change his mind and put him over in light of the crowd response. Ouellet rejected the request, so Nash continued to play the antagonist until they did the planned double count out that had been agreed.

Immediately after the show, Ouellet, fearful of the backlash, announced he was resigning. He was eventually talked into returning for a match the next night in Quebec City, where he and Nash were booked to work with each other again. Ouellet apologised to Nash for the previous night, and the office gave them another count out finish in order to avoid further issues. Things were going fine until Ouellet went for one of his trademarks; a legdrop from the top rope. He had done the move hundreds of times before and never had any problems, but on this night of all nights he landed wrong and accidentally caught Nash square in the face with the heel of his boot.

In Nash's mind, the timing was too coincidental for it to be anything other than intentional. He figured Ouellet was trying to get a cheap shot in on him, so he stopped selling and started lacing the pirate with hard punches, then called for his powerbomb and warned him to stay down. Ouellet realised what he had done and knew better than to try and kick out of the move; he had enough heat on him as it was. Instead, he decided to settle things backstage, and jumped Nash as soon as he walked through the curtain, but the two were split up before it could get serious.

By the time the crew arrived at Toronto's Maple Leaf Gardens the next day, there was a very real threat of a full-scale locker-room brawl. Nash had The Kliq on his side,[42] while Ouellet had talked to his own friends and he knew they had his back if anything happened.

Ouellet prowled the building like a caged animal, fully expecting one of The Kliq to jump him. He was ready to fight them, all of them if he had to. Fortunately, it didn't come to that. Of the two, it was Nash who ended up being the bigger man, standing up in front of the locker-room and diffusing

---

[42] Including Peter Polaco, though not Scott Hall, who had been working on the 'B' show loop in Florida in main events against Sir Mo, in front of embarrassing houses that didn't even manage to reach four figures.

the situation. He cautioned that they were all adults and the petty squabbling and in-fighting needed to stop immediately. It was the kind of speech the WWF champion *should* have been making, and the agents at the arena certainly appreciated not having to deal with yet another incident. Jim Cornette however, was not entirely convinced that Nash's reason for quelling the issue was all that noble, "A fucking mad, fresh Pierre wouldn't be someone Nash would want to fight after he had spent twenty-four hours stewing over things, especially if he had Jacques on the phone goading him all night. Nash calmed things down because he likely realised he could have got his ass kicked."

In order to ensure that there were no more problems between the pair, the agents switched up the card and put Ouellet in with Fatu, and Nash with Dan Spivey, who was winding down his career as the ahead-of-its-time Waylon Mercy character. As a punishment for the previous few nights, Ouellet was booked to lose cleanly, and with the BSKs out in force on the tour he had few complaints about doing the job.

Nothing was said about the incidents for the next few weeks. After the Fatu defeat, Ouellet continued to win matches on the road, beating Kliq sixth man Aldo Montoya routinely at house shows, which didn't sit well with the group. Shawn Michaels wouldn't let it drop, and called Vince at his lavish Connecticut home to express his feelings about the WWF's resident buccaneer. Michaels demanded that Vince fire Ouellet, and while McMahon was not happy with having been held to ransom, he felt that firing him was too harsh a punishment for the crime, so he refused. Instead he levied him with a $1,000 fine, which he felt was enough. It seemed like Ouellet had beaten The Kliq again.

THE REDUCED price, two hour *In Your House* concept continued on September 24th at the Saginaw Civic Center in Saginaw, Michigan. The third edition of the show featured a unique all-titles match pitting WWF Champion Kevin Nash and Intercontinental Champion Shawn Michaels against WWF Tag Team Champions Yokozuna and Owen Hart in the main event, but only managed the same buy rate as the previous *In Your House* show, despite the rare promise of a guaranteed title switch.

Vince had booked himself into a corner. He knew that the prospect of the title change would attract viewers, but that meant actually changing one of his champions, which proved difficult. He had no intention of ending Kevin Nash's near year-long reign in a tag team match on a 'B'-pay-per-view,[43] and talking Shawn into dropping his belt was a headache he could do without. That only left the tag titles, which were easily the most expendable of the three, but that meant The Kliq holding all of the WWF's on-screen gold and he knew the locker-room would likely revolt at the prospect.

Instead, Vince reverted to his carny roots and decided to pull a bait-and-switch, running a show-long angle with Owen Hart that saw him pulled from the match and replaced with his brother-in-law Davey Boy Smith. When Owen later made it to the match and dropped the ball for his team by getting pinned, it gave Vince a way to overturn the result the next night on *Monday Night Raw*, fully short-changing the fans who had paid to see the pay-per-view.

IN YOUR House 3 also marked the pay-per-view debut of Dan Spivey's avant-garde Waylon Mercy. Inspired by Robert DeNiro's celebrated portrayal of Max Cady in Martin Scorsese's *Cape Fear*, the legitimately tough Spivey's depiction was dark and sinister. He acted like a babyface by smiling and shaking hands with fans, but had a wild-eyed and ruthless vicious streak that betrayed his outward gentlemanly demeanour. Speaking almost in riddles with a quiet, hypnotising Southern drawl that engaged the viewer in a manner not seen since Jake Roberts, Waylon Mercy was one of the more edgy and intense personas that the WWF had experimented with. He was a far cry from the clowns, day job specialists and superheroes that Titan had recently promoted, and was a sign that things were beginning to change.

Unfortunately, Spivey, who had been a star in the eighties, was breaking down physically. In his younger days he had thrown himself around the ring in a manner uncommon for someone standing six-foot-seven, but his athletic, physical ring-style combined with a football career at the University of Georgia, had left him in constant pain. He was now moving much slower than in his heyday and was struggling with the rigours of being on the road.

Even so, it was a surprise for many to see Waylon Mercy lay down and lose on his pay-per-view debut to midcard performer Savio Vega. Common convention in Titan and across all of wrestling was that the new guy would establish some victories prior to going out and putting over the bigger stars, so that when he eventually lost it would carry a greater gravitas. Having him beaten right out of the gate was a clear sign that his tenure with Titan was going to be short-lived. Before he had the chance to really develop as a personality and explore the vast possibilities that his unique character

---

[43] The WWF title wouldn't switch at an *In Your House* event until February 1997, which was only necessitated because Shawn Michaels had vacated the belt a week before the show and the WWF needed to crown a new champion going into *WrestleMania 13*.

presented, Spivey called time on his career in October, and unlike so many others in the business, he never attempted a comeback.

WHEN SHAWN Michaels stole the show at *In Your House 2* against Jeff Jarrett, it frustrated Bret Hart. Not because he was jealous of Michaels or envious of his skill - he wasn't - in his mind he was every bit the performer that Michaels was. Rather, Hart was annoyed that he wasn't even on the card, having had the best match on the show with Hakushi at the premiere edition of the event. Determined to make up for it and wanting to outdo Michaels so that Vince could see that he was the horse to be betting on, Hart vowed to have a great match with Kliq nemesis Carl Ouellet at *In Your House 3*.

Prior to the match, one of the boys backstage joked to Hart that even he would have a hard time getting a good match out of a one-eyed pirate. "No I won't," he coolly retorted, "I'm Bret Hart." As much as the response induced eye-rolling from some, it was not an unexpected one; few took the business as seriously as Hart. Being the son of legendary promoter and wrestler Stu Hart, a man feared for his ability to stretch people with intricate *shoot* (legitimate) holds rarely seen in modern wrestling, Bret's attitude and demeanour were no surprise. He was stoic and focused on his job, determined that his oft-repeated catchphrase of being, "The best there is, the best there was and the best there ever will be," would be an accurate boast and more than just a slogan used to sell t-shirts.

Fortunately for 'the Hitman', Ouellet also had a point to prove in the ring that night. Like Hart, he wanted to go out and have a great match, feeling it would improve his standing with Vince following the Montreal incident with The Kliq, which was fresh in the memory having taken place just a week earlier. Also like Hart, Ouellet's roots were in a Canadian wrestling hotbed, with the likes of Édouard Carpentier, Pat Patterson and The Rougeau Brothers having paved the way for French-Canadian wrestlers in the WWF. Powerful and hard-hitting but safe in the ring, Ouellet was from the same mould as Hart in that he liked to work snug and make his matches appear believable. That night, they were perfect opponents for one another.

Hart was far from inspired by the storyline that Vince's writers had conceived to set up his rivalry with Lafitte, in which the pirate had stolen his leather ring jacket and Hart wanted it back. "It was pathetic. It was probably the lamest storyline of my entire career. Why wouldn't I just go out and buy another one?" he later quipped. At the time though, Hart wondered exactly how he was supposed to convey much in the way of anger to build an intense story based around an act of petty larceny.

Ouellet was already in the ring while Hart was desperately trying to generate interest in their issue with a live backstage promo. Clad in blue velour trousers and knee-high leather boots, with wet, scraggly hair and an eye patch covering his genuine glass eye, he looked every bit the pantomime villain that most of Vince's heels had become.

Hart made his way to the ring exuding a cool air of confidence and determination, but he was worried that the dire angle would have an impact on the crowd response. Concerned that their contest would unfold in front of silence, Hart hatched a plan. He had watched Shawn Michaels deliver a dangerous looking but undeniably exciting plancha against Jeff Jarrett at July's *In Your House*, and he intended to put his own spin on it. He wanted to prove that anything Shawn could do he could do equally well, as well as start the match on an immediate high.

As Lafitte wandered around ringside arguing with fans, Hart launched himself to the outside between the top and middle ropes, landing on the pirate with a move known as a topé. It was spectacular, and instantly the fans were invested in the bout. Suddenly no one cared that the reason they were fighting was so insipid; they just wanted to see a good old-fashioned brawl.

The match unfolded with both sticking to their principles by working a snug match. Every move they delivered connected with purpose. They were working safely but firmly, and both knew that the next day they would be sore. At one point Hart instructed Ouellet to move as he charged the corner, then dived through the gap between the turnbuckles and shoulder-first into the ringpost. It was an impressive looking move that always garnered a response, but in reality the vicious-sounding noise came from Hart smacking the post with his hand. It was a trick he had used to great effect before, and to the fans it added an element of risk that he might be beaten, as he now only had one arm to wrestle with.

But Hart knew they needed more than that. After all, he was a former two-time World Champion and had been one of the top guys in the WWF for four years, whereas the Jean-Pierre Lafitte character was still new. Fans didn't see them on anything like the same level and expected Hart to easily dismantle him, but that wasn't how 'the Hitman' operated. He wanted Lafitte to look good, because when he did beat him he would look even better.

Hart instructed Ouellet to grab him by the seat of his tights and throw him into the post again, then instructed that he be thrown into the corner so he could charge chest-first into the buckles at speed. It was another little trick that Hart had used repeatedly over the years, and one of his favourites because he could hit the corners at full speed and actually move the ring without suffering a great deal of pain outside of minor rope burn on his inner arms.

Even then Bret wasn't finished, because he knew that the angle the match was built on was so weak that he needed to really take a hammering to generate enough sympathy for Ouellet to be taken seriously. He allowed himself to be thrown into the hollow steel steps at ringside, which made a loud booming sound, though their bark was considerably worse than their bite.

Satisfied he had placed his character in enough peril that the fans would be firmly behind him, and moreover, to guarantee they would be into the bout due to the now realistic possibility of Lafitte winning, Hart let Ouellet place him in a chinlock so he could catch his first breather of the match. Ouellet was a jacked up physical specimen, and like all gym guys he was prone to tiring easily. Hart had no such problems and had stamina unmatched by almost anyone else in the business, but he knew that the rest of the match would be a struggle if he didn't let Ouellet convalesce, so he sat in the hold and waited for the next stage of the bout.

Even in a chinlock where his movement was limited and his facials were blocked by his opponent's large muscled arm, Hart knew that he could still keep the crowd invested. He was well aware that the best babyfaces were the ones who constantly showed fight and signs that they were still "alive" in a match, so set about continually mounting comebacks, only for Ouellet to club him back down and return to the hold.

Suitably rested and sensing the time was right to increase the impact levels, Ouellet climbed the top rope and flew off with a legdrop, the same one he had accidentally potatoed Kevin Nash with a week earlier. The crowd in Saginaw were now worried for Hart, and when Ouellet raced up the ropes again looking for his cannonball finishing manoeuvre, they were holding their breath. But as planned, Hart moved out of the way, and Ouellet came flipping down into the ring back-first on the hard mat.

With the crowd beginning to bite, Hart set for his famous sharpshooter finishing hold, a move that would see him grapevine his opponent's legs and cross them over each other, before turning them and sitting on their back as he stretched them. It looked painful, and often it was. Ouellet didn't have to find out, because Hart allowed him to power out of the move before he locked it on, sending him tumbling through the ropes to the floor.

Ouellet had also seen Shawn Michaels' dangerous bumps at the last *In Your House*, and he too wanted to outshine him. Taking a run up from the ropes, he launched himself to the outside of the ring with a flip plancha, an impressive variation of Shawn's standard version of the move. As Ouellet had instructed, Hart moved out of the way and the pirate came crashing down to the floor with an incredible thud. The bump was a hard one, but Ouellet knew that it would look good to viewers at home.

Mirroring what Ouellet had done to him earlier, Hart threw his opponent hard into the ring steps before rolling him back in the ring. Bret was known for his fondness for a particular sequence of moves as his matches reached a crescendo, and he launched into them at speed. Ouellet kept with him and reversed a whip into the corner, with Hart looking to leap backwards over his opponent and into a pin attempt. Ouellet didn't quite get the timing right, but the veteran Hart seamlessly saved the spot from going wrong by calling out instructions on the fly, and no one was any the wiser.

The bout was beginning to reach a climax, and Hart tried for a bulldog only for Ouellet to push him away and into the buckles, with Hart again taking his high impact chest bump into them, writhing around in apparent pain to sell the effects. But he was not out it yet, and connected with a forearm blow to the face that resonated around the building with a loud smacking sound.

Hart was upping his game, trying different things to what people were used to seeing from him, and even commentator Jim Ross noted as much. His next impressive visual was flying at Ouellet, only for him to move and cause Hart to land in the ropes, tangled up helplessly like a kite trapped in electrical cables.

The breathless encounter finally came to an end when both men hit simultaneous clotheslines and crumpled to the mat together. As they lay selling their very real exhaustion, Hart called over to Ouellet, "Let's take it home kid," before expertly threading his leg through Ouellet's and intertwining them like a sailor's knot. In one quick movement, Hart slipped into the move he had used to beat opponents for the last half-a-decade, his sharpshooter. Hart held onto Ouellet's foot and yanked back, leaving the pretzeled pirate no choice but to call it quits.

Cheers echoed around the Saginaw Civic Center as Hart lay face-first on the canvas, deeply inhaling as he soaked in the response. He felt a sensation of deep satisfaction envelop him. He knew both of them had worked a herculean shift and delivered the excellent match they had envisaged. Hart was proud that once again he had been able to take an unheralded performer on a much lower level than him on the totem pole, and make him look like a bigger star in defeat than he had been coming in.

THE MOST notable thing coming out of *In Your House 3* was a backstage announcement from Vince McMahon prior to the event that there would be a new man solely in charge of the creative team: Bill Watts. While Watts had been working with the company since August and his fingerprints were all over the *In Your House* show, this was the first time that it was acknowledged to the talent that Watts would be exclusively responsible for the company's creative direction. In the meeting, McMahon announced to the roster that he was resigning as head booker to focus more on being a corporate executive, and described Watts as, "The brightest mind in wrestling."

McMahon and Watts both addressed the assembled talent, with McMahon discussing the Monday Night Wars and the WWF's own change in philosophy regarding the way their television would be presented, hyping soap-opera style "next week" teasers to get people excited to tune in and watch the storylines progress over time. For his part, Watts decried the lack of a top African-American babyface and then noted that recent signing Tony 'Ahmed Johnson' Norris, would be pushed heavily when he made his official debut (Norris was in attendance, having beaten Chris Candido in a dark match before the show). He also hinted that Bret Hart would be the next WWF Champion and that the overly-gimmicked characters would be toned down and phased out in favour of more realistic personalities.

Watts realised that if the WWF wanted to return fire in the war with WCW, then a refresh of the stale product being presented was vital. Other than the personnel, not much had changed in the company for years, whereas over in Atlanta WCW had received a significant update from its tradition of being a Southern-style wrestling promotion. The shift had lost them a lot of older fans, but on the flipside their product was hotter than it had been in years. WCW had rarely been able to compete with the WWF before, not since the NWA days, so there was obviously some merit to Bischoff's decision.

Bill Watts knew that something similar needed to occur in the WWF, though ironically enough, a shift back towards good, old-fashioned wrestling was just the tonic he felt was required. The hard part, he realised, would be convincing Vince McMahon to get on board with that, and thus rethink his entire modus operandi. With WCW in the ascendancy, the stakes were different to what they had ever been, so if that was ever going to happen, now was the time.

TEN

VINCE MCMAHON WANTED TO FIGHT Eric Bischoff and WCW, but he was creatively throttled by one of the WWF's own corporate manifestos; a document titled *The Principles*. The entertainment industry had come under increased pressure from Congress to reduce the amount of violence on pre-watershed television, lest a directive be passed that shunted all programming of its kind to undesirable late night slots. For the WWF that would have been commercial suicide, as their key target demographics were children and young adults. Both for his own company's prospects and for his sponsors and advertisers, Vince had no choice but to adhere to *The Principles*.

Titan had already lost a number of key advertisers during and since the steroid trial, and the WWF Vice President for Distribution Michael Ortman realised that the company needed to act first before any legislation was even passed. He decided to go on a charm offensive in order to change public opinion of the company and avoid alienating future potential partners.

With the issue of excessive violence front and centre of the public consciousness, Ortman decided that the smart thing to do would be for Titan to actively distance themselves from the prevailing perception prospective suitors had of them, and champion a new set of principles, hence the title of the corporate document. These would see the company promise to ban, among other things, any blood on television, overt portrayals of sexuality, the use of weapons, and all violence towards women. The intention was to deflect the outrage to WCW, so that Ted Turner came under pressure from the only people he needed to answer to: his stockholders.

For Vince, *The Principles* were a necessary evil. While on one hand he hated to be restricted in what he could do with his own company, it was also imperative that he stuck to the guidelines set out in the document. The last thing he needed was for his wounded Federation to be coming under scrutiny, especially with the added pressures caused by the recent success of WCW's *Monday Nitro*.

Ortman was confident that the WWF's reputation could be rebuilt, and spent the next few months trying to smooth over Titan's concerned existing business partners. But as WCW continued to hold their own against Vince, Ortman frequently found himself having to explain his employer's actions.

He noticed that things directly violating the promises of the manifesto- little things at first - were slowly creeping back in.

ON THE October 16[44] episode of *Monday Night Raw*[44], blood (*colour*) stained a WWF broadcast for the first time in over two years, courtesy of Jerry Lawler.[45]

In the past, guys had always got colour from the somewhat barbaric act of self-mutilation known in the industry as blading. The practice would see a wrestler cut their own forehead during a match with a sliver of razorblade in order to draw blood, theoretically increasing the drama in his match. It was often an effective tool when used sparingly, but had been banned in the company for years. Bleeding in the cartoon world of the WWF was considered a thing of the past, consigned to history for good.

And then Jerry Lawler changed all of that. On this night, it wasn't a blade that caused Lawler's flow of claret, but rather a long-standing condition caused by years of taking shots to the face, *potatoes* that served as receipts from years of dishing out paltry pay-offs while running his Memphis territory. Lawler had been walking around with a deviated septum for over fifteen years, causing one of his nasal passages to be permanently smaller than the other. He had always put off the corrective surgery because he had heard it was very painful and couldn't face the ordeal. Instead he combated the occasional difficulties he had breathing with a strong nasal spray, which would cause his nose to scab on the inside.

That night on *Raw*, 'the King' was involved in a cage match between Glenn 'Isaac Yankem' Jacobs and Bret Hart, with a stipulation ordering him to be raised above the ring in a small shark cage to prevent his interference. The gimmick was a staple of wrestling that had been used for decades throughout the territories, though its effectiveness was dependant on the budget of the group promoting it. As Jim Cornette recalled, "In some places there was nowhere you could physically hang the cage from so they brought in a cherry picker, in others they had a pulley system using a chain. At the Houston Coliseum, a big arena, they put a rope on the ceiling and had four guys pull me up. Every time the rope would stretch slightly it would feel like it was falling!"

---

[44] The show was taped three weeks earlier on September 25th

[45] Though, it wasn't the first time someone had bled in WWF rings that year. On a house show in Tampa on July 16th, Fatu bled in a match with Tatanka. Many in attendance claimed that he had bladed because of how Fatu played it up, but the cut was actually accidental.

The concept was one of Bill Watts' favourites. He had used it to great effect in the past, and he knew that Lawler would be the perfect man to have locked inside the contraption. For his part, 'the King' knew just what was needed to increase the drama: blood. Lawler was mic'd up so he could convey his distress to viewers watching at home, and once hoisted in the air he claimed to be scared of heights. Lawler begged Vince, who was sat doing commentary at ringside, to get him down. "I'm getting sick. I'm going to get a nosebleed," he pleaded as he pretended to wretch.

Suddenly, a tiny drop of blood splattered the canvas twenty feet below. Jacobs and Hart carried on with their match, not even realising that any blood had fallen. Moments later, there was another drop, then another. Lawler continued to exaggerate the situation for the viewers at home, "Get me down, I've got a nosebleed! I'm scared of heights! I'm gonna get sick," he whined. By now Vince had noticed Lawler's bloody nose and the timbre in his voice changed ever so slightly. He assured Lawler that he would be okay, but he knew that Mike Ortman would have a lot of questions about claret staining the mat.

Like everyone else, Vince assumed Lawler genuinely was scared of heights, not for one second guessing that the wrestler had picked the small scab on the inside of his nose to intentionally draw blood. Lawler kept the truth quiet, knowing that Vince would be furious if he found out he had gone into business for himself.

It didn't seem like a particularly notable thing at the time, and the blood was minimal, but it turned out to be fairly monumental. As Lawler remembered, "It was a huge deal to have blood back on the TV [show], and soon after that the WWF started letting guys bleed again."

AS HE had proven time and again, Shawn Michaels had a tendency to run his mouth off to anyone and everyone, with little regard for their stature, physically or politically. Usually, because he was Shawn Michaels and had a band of brothers to protect him, he could act with impunity. But on October 5th at Madison Square Garden, whilst his running buddies were on a different loop, Michaels got a little too smart for his own good with the burly Harris twins, Ron and Don.

The duo were on their way out of the company a week later having recently handed in their notice, and discovered that Michaels had openly mocked their performance that night against The Smoking Gunns, commenting that the two *stiffs*[46] wouldn't be missed when they left. Ron in

---

[46] Wrestling vernacular for a cumbersome, uncoordinated worker

particular was annoyed about the remarks, but the pair in general were already sick of Michaels' attitude. With their impending departure freeing them from any repercussions, the twins seized the opportunity to confront Michaels alone.

Acting quickly while Shawn showered, Don spotted a chair in the corner of the room and made his move, lodging it under the locker-room door handle to barrack it shut. The twins wanted to deal with Michaels alone; they didn't want anyone stopping them until they had shaken him up a bit first. When Shawn exited the shower, Ron darted forwards and lifted him up by the throat, then aggressively slammed him against a wall, daring Michaels to say something else derogatory to his face.

Shawn realised he was in danger, and for once in his life, wisely kept his mouth firmly shut. Ron wasn't finished and bellowed, "You know what? I would beat the fuck out of you motherfucker, but you are such a piece of shit that you ain't worth my time." With that, the twin slapped the petrified Michaels hard across the face before letting him go, satisfied that his tormentor had been sufficiently traumatised and would think twice about mouthing off at them again.

FOR VINCE, the backstage altercation involving Michaels was the start of a dreadful week. Two days later in Rhode Island, Mark 'The Undertaker' Calaway and Nelson 'Mabel' Frazier, Jr. were headlining a house show for the third night straight, sleepwalking through the same routine they had been doing in the other towns. Whether down to tiredness from a hard couple of days on the road or a lack of concentration due to their insouciance, tonight their timing was awry. Frazier threw his arm out for a clothesline, but realised too late that Calaway was further away than he had anticipated. His errant fist accidentally connected hard with Calaway's eye, smashing his orbital bone. Even though both men were equally at fault for the mistimed manoeuvre, for Frazier it was yet another casualty to add to his rapidly expanding litany. Calaway worked through the pain for the next three dates in matches with Glenn Jacobs, before having to quit the road and undergo surgery.

Vince had to act fast, and rather fortuitously he had already shot an angle at the *Monday Night Raw* tapings two weeks earlier, where Mabel had crushed The Undertaker's face with a series of legdrops. The episode with the attack went out two days after the real injury, before the extent of the damage was known, so no mention was made of Calaway's condition on the broadcast. But on the next week's taped show - thanks to the magic of post-production - Vince was able to announce that The Undertaker had been injured as a result of the televised Mabel assault. He had turned a negative into a positive - one of his favourite sayings - for his future storylines, but The Undertaker would still be unavailable for the upcoming *In Your House 4* pay-per-view. His scheduled match against Mabel would have to be changed.

LESS THAN three weeks following the talent meeting in Saginaw detailing Bill Watts ascension to head booker, 'the Cowboy' resigned. Vince had grown restless at not having full autonomy over every aspect of his business, and was unable to ever fully cede control to Watts. Despite his promise to oversee rather than overrule, Vince had continued to do the latter. It just wasn't in his nature to be a mere observer, especially when his family's future was at stake and could potentially hinge on one bad decision.

"Bill was trying to bring some actual *wrestling* to the wrestling promotion," remembers Jim Cornette, "I could never get excited about performing there because it was just WWF style wrestling, which I had always hated anyway, but I started briefly getting more interested in what I was doing in the WWF when Watts was there. Unfortunately he then quit over an angle, one I was involved in."

The angle in question was a very un-WWF-like heel assault on three of the top babyfaces, Shawn Michaels, Diesel and The Undertaker, which aired on the October 9th episode of *Monday Night Raw*. Crafted by Watts, the attack from Davey Boy Smith, Owen Hart, Yokozuna, Dean Douglas and Mabel was so brutal that it had left the three faces out cold, with no big comeback or any indication that they would even be okay.

Vince had always believed in the all-conquering babyface hero and had never let his good guys be left in such a manner of peril, so this was a radical change for the WWF. But instead of increasing the angle's impact by closing the show with it as Watts had planned, Vince decided to air it first so the broadcast would not end on a low note. He was so used to doing things a certain way - his way - that he couldn't deviate from the norm even once.

While Cornette attested that Watts left because of that specific angle, according to Bret Hart the straw that broke the camel's back was a disagreement over the direction of the WWF Championship. Watts wanted Hart to be the long-term future of the WWF and the man the company was built around, as he had hinted at in the Saginaw meeting. For Hart, who had been frustrated all year, Watts' stance was music to his ears. But McMahon was already enamoured with Shawn Michaels, despite his numerous personality flaws, and wanted him as the company's champion as of

WrestleMania XII the following March. Watts disapproved, he felt that Michaels was too small and scrawny to be the top guy, plus he didn't respect the rest of the boys or the business enough to justify that level of push. Both men were stubborn to the core and were intransigent in their opinions, so neither budged on their stance.

"Well, what are we going to do about it?" asked McMahon agitatedly. "It's easy," Watts replied, "You're the boss and I'm going home." It was an entirely amicable parting, with no bad blood between the pair, and 'the Cowboy' received a healthy pay-off for his services, even in the tough economic times. Watts had been in McMahon's shoes as a company owner before, and admitted that he too would have had a hard time delegating authority to anyone else, and so empathised fully with Vince's position. "Vince just can't stay away," Watts would later say, "I respect that and I feel the same way."

Watts could have stayed on with a reduced role, but he had no intention of being yet another yes-man to McMahon, something he felt the chairman had more than enough of as it was. He also wasn't going to sit and wait for Vince's approval before he made a decision. "It just wasn't worth it to me," he reflected, before recalling what he had told Vince when he first came in, "I will either make you money or cut your losses, but give me total control or don't talk to me."

McMahon's wife, Linda, was disappointed that things didn't work out with Watts in the WWF, because she saw the stress and pressure her husband was under and could see that Watts' influence and involvement was helping to reduce the load. She expressed her wish that he should stay, but as Watts tersely surmised in a letter of thanks that he later sent to Linda, "There is only room for one 'titan' in Titan Sports."

LATER THAT same night, Shawn Michaels, one of Vince's top stars, was involved in a real-life altercation that ended up putting him out of action for a month.

Following a house show in Binghamton, New York on October 13th, Michaels made the seventy mile trip to Syracuse, the location of the next night's live event, along with Sean Waltman and Davey Boy Smith. Michaels's usual babysitter cum bodyguard Kevin Nash was in Europe, and minus his surrogate big brother he was like a lamb to the slaughter. Arriving after midnight, the wrestlers checked in at Motel 8 on Seventh North Street. Some wrestling fans in the lobby, having overheard the trio talking about wanting to party late into the night, offered to drive them to a hangout called Club 37 in the north of the city. "We used to do stupid things like that then," recalled Michaels, ignoring the old New York adage that, "Nothing good can happen after midnight."

They weren't at the club for long. The three felt like they had to make up for lost time, and with only an hour left before the venue closed, they quickly loaded up on a potentially lethal concoction of shots and somas. Shawn quickly hunted a hook-up for the night, and soon took a shine to a pretty young girl on the dance floor. He began to make his move, flaunting his fame and causing a minor scene with his presence as he attempted to woo her.

Also in the club that night was twenty-three year-old Corporal Douglas Griffith, a soldier from the 10th Mountain Division at Fort Drum, 85 miles north of Syracuse, who was enjoying a rare night off along with some of his comrades. He used to date the girl Shawn was now pursuing, and although the two were not together, it still irked him that the wrestlers were getting so much attention from her and a lot of the other patrons.

As Shawn remembered, "Everyone in the club knew who we were. It was one of those places where I felt like Fonzie. The women were all over us, which I'm sure didn't endear us to any of the other guys there." It certainly didn't endear them to Griffith. He had no time for wrestling, which he considered to be phony, and decided to interject.

Overcome with irrational jealousy, he stepped in and politely but firmly told Michaels that he and the girl were something of an item, and that it would be in his best interests to just leave her be. Shawn, belligerently, ignored him. With his words becoming increasingly slurred, Michaels continued to drunkenly pursue the girl, imploring her to come back with him to his hotel room.

Club bouncer Tony Alberti was always a step ahead when a problem was about to occur. He had a sixth sense for potential trouble, finely honed from years of bouncing in dangerous New York hotspots. He had seen situations like this one flare up out of control if not swiftly dealt with, and he could smell an incident brewing. He noticed that the wrestlers had become friendly with another of the patrons, wrestling fan Richard Jones. A star-struck Richard had introduced the drunken troupe to his sister Donna Jones, a twenty-one year-old care worker from North Syracuse who used to waitress at the club, and also happened to be Alberti's girlfriend.

Alberti suggested to Richard that it would be wise for the wrestlers to leave before the situation got out of hand. But they had a problem; it was 2am on a Friday evening in Syracuse, kicking out time for most bars, and all cabs were fully booked. Alberti, who was aware of who the trio were and didn't want a confrontation to occur on his watch that would end up appearing in the local papers, asked Donna if she would drive them back to their hotel, as she was the only one who hadn't been drinking. Richard offered to ride with them to help get a now passed out Michaels in and out of the car and into his hotel room.

The three men that remained conscious hauled Michaels to Donna's two-door Pontiac Sunbird and placed him in the front seat, before making their way around to the driver's side and piling in the back. Given his size, Smith took the middle seat. Then from the shadows, a still wound-up Griffith and two of his fellow servicemen appeared and surrounded the car.

Griffith already knew Donna, as she was friends with the girl Shawn had pursued. He leaned into the open car window and accusingly yelled to her, "What are you hanging around with those loser wrestlers for? They are all a bunch of *fakes*." That was enough for Davey Boy, who acted before thinking and threw a glancing drunken punch at Griffith from the back seat.[47] Stunned, Griffith reared back just as a barely conscious Michaels escaped his seat and threw a weak shot of his own in Griffith's direction.

That was all the excuse the soldier needed, and he yanked Shawn's semi-conscious body from the car. Michaels couldn't stand on his own volition and crumpled to his knees in a heap, so Griffith grabbed him by his jacket and hurled him into the car, then slammed the vehicle door into his head. Michaels fell to the floor, where Griffith proceeded to kick him in the face with his army issue steel capped boots.

Meanwhile, Smith and Waltman struggled to escape the car to help Shawn, but the lack of rear doors and their intoxicated state made it difficult, not to mention Griffith's two friends acting sentinel by the front doors to prevent their escape. Eventually they prised them open and broke free, after which a barely standing Waltman threw some pitiful worked karate kicks that caused him to tumble to the ground in an embarrassing drunken heap. Smith did briefly succeed in dragging Griffith off of Michaels, but the other two soldiers grabbed him and restrained him, and in the fracas nearly inadvertently poked out his eyeball as they heaved him away.

Panicked, Donna ran into the club and told Alberti, who rushed out with another bouncer and started throwing punches, which finally broke up the fight.[48] Rather than risk the assailants returning and doing more damage,

---

[47] According to the written statement Donna submitted to the police over a month after the incident, Griffith had shoved her and then threw a punch at Smith to trigger the assault, but other witness accounts strongly suggested that Smith threw the first punch.

[48] The alleged story is that the solders then jumped into a white Ford Bronco to leave,

Alberti called an ambulance while Donna and Richard took the three wrestlers back to their hotel, where they were met by the paramedics and taken to the nearby St. Joseph's hospital. Michaels ended up suffering a torn eyelid, cuts to his face, two black eyes and bleeding from his ears where his earrings had been torn out. Smith needed stitches in his face and had a bloodshot black eye, but Waltman escaped unharmed.

When the rest of The Kliq found out, they were furious but hardly surprised, because incidents like this had nearly happened before. According to Paul Levesque, "There were a million times where we had been out places and Shawn would do the exact same thing. But I was there, or Kev was there or Scott was there, you know, it was different," he reflected. When they got home from Europe, Nash and Hall berated Smith and Waltman for not having taken care of Shawn properly, but the pair pleaded their innocence and admitted that they were almost as inebriated as Shawn and could barely remember anything from the night either.

Vince was irate when the news got back to him. He was growing tired of Shawn finding himself in these situations due to his adolescent behaviour, and he was also livid that babyface Michaels and heel Smith had worked a match together and then gone out socialising with each other following it. Years earlier, promoters used to fire performers over similar infractions, but he had no intention of doing that. Details were too sketchy to ascribe blame to any of the wrestlers, and he was certainly not willing to lose two of his main event performers over it.

To many old school veterans, even worse than the kayfabe breach was that Michaels had lost the fight, which in the territory days of wrestling had been a cardinal sin. As Jim Ross noted, "If you lost a bar fight back in the day, you got your notice." Bill Watts later said he would have fired all three of the wrestlers for having been on the losing side if he were in Vince's position, and would have pressured the chairman to do the same had he not resigned.

When Vince eventually calmed down, he realised that yelling at Shawn would achieve little, and instead wrapped a fatherly arm around him, advising him to rethink the way he lived his life. "You shouldn't be out doing that stuff," McMahon told him, before adding he was worried that one night things would go too far, even further than they had in Syracuse.

---

but turned around and tried to knock down Alberti before fleeing the scene. This was never verified and other than confirmation from Griffith that he did leave in a white Ford Bronco, the incident didn't appear in any of the written affidavits taken by the Onondaga County Sheriff's Department. Griffith's defence attorney Bob Mascari later noted that there was, "no credible evidence to support that".

"I don't want to see you in an early grave, Shawn," Vince told him pensively. Michaels simply brushed it off; he had no intention of changing anything about himself. He didn't even remember the evening of the assault; he was practically asleep when the beating took place.

Michaels, in an attempt to save face, claimed in his own written testimony given to police in late November, that up to eight assailants had been involved in the attack, all of them US Marines. It was a number and story that the WWF parroted on television.[49] In the affidavit, Michaels flatly stated:

> We had no problems with anyone at the club. I don't remember much that happened, but I know I suffered head injuries and lost consciousness. I am told by my fellow wrestlers who were in the back seat of the vehicle that seven or eight men pulled me from the car and beat me up. I did not provoke these men in any way and they had no right to beat me up. I do desire prosecution on the matter. I give the Onondaga County Sheriff's Department permission to obtain any and all medical records relating to my treatment for the injuries I sustained on October 14, 1995

Griffith in his own statement told a different story of the evening's events and expressed regret for what had occurred:

> This wrestler, Shawn Michaels, came at me, we swung at each other and I was able to take hold of his jacket and I ran him into the side of Donna's car. This Michaels is a big guy, 250lbs, and I was trying not to get hurt by him. I am sorry that this happened. I didn't mean for anyone to get hurt. My friends were with me but I didn't see any of them get into the fight.

Griffith was to be charged with second degree assault in connection with the incident, and the case was due to go before long-serving veteran Judge Herman L. Harding in the town of Salina. With thirteen years of

---

[49] Donna told the *Syracuse Post Standard* that there were ten assailants, a claim backed up by Waltman's report to the police. But as he later admitted, he couldn't remember much from the night, so his claims may well have been fabricated. A month later, Donna wrote in her affidavit that there were "about four or five" guys involved in the assault, with the contradictory halving of her number serving to make both of her testimonies unreliable.

experience in the field, Syracuse-based lawyer Robert Mascari was hired as Griffith's advocate.

Mascari had represented hundreds of clients over the years and had a keen nose for sniffing out the genuine articles from the fabulists. For him, Douglas Griffith fell firmly into the former category. Years later, the lawyer said of the soldier, "He was a real nice, genuine guy, the perfect client in many ways. But, as a defence lawyer, one of the worst clients you can have is actually one that you believe entirely. On the other side, as a prosecutor, you have lots of discretion, with the only goal to see justice done. That might mean trying to put someone in jail for life without parole, it might mean dismissing a case. You review a file, do your interviews, then make a judgment that leaves you with a clean conscience. But as a defence attorney, my role was to be a fact-checker. It was my job to make sure that my client received a fair trial and that the prosecution proved their case beyond a reasonable doubt. If I did that fairly and zealously, I fulfilled my task no matter what the outcome. But when you have that rare client who you believe was actually innocent - as opposed to not guilty beyond a reasonable doubt - no outcome other than an acquittal or a dismissal will let you sleep at night. That's why an innocent client is the worst; because only one outcome is acceptable. Out of thirty-two years as an attorney, I can probably only think of two or three clients that I was absolutely, positively convinced were telling me the whole truth. The soldier was one of them; I totally believed his story."

Mascari had more insight than anyone into the case, having talked with several other witnesses who were not interviewed by the Onondaga police. He had complete conviction in Griffith's account of the events, which he noted were corroborated by his witnesses. Those he interviewed included other patrons who were in the bar that night, and military personnel from Fort Drum who served as character witnesses. All certified Griffith's version of events. As Mascari remembers, "Almost unanimously, they all told me that what he had said happened, happened."

On the other hand, the statements from Michaels, Jones and Waltman were full of holes. The unreliable nature of the testimonies was something that Michaels himself later admitted. He had received wildly differing accounts of what happened that evening when he asked Davey Boy and Sean about it the next day. "They had a bunch of different stories," he noted, "And after a bit, I knew I wasn't going to get a straight answer out of them."

With the case due to go before a grand jury and to trial, Mascari set about gathering evidence against Michaels, and with the very public steroid trial against the WWF having occurred little over a year previous, he knew exactly which weak spot to probe at. "The steroid issue was already in the national consciousness. I was of course aware of the trial against the WWF, but it was a very obvious thing to target," he recalled.

Mascari talked a number of times on the phone with the case prosecutor, who he happened to know already from his previous job as a government attorney. He warned that from his findings, Michaels claims on television regarding the number of assailants would be exposed as a lie, and he would look foolish for having been beaten up by one person a third of his size rather than the group of highly trained Marines that he had claimed. It was an account of the incident that was strongly backed up by the data he had collected from witness testimonies, all of which differed greatly from how the assault had been presented on WWF television.

During another informal conversation with the prosecutor, this time face-to-face, Mascari delivered the news that he intended to bring up the effects of steroid and drug use in wrestling as part of the defence strategy, as he had numerous accounts from the evening that confirmed Michaels was acting under the influence of more than simply alcohol that night. Mascari then advised the prosecutor that if the case went to a grand jury, his client would not only testify, but he would also request to subpoena Michaels's medical records and have witnesses brought in to testify about steroid use amongst professional wrestlers. Just as he expected, this caused ripples of concern within Titan offices when the information filtered through to them.

According to Mascari, this is what led to the case's abrupt dismissal. The belief was that Vince McMahon had gotten into Shawn's ear and advised him that for the good of the company he should cease pursuing prosecution, warning that the revelation of his drug-fuelled state that night in Syracuse would make headlines once it became public knowledge. By the time the case was scheduled to be heard in mid-1996, Michaels was the new WWF Champion, and having his image potentially shattered in such a way was not something McMahon could risk. With media interest in relation to steroids and illegal drugs in the wrestling business at its lowest in years, the timing would have been a real blow for Vince if one of his top performers had been exposed in such a manner, and might have blown the whole inquest against the WWF wide open again.

As Mascari remembered it, the time between the prosecution finding out his intended mode of defence and the dismissal of the case was brief. "They were looking for a guilty plea, anything so that they could say Shawn was attacked. When they didn't get that, they walked away. Actually, it was more like they ran away. The turnover was very quick in that happening, but from my experience that was no surprise. Very few things in the world are coincidental when it comes to fact patterns and the law. The prosecutor in the case was aggressive, but he was fair. If he had thought that the case could go forward, he would have done so. In law we distinguish between stupidity and criminality. Was there some stupidity to what my client did? Probably, yes. Criminal? No."

In May 1996 Michaels officially decided against pursuing legal action any further and requested that the District Attorney drop the case, resulting in the following being submitted to Judge Harding by assistant D.A. Nicholas DeMartino:

> The victim, a resident of Fort Worth, Texas, the victim's attorney, and the victim's representatives have informed this office that they do not wish prosecution of this matter and that it is their desire to "Put this matter behind them". The People are, therefore, moved to amend Assault 2nd Degree to Assault 3rd Degree. Upon the court granting said motion, the People would move to dismiss said amend charge pursuant to [C.P.L. Section 170.30 (1) (f)].

The WWF made the most of Shawn's injuries, weaving his condition into an angle, using the real-life incident as a way to generate sympathy for the Shawn Michaels babyface character. In doing so, Vince established him as a man who could overcome seemingly insurmountable odds. "Vince McMahon is a genius, regardless of anyone's personal opinion of him," admitted Mascari, adding that, "The whole thing worked out well for him and Shawn, it made them both millions."

ELEVEN

VINCE'S FAILURE TO PRODUCE ANY legitimate new heels at the top of his card meant he was short on options as *In Your House 4* from Winnipeg, Manitoba approached in October. Needing a worthy foe for dead-in-the-water champion Nash, Vince turned to Davey Boy Smith. The man also known as the British Bulldog had spent his entire WWF career as a babyface hero prior to his heel turn the previous month, which came about in order to freshen up his own played out character and simultaneously inject some life into the WWF's weak heel division. Smith was still finding his feet in the role; struggling to adapt, his usually smooth work had become more wooden and clunky and he hadn't yet honed the villainous side of his persona, but he was still Vince's best option.

McMahon's problem was that he didn't want Davey to lose and kill the momentum his turn had given him, because despite the slight drop in his performance levels, the switch had at least freshened him up and catapulted him back into the main event bracket. As with two of the previous three *In Your House* presentations, Vince again decided to get out of having booked himself into a corner by short-changing his viewers with a cheap finish.

The man he used to help him do that, Bret Hart, was once again forced to sit out the televised portion of the show, despite having entered a great performance at the previous event. He had to settle for beating Isaac Yankem D.D.S. in a post show dark match, as well as interfering in the Smith-Nash bout to give McMahon his booking escape route. For Hart, not being on the live broadcast of the show was especially frustrating. He was next in line for a WWF Championship match, and wanted to garner some momentum going into the bout so that fans would be behind his chase for the gold. To him, it made no sense that he was kept off the broadcast when he should have been one of its focal points.

Hart wasn't the only one bemused with a lack of television time. Bob Holly (who defeated Louie 'Rad Radford' Spicolli in the un-broadcast opener) was increasingly demoralised by the WWF using him as a warm-up act. As well as the Winnipeg show, Holly had worked at the first and third *In Your House* shows before the cameras were switched on, doing jobs for guys not even on television at the time, and it was getting to him. He felt like management thought he was good enough to wrestle in front of an audience, but not worth paying to see.

He had fallen into the trap of having proven himself to be a good, dependable and consistent worker, but one unwilling to play the political game. Doing his job (and in-ring jobs) without complaint, the view in the office became, "Bob's a good hand and makes people look good, so let's keep him in that role and use him to work with newcomers or guys we need to get over."

ONE NEW character debuting that night who would soon be the cause of many headaches for Mike Ortman was Goldust. The creation was Vince's latest bizarre brainchild; an androgynous character that channelled fifties icon Gorgeous George and was loosely based on an Oscar statuette. Goldust would be dressed head-to-toe in an all-gold skin-tight jumpsuit that left little to the imagination, with a painted up face, a long blonde wig and a penchant for quoting movies. Some thought Vince had finally gone too far, and in a year filled with bad gimmick ideas, Goldust seemed like it might be the worst of them all.

The man chosen to play the role was former WCW star Dustin Runnels, the son of Texas-born wrestling icon Virgil Runnels, better known as Dusty Rhodes. Dustin had been fired by WCW in March after a match with Barry 'Blacktop Bully' Darsow at the roundly criticised *Uncensored* pay-per-view, because both men had violated company policy by blading. The match was unique, a "King of the Road" match that took place in a moving truck, and was actually taped two days prior to the pay-per-view.

There was a lot of controversy surrounding the dismissal, as the pair were instructed to juice by road agent Mike Graham. He had even provided the blades. Even though bleeding was strictly banned by WCW, Runnels and Darsow were being instructed to do so by a superior on a show that WCW had been advertising as "anything goes". They assumed that the pay-per-view was a one-off exception and that the company were softening their stance for the event. It was taped anyway, they reasoned, so if they went too far they could always go back and edit bits out or censor them. Not only that, but Hulk Hogan had bled in a match with Vader less than two weeks earlier on a Chicago house show, from which no issues arose. The pair didn't think anything more of it and went on to have the match.

Less than a week later Runnels, Darsow and Graham were all fired, leaving many in the company immediately suspicious. It seemed like the trio had been entrapped so that WCW could get them off the books. With the group looking to slash their wage budget, all three were considered expendable. For Darsow that was the end of his run in the mainstream, but luckily for Runnels, Vince McMahon and the WWF came calling six months later.

"Are you sitting down?" Vince asked Dustin over the phone, before he laid out the proposed new character in fine detail. Runnels was apprehensive but Vince assured him, "I'm going to be behind you no matter what, Dustin. There's going to be a lot of people talking..." Runnels agreed to give it a shot, because for him it was the chance to do something other than be known as, "Dusty Rhodes' son" and a way for him to carve out his own niche. His relationship with his father was fractious - the two had been at odds for a long time - and a part of him enjoyed how much Goldust would make Dusty squirm. It was not the way he expected to make a name for himself in wrestling, sure, but he knew it was certain to get people talking.

Goldust started out on the road in August and made his television debut a month later at *In Your House 4*, but at first the character didn't really click. *Power Slam* magazine editor Fin Martin said of his grand unveiling:

Dustin, how could you? How could you go through with it? That *Lost in Space*-like get-up, that gold face paint and those black ears! To say Goldust's pay-per-view debut was unimpressive would be quite the understatement. Runnels looked very uncomfortable under his new guise.

Most others didn't understand the gimmick either. In truth neither did Dustin, who was out of his depth. "At first I didn't even know what androgynous meant - I had to look it up in the dictionary! I was dressed the part, but didn't really understand how to act the part," he later admitted. It wasn't until he worked with Savio Vega that a frustrated Runnels stumbled into the answer. During one of their matches on the road, Vega grabbed Runnels in a waistlock. "Switch and then stroke my chest," instructed the Puerto Rican. Dustin was slightly taken aback but went along with it, and instantly the fans reacted. For the next spot, Savio called for Dustin to whip him into the buckles and then back his ass up towards his crotch. Again, Runnels was apprehensive and reluctant, but he did it anyway and the crowd response was volcanic.

The heat generated was very much of a homophobic sentiment, but Dustin saw Goldust getting over and continued down that path. Soon the character became all about camp theatrical gestures, sexual innuendo and unabashed homoeroticism. Dustin became so good at playing Goldust so quickly, that Vince actually had to tone him down a little. McMahon's tactic to try and sidestep the issue that he was blatantly exploiting his audience's inherent homophobia, was to frequently refer to Goldust's unusual traits as "machinations", dismissing them as mere mind games.

Steve Austin had been friends with Dustin since they were in WCW together at the start of the decade. As he remembered it, "Dustin was the hottest heel in the world. He had so much heat and they were dumping a lot of gasoline on him and keeping him hot." The backlash against the persona was almost immediate, with Vince receiving conflicting criticism from both sides of the spectrum, via gay rights movements and concerned parent groups, and the Titan offices were soon flooded with hate mail and constant phone calls complaining about the character. Vince wasn't worried about that at all, because to him any publicity generated by something he was doing on-screen rather than off it, was good publicity. If people were outraged enough to make their feelings known, it meant they were watching.

It wasn't just the fans who were uncomfortable with the gimmick; Dustin had a lot of heat with the boys too. Scott Hall didn't hide the fact that he was uneasy working with Goldust. He complained that he had kids at home and he didn't want them to start asking awkward questions about his own predilections, or get bullied at school because their dad was a "homo". Others expressed similar sentiments, with some so convinced by Runnels' portrayal that they thought he was enjoying it too much for their liking, and made sure to beat the tar out of him during their matches. He had supporters too though, with Bret Hart believing Goldust to be the best character that the WWF had created in some time, praising Dustin for playing the role with such gusto and conviction.

All Mike Ortman could see in Goldust was the outrage he was causing, and he didn't share McMahon's views that all publicity was good for the company. He would have a hard time attracting business partners and sponsors if the WWF was enduring hostility courtesy of an insensitive and ill-conceived character. McMahon had been canny with the act as it didn't technically violate anything written in *The Principles* document, but he was still intentionally treading a fine line between acceptable and inflammatory.

Executives at *USA Network* were equally worried about Goldust, and wondered just what was going through McMahon's head when he came up with the character. They were no longer sure that he could be trusted to behave rationally, and suspected that the pressures of competing with WCW were beginning to affect him. It was also becoming clear to Ortman that Vince McMahon on a leash, especially when he was under duress, was potentially even more dangerous than when he was allowed to creatively roam free.

ELSEWHERE ON the *In Your House 4* undercard, Yokozuna was drafted in to replace The Undertaker in his scheduled match with Mabel. The goliaths did battle in a bout that was typical Vince, as he once again satiated his need for size by making the two biggest men on his roster square off. "I don't imagine there was any thought process behind it other than, 'Let's make two big guys fight'," noted Yokozuna's on-screen manager Jim Cornette.

Ordinarily programmed as a heel, Yokozuna received a smattering of cheers prior to the bout, largely due to Mabel having been given the storyline credit for putting The Undertaker out of action. The two behemoths slugged it out with a whirl of flapping arms, as the crowd ooh'ed at the sheer spectacle of mass on display.

As Mabel took on the role of the aggressor and crushed his mammoth foe in the corner with a squishing splash, announcer Jim Ross offered his honest assessment that the bout was, "technically imperfect." Both then missed elbow drops that might well have flattened the other had they connected, and limited with what else they could do to one another, resorted to punches and headbutts.

They allowed themselves to fall out of the confines of the ring and continued their lethargic brawl on the outside. Yokozuna then threw Mabel into the ringpost to knock him down, but accidentally tripped over manager Jim Cornette and pancaked him, leaving him struggling and gasping for air like a speared fish out of water.

According to Cornette, his reaction was pure theatrics. "Yoko always took care of me," he remembered fondly, "One night in Indianapolis after he had turned babyface, he was told to give me his Banzai Drop. I had seen how he would fucking kill those jobbers when he did it to them, so I was obviously apprehensive. I didn't object, I just jokingly said to him, 'Please big man, I gotta go home tonight.' He reassured me, 'Brudda, don't you worry about a thing.' When he did it, it felt like someone dropping a bed pillow on me, though if I *had* complained about taking it then it might have been different!"

The result of the contest saw both men counted out after just five-minutes of combat, which the crowd instantly turned on. As one unimpressed critic put it:

What paying customer wanted to see this? Two immobile hulking beasts in a lardy slugfest that went nowhere, cutting a pace that could politely be described as "slow". It was more akin to watching two guys in sumo suits grappling at a party than anything you might recognise as professional wrestling.

"Horrible match with a horrible finish and a strong candidate for worst match of the year," griped *The Wrestling Observer*, and most watching agreed with the evaluation. This kind of insipid non-action with two fat guys flopping around the ring, was simply no longer acceptable to the modern wrestling fan. Their eyes had been opened to a new, quicker, and much more high impact style thanks to the likes of Dean Malenko, Rey Misterio, Jr., Chris Benoit, Eddie Guerrero and Sabu being given screen time by ECW and WCW. Vince McMahon was going to have to evolve his long-existing preferences regarding how wrestling should be if he hoped to keep up with the rapidly changing times.

THERE WAS no doubt that Shawn Michaels suffered injuries in the Syracuse fight just over a week prior to *In Your House*, but just how badly he had been hurt was where controversy arose. Michaels was scheduled to defend his Intercontinental Championship against Kliq adversary Dean Douglas, and according to Troy Martin, Shawn was booked to lose the belt to him.

When Michaels turned up for the show in Winnipeg sporting a five o'clock shadow and with his face all bruised up, Martin instantly assumed foul play. "The makeup girl made him up like that, he wasn't hurt at all," he attested of Shawn's injuries. Sure enough, the news soon filtered through to Martin that the scheduled match was off, just as he had suspected.

This was especially galling for him, as just twelve days earlier, he too had suffered an injury (an as yet unspecified back injury which later turned out to be a herniated disc), but the reaction to him skipping a match against Scott Hall in Köln, Germany was somewhat less sympathetic.

Paul Levesque ended up having to work twice because of it. First he defeated Henry Godwinn, before losing to his Kliq buddy Hall while serving as a stand-in for Douglas. The Kliq were furious and thought Martin was faking the injury just to get out of having to lose to Hall, and they weren't the only ones with such an opinion. Guys were picking up knocks all the time and working through them; it was simply the old-school way of doing things in an era when taking time off for injuries was frowned upon.

At the start of the year Tatanka had injured his ankle in a match with The Undertaker, but he didn't miss a single show. In May, Kevin Nash tore his triceps while working with Kama, an injury that would usually cause a performer to miss six to eight months. He rehabilitated it for a month, then taped it up and carried on. Others were banged up and hurting too, but the attitude at the time was that if you can make it to the building, you can work.

Rather than The Kliq, it was Rodney 'Yokozuna' Anoa'i from the Bone Street Krew who tore into Martin, "Yo motherfucker, you watch that match?" he demanded, blindsiding Martin while he clambered aboard a coach chartered to take the entire crew from town to town. Martin was caught off-guard and wasn't sure what he meant, so cautiously asked the giant Samoan to repeat the question, "You watch Scott's match with Hunter?" Anoa'i impatiently asked again. "Err, no," offered Martin meekly. Anoa'i was tired, sore and burned out from a long tour and in the mood to vent his frustrations. In front of an amused roster, he chewed out a flustered Martin, "Well motherfucker, if you'd watched the match, maybe you would realise what Scott needs out there. They fuckin' tore the house down. And another thing; there ain't no fuckin' days off in this fuckin' shit. We're all hurt motherfucker. And if you ain't fuckin' paralysed, then you take your motherfuckin' ass out there."

For Martin, the hypocrisy of the criticism he received was brought into sharp focus a month later during a *Monday Night Raw* taping in Richmond. While working against Hall again, he aggravated his already damaged back, and Hall complained to anyone who would listen that he was faking it. Martin couldn't understand why he was getting so much heat for being legitimately hurt, especially as Hall himself had missed *King of the Ring* in June because of a rib injury, and he hadn't had to deal with anything remotely like this.

At Madison Square Garden five days later, a still furious Martin spotted Hall in the corridor and shouted over to him that he was, "A no-good piece of shit." Hall had no interest in getting into a confrontation with Martin, and carried on walking. Later that night the arena doctor diagnosed Martin with having a herniated disc, and said that he couldn't wrestle. Vince, who considered it almost a personal affront when his performers would pull out of working at the Garden, pressured the doctor to change his opinion and let Martin compete. He turned to Martin and asked him if he agreed with the assessment, but the wrestler simply laughed. "You are putting me in a very uncomfortable position," he told the chairman, "I'm not qualified, I can't agree or disagree." McMahon had heard enough and stormed out of the room, replacing Martin on the show for his match against Savio Vega with Isaac Yankem.

While that incident caused Vince to wash his hands of Troy Martin, The Kliq had been sour on him from the start of his run. There was no particular reason for it, outside of him being a new face who had done well elsewhere. "He was a dirt sheet hero. They built him up like he was the second coming, but he had little talent," observed Shawn Michaels. "Whatever he had in ECW, he didn't have in the WWF. From what I have seen he just used to cuss a lot in promos. He would use words like 'fuck' and 'ass', and to me that's not a good interview," Shawn decreed. Kevin Nash added, "It wouldn't have mattered what his gimmick was, he was dead, he was the indy guy. It wouldn't have mattered if he wanted to get over, he wasn't gonna get over."

After working a subpar match with Martin on Dean Douglas' WWF in-ring debut on August 28th, Kliq talent gauge Sean Waltman turned to Shawn Michaels and said, "Isn't going to happen. I just don't get him, man, I heard so much about him." Michaels suspected the gimmick was hurting Martin and that he wasn't comfortable in the Dean Douglas role, but it didn't matter. He had been given The Kliq thumbs down and added to the list of "deadwood" guys that the group didn't want to have any part of. Nash confirmed this, "He was fucked; he didn't have a good match with Kid. He gave him the stamp of death, and it was over from there."

At *In Your House 4*, the official story from Titan was that Shawn Michaels was still suffering the effects of a concussion from the Syracuse incident, and doctors had not cleared him to wrestle. Martin believed the assessment of Michaels' condition to be a cover-up, and instead cited a backstage episode as the reason for him pulling out of the match. According to Martin, Shawn - in one of his trademark venting rants - had ran his mouth in the dressing room about Dean Douglas being, "An embarrassment." When Martin got wind of the comments he told Davey Boy Smith that he was going to stretch Shawn if given the chance. He believed that Michaels then called in sick on the *In Your House* match because he found out and was fearful that he would get hurt. Shawn later refuted this, claiming that Vince was concerned about his condition and steadfastly refused to let him wrestle on the show.

With Shawn no longer putting Dean Douglas over, Vince now needed a new plan for his secondary title belt. Because he didn't know how long Michaels would be out, he decided that he would forfeit the Intercontinental title and award it to Dean Douglas, a move that Martin considered, "A farce." It would mark the second time in his career that

Shawn had given up the belt without losing it, and set a pattern for an unprecedented amount of career title belt forfeits that prevented him having to lose them in the ring.

THE WAY the surrender of the belt played out on television was scripted WWF drama at its finest. Dean Douglas was already in the ring alongside on-screen WWF President Gorilla Monsoon and announcer Dok Hendrix when Shawn Michaels' music played. Fans cheered as usual, but Shawn's look and demeanour were anything but normal. He trudged down the aisle clad in an expensive and colourful *Pelle Pelle* leather jacket, with accompanying smart charcoal grey trousers and leather loafers. Instead of the part-strip dancer, part-Adonis that fans were used to seeing, this was a Shawn Michaels who looked for all the world like a forlorn puppy who had lost his master.

Once he made the ring, Shawn cradled the title belt like it was his most treasured possession, staring deeply into it and grimacing slightly at the bruised and battered reflection it shot back his way. He soaked up the sympathy of the crowd as they begged him not to go through with the forfeit, with some perhaps hoping that he would nail Douglas with his trademark superkick and flout the authority who had told him to give up the title.

But that didn't happen. Instead Shawn slowly inched towards Monsoon, each step slower and less assured than the one it followed. As Michaels got closer, he finally gave one last longing glance at the gold, and had seemingly found the inner strength to go through with it, only for 'The Dean' to step in and snatch the belt from his grasp. "That was easy," barked Douglas into the camera.

Shawn could only look on heartbroken as Douglas paraded around with the title. Michaels shot him an expression of extreme despondency, as if devastated that his enemy was stealing his love away from him. Unable to take any more, Michaels made a slow and sombre walk back up the aisle, stopping at the entranceway to take one final look at what he had been forced to give up, before departing without having uttered a word.

IN ORDER to appease the pay-per-view audience who had been promised an Intercontinental title match, Vince made the decision to run a bout immediately between Douglas and another Kliq member, Scott Hall, in a rematch from *In Your House 2*. There was lingering bad blood between the two, but because Hall was much bigger than Shawn there was little risk of

Martin trying something with him like he might have had he worked with Michaels.

Martin was booked to lose to Hall and drop the strap right away, keeping the belt firmly entrenched within the confines of The Kliq's political circle. Bret Hart saw Hall being given the title as another example of The Kliq looking out for themselves and keeping the money spots within their group, a feeling that was echoed throughout the locker-room.

Shawn Michaels later refuted claims that it was a political power play, stating, "It was the office who decided Scott would win the title. There was no great conspiracy on our part to keep the belt within The Kliq. With all due respect to Shane, he wasn't getting over. They (the office) had already given up on him." Martin invariably had a different opinion, telling how Michaels stormed into Vince's office while the chairman was in the middle of a private meeting with Rodney Anoa'i and Harry 'Mr. Fuji' Fujiwara. Michaels told McMahon there was no way that Martin was winning the Intercontinental belt, because he was too limited in the ring and couldn't get heat.

Martin had little choice but to accept the booking, reluctantly agreeing to put Hall over, though not before first expressing to McMahon that he thought the storyline was hokum. The Kliq believed Martin's complaints were down to a reluctance to do the job for them, and took it as another sure-fire sign that he was someone they couldn't trust to do business. Because of that, Hall set about making him look as bad as possible. Every time Martin tried something, Hall reversed it, dominating the bout from start to finish.

For eight minutes of the match's eleven minute duration, Hall was in charge of the contest and made sure to look thoroughly bored and uninterested throughout. Dean Douglas looked for all the world like an out-of-his-depth enhancement talent, and the crowd were completely indifferent to what they were being presented with. Martin knew the match was bad too, and sniped, "I was in there with a guy who was very limited. When you're working with someone who has three moves, there are very few things you can actually do."

Hall's unprofessional behaviour irked many of the boys, but for the most part they were too worried about their own spots to speak out and say anything in support of Martin. Scott Bigelow later shared his belief that the bad matches Martin was having with The Kliq guys were by design. "They used to sandbag Shane and botch spots with him on purpose, then bury him for not being able to work. He would get heat from the office because of it," Bigelow noted. Bob Holly shared a similar view, pointing out that

Hall wanted to work with his buddy Paul Levesque rather than Martin, so he was purposely trying to make Martin look bad in order to get his program changed. Shawn Michaels thought the claims were ludicrous, "Who goes out there to purposely have a bad match? That makes no sense at all," he sneered.[50]

After beating Dean Douglas and winning the Intercontinental Title for a record fourth time, Hall could barely even manage a smile. He had been deeply dissatisfied with his creative direction for the past few months, partially because of having to work with Martin, but also because he saw the Intercontinental title win as career stagnation. Much like when his heel turn and program with The Undertaker at *WrestleMania* was nixed, he was angry that he was still stuck in the same spot that he had been in years ago. It was yet another of many moments that would ultimately play a part in his decision to leave Titan and jump ship to Turner in 1996.

The finish of the match with Hall - designed by Martin and agreed to by Vince to ensure Dean Douglas retained some heat for a series of rematches - saw the evil teacher get beat with his feet under the ropes so that he had an "out" for losing. It never came to anything and wasn't even acknowledged on television, rather just quietly forgotten about. At that point it became evident to Martin that his career was going nowhere in the WWF and he was simply spinning his wheels. *In Your House 4* could have been his breakout night, but Shawn's refusal to work with him had ruined that, and had in turn ruined his WWF career. Ultimately, The Kliq had gotten their way.

IN THE main event, Kevin Nash defended the WWF title against Davey Boy Smith, with Bret Hart watching from ringside as the guest commentator. The two combatants failed to mesh and had a dreadful match, defined by Smith applying a series of repetitive leg locks. His strategy was to chop the champion down, much as Hart had done with Nash at the *Royal Rumble*. But Smith was not a technical wrestling master

---

[50] Fans who were still watching a decade later may well point to Shawn's match with Hulk Hogan at *SummerSlam* in 2005 - a match billed as a once-in-a-lifetime battle of legends - as an example of Michaels doing exactly that. In this case it was the very opposite of sandbagging, with Michaels purposely going out of his way to take the most absurd and phony looking bumps possible in order to show up Hogan as being a decrepit relic. The issue between the two was down to Hogan's refusal to put Shawn over, and Michaels briefly dropped his guard and his recently adopted Christian values of "turn the other cheek..." to put in a performance that harkened back to the Shawn Michaels of the nineties rather than the apparently reformed model of the new Millennium.

craftsman like his brother-in-law, and the crowd sat in bored silence for the near twenty-minute affair.

"It was one of the worst matches in the history of pay-per-view. I was fucking bored, and I was actually in the thing!" complained Jim Cornette, who was forced to suffer the contest while acting as the new manager of Smith. "Davey Boy was like a British version of Dick Murdoch; if he wasn't motivated he could have some awful matches," he explained. Cornette continued, "At one point Nash ended up out on the floor, so to try and give the match some heat, I grabbed his foot and started to elbow his leg, but it got a huge fucking pop! The heel manager's offence got a bigger reaction than the rest of the match! That's when I knew that we were in trouble."

After enduring the tedium of the contest, the crowd were then presented with a deeply dissatisfying disqualification finish following Hart's predictable involvement. The Canadians were furious and turned on the angle, going against the WWF's script and peppering the incumbent champion with rejective boos. They cheered raucously for Hart as he engaged in a pull-apart brawl with Nash to end the televised show.

McMahon couldn't understand the response; he was expecting a split crowd. After all he had spent the last year building up the Diesel persona as the WWF's top babyface. He should have known better. Not only had he tried the play before - with Hart and Lex Luger in 1994 - and experienced the same outcome, but this show was in Canada, where Bret Hart was the closest thing to a national hero that a wrestler could be.

Already strained because of WCW's resurgence and the trying week he had just endured, Vince was appalled with the show and realised that from top to bottom it was one of the worst that Titan had ever presented. Following the woeful championship match, an exasperated McMahon threw down his headset and glasses, loudly muttered, "Horrible," then stormed backstage. As well as the flat main event, he was angry that the crowd hadn't responded to other key angles as he had wanted.

Cornette felt guilty for his involvement in the main event, which he considered to be one of the worst that he had ever been involved in. Mortified to have been associated with the debacle, he felt like he had let down his long-time followers who only associated him with great acts like tag team The Midnight Express, a tandem that was routinely involved in the match of the night during their pomp. Cornette was the first person that an irritated Vince McMahon bumped into after the contest. Feeling like he owed his boss an explanation, Cornette offered an apology for his involvement. It took Vince a little by surprise, as it was rare for one of his charges to say sorry for their performance. He dismissed it in his usual, nonchalant way. "No pal, you were fine," he assured the flustered manager.

The *In Your House 4* card was roundly panned by critics, with *The Wrestling Observer Newsletter* stating:

Although the poll would indicate otherwise, as this was the worst poll reaction to a WWF show in history, I'd say it was very bad but not overtly offensive or horrible. Based on the reaction and not just the percentage, but the vehemence of the negative complaints after the show, it was one of the worst reactions to any show in a long time.

In Your House 4, the first WWF pay-per-view in Canada for half a decade, had seen the fans turn out in force with a crowd of over 10,000 in attendance. Unfortunately for Vince, the increased live attendance didn't translate to pay-per-view buys, and the event did an all-time company low 0.4 buy rate. Put into context, only 90,000 people ordered the show, half the number of the first instalment of the series from only five months earlier.

There was no hiding from the truth for Vince; very few wanted his cut-price monthly pay-per-views. After just four of the presentations, fans had decided that the majority of the action they were getting wasn't worth paying for. The few fans who had ordered *In Your House 4* were left feeling much the same way following the cheap main event finish. It seemed as though the series was doomed to fail less than six months into the venture.

TWELVE

FOR THE KLIQ, THE MONTREAL incident in September with Carl Ouellet served as a catalyst for discontent. Because of the way it was handled, they believed the office "didn't have their backs," and on November 5th in Indianapolis, they decided to make their feelings known by threatening to go on strike. Vince had once told Shawn that he was only aware of the locker-room climate amongst the boys if others told him, because he wasn't always around and few were ever straight with him. Having been assured by Vince that he was open to a call at any time, Shawn decided to take advantage.

Michaels bluntly told McMahon that The Kliq thought everything the company was doing "sucked," and things needed to seriously change. He added that they were so unhappy, they wouldn't wrestle that night at the Market Square Arena. Worried that he was on the brink of losing three of his biggest stars, not to mention two stellar hands from the midcard, Vince offered to fly to Indianapolis and meet with them to discuss ideas.

Vince sighed as he put the phone down. The inmates were starting to run the asylum, and he was conflicted. On one hand he hated yielding to anyone, especially a group of his talent, but on the other they were key personnel, the best he had. But what really resonated with him was that he knew there was truth to their complaints. The WWF had been poor creatively all year, and commercially numbers across the board had suffered a dramatic fall in the twelve month period.

He knew meeting with The Kliq in a private confab would cause even more tension in an already fractious locker-room, but that wasn't necessarily a bad thing. In some ways, the heat The Kliq had with the rest of the crew was beneficial to him, as it diverted their attention away from more pressing concerns to petulant back-room squabbling. The unrest that The Kliq caused in the locker-room meant that the boys would have something other than their all-time low pay-offs to complain about, and to Vince that was a welcome boon.

Vince grabbed his closest aide, Pat Patterson, and the two landed in Indianapolis within a couple of hours of the call, then immediately headed to meet with the frustrated performers in their hotel room. Paul Levesque was still new to the company and Kevin Nash had advised the rookie prior to Vince's arrival that he should probably stay out of the argument; it wasn't worth the hassle it would cause his fledgling career. When Vince arrived at the hotel, Levesque tried to excuse himself politely, but Vince wasn't in the mood for standing on ceremony. "No!" he demanded, "You are in the room too, you are going to weigh in as well." The meeting was tense, Vince had never been backed into a corner like this before by anyone, and it made him uncomfortable. But as he listened to The Kliq's side of the story, he found himself gradually persuaded by their assessment of the talent pool and views on the WWF's general direction.

According to Kevin Nash, the issue was not about money or wanting to run the company, but rather, they just wanted a direct meeting with Vince to hear his feelings and to share their own. The group wanted changes to the WWF that would improve it as a whole, and sure enough, the meeting had its desired effect. Within days of the summit, there *were* noticeable changes inside the company. Mostly they were subtle, though still significant, such as a slightly increased level of violence, and willingness to show a little more graphic content. The angles improved too, with a lot of the goofier gimmicks repackaged, renamed or released, as a more realistic style of storytelling came to the fore. The pressure exerted from The Kliq was starting to pay dividends, and for once, not just for their own benefit.

WHILST HE was in Indianapolis, Vince figured he might as well attend that night's house show and give other members of his roster the chance to talk with him directly if they so desired. The attitude in the locker-room was that of anger. The majority were furious that Vince had granted a private meeting with The Kliq, and used it to further embellish their own paranoid theories about the group's stroke within the WWF.

Shawn Michaels' later insisted that no one was fired as a result of the Indianapolis meeting, and Kevin Nash claimed the group had no intention of costing anyone their jobs. He maintained that they had actually put over the likes of Scott Bigelow - someone they admittedly didn't like personally - as someone who could "play on their team." Nonetheless, it didn't go unnoticed amongst the boys that there were a series of casualties within weeks of the Indianapolis stand-off, and a number of notable Kliq targets were gone from the WWF before Christmas.

Less than a week after the meeting, on November 10, 1995, in Long Island, Jean-Pierre Lafitte wrestled his last match for the WWF.[51] He had

---

[51] With Nash and Hall long gone from the company, Carl Ouellet would be brought back for one final run in 1998, once again alongside Jacques Rougeau. The duo seemed out of place in the WWF's edgy Attitude Era, and made little impact. Rougeau departed after less than a year, leaving Ouellet with little to do. He was sent to the WWF's

become sick of the backstage politics and wanted out. Ultimately, The Kliq *had* got the last laugh and defeated him, even if he had jumped before he was inevitably pushed.

Later in the month, Darryl 'Man Mountain Rock' Peterson was let go. Once a renowned gritty brawler in WCW under the handle of Maxx Payne, Peterson had suffered a troubling run with Titan. As well as possessing a guitarist gimmick that had little chance of propelling him beyond the undercard, injuries and drug problems also blighted his time with the company and led in part to his release. Most of the locker-room were relieved, because Peterson had caused some unease by shooting footage of the boys on the road with his home video camera. Among other things, he caught a wasted Louie Spicolli struggling to open his hotel room door, Kevin Nash pulling a vast quantity of prescription pills out of his pocket and joking about them being a prerequisite of WWF road trips, and many of the boys abusing other substances and partaking in solicitation. For many years afterwards, Peterson threatened to release the footage as a documentary, but he never followed through with it for fear of the legal repercussions that would surely have followed.

Dean Douglas too was gone from the group before the year was out, by his own volition, but thanks largely to the way his career had nosedived after butting heads with The Kliq. After learning of the meeting in Indianapolis, he too jumped before he was pushed. The sharks had claimed another victim, and within just months of signing with the WWF, Martin asked for his contract release. He lasted a few more months, competing at *Survivor Series* (in what was his only televised outing opposite Shawn Michaels) before making a final appearance at *In Your House 5*, then left never to return.

The politics had been too much for Martin to deal with, but he was also struggling financially with his WWF deal. With bills mounting and no cheques to cash from Titan, Martin went to the source. He told McMahon that he was losing money working for him, and was eating into his personal savings just to pay his bills. "There is money coming," Vince told him, but was then taken aback when Martin pointed out that his mortgage was due that day and he needed money now. "I don't know what to tell you," Vince replied, so Martin asked for his release.

Vince was not in the habit of releasing genuine talent during the Monday Night Wars, but he realised that Martin had no future with the company due to his political enemies and the fact his gimmick had been an

---

developmental groups and repackaged as Kris Kannonball, but rarely worked on television before his release in 2000.

unmitigated flop. Martin theorised that he was allowed to leave because he had threatened Vince with a date in court on the charge of "fraudulent inducement", (that McMahon had promised Martin the world but not delivered on any of it) and he didn't believe McMahon could afford a lengthy court battle with him.

Of course, Vince had just fought the Federal Government in court and won, so a lawsuit was totally irrelevant to him. Rather, releasing Martin would alleviate some of The Kliq's lamentations, at least until they found their next target. In addition, getting a character off the wage bill that obviously wasn't working and was unlikely to ever be profitable, was just smart business sense to him.

Scott Bigelow felt much the same way as Martin; he believed The Kliq had thwarted his promised main event run and irreparably damaged his career, so he too moved on. Bigelow wrestled his last match for the Federation at the *Survivor Series* show in November before taking a full-time job in Japan, eventually resurfacing in North America via ECW. Just eight months earlier he had headlined *WrestleMania* and became one of the most recognisable wrestlers in the world. It was as rapid a descent imaginable.

Jim Cornette felt that Bigelow likely left before he was forced out by The Kliq's political manoeuvrings, and that the group were fearful of him. "Bam Bam didn't put up with any bullshit and he would have waded through that fucking group," believed Cornette, "He was a great guy if you didn't try to fuck with him, but they fucked with him. I wouldn't be surprised if he had told Vince where to go too."

Nelson Frazier was another who had headlined a pay-per-view that year, only to quickly find himself no longer employed by Titan. His final appearance (until he returned full-time in 1999) came at the *Royal Rumble* in January 1996, but Vince had already begun phasing him down prior to that. It was no coincidence, many thought, that he was released just a few months after hurting Kevin Nash at *SummerSlam*. It seemed to most like The Kliq were winning in their quest for wrestling dominance.

AS VINCE had anticipated, The Kliq meeting had caused intense paranoia within the locker-room, and the powder keg environment threatened to blow just days later with an announcement that 'B' shows (house shows featuring a crew of mostly not over or inexperienced wrestlers, and only a few marquee names with frequent television exposure on top) were discontinued. From that point onwards the WWF would only be presenting eighteen 'A' shows per month, and spots were limited. It was bad news for the already stressed undercard workers, many of whom were already living hand-to-mouth as it was. For them, no 'B' shows would mean they weren't being used, which in an era before guaranteed contracts meant they weren't getting paid. "Guys were starving," Kevin Nash remembered, "They were living off their draws."

A draw was an advance on a performer's salary, given upfront by the agents at live shows to pay for road expenses, which was then deducted from the final pay-off for the show that the wrestler would receive months later. A standard draw was $200, though could be higher depending on the status of the talent. The rule in the locker-room was, "Always get your draw," as then there was a guarantee for the boys that they would get at least something from the show in times of financial struggle.

When the business was booming the draw was a nice bonus to keep the drinks flowing in the bars after shows, but in 1995 when it was in a terrible state, many were using their draws to pay their bills. Subsequently, when they were on the road, the boys would eat cheap, stay in run-down hotels in groups, and squeeze as many people into a single car as possible. It was a stark contrast to the way the wrestlers were presented on television as "superstars".

Jim Cornette didn't believe the crew were in as much trouble financially as some claimed. "The underneath guys weren't doing too well, but it was all in relation," he said, "I'm sure most wrestlers on the scene in later years who were not with the WWE would have loved to have made that sort of money." As he remembered it, there were still bonuses given out, which could be earned for anything ranging from a particularly good performance to agreeing to do something humiliating. Cornette shared how one night he was given a $500 bonus for allowing Davey Boy Smith to drag him all the way back to the locker-room by his feet, after having been given a Banzai drop by Yokozuna on instruction from the agents. It was obviously a rib, but he played along without complaint and was given the bonus for taking it all in good humour.

Tom Prichard too downplayed the severity of the financial situation amongst the boys. As he remembers it, "We were making okay money compared to Smoky Mountain, obviously, though we weren't exactly making *WrestleMania* money. The thing is, there was nowhere else to really go, because unless you knew someone in WCW then it was hard to get in there. There was ECW, but then you had to deal with Paul Heyman's lies and his bullshit. And if you did manage to get paid, just how much was it really going to be? The indies were not exactly thriving and there wasn't much money to be made on them, certainly in relation to the WWF. It was where everyone wanted to be, even when business was struggling."

Even so, Vince came under immense pressure from his undercard during another tumultuous week, which saw him attend further house shows in Columbus on November 8th and New Jersey on November 12th, in an attempt to smooth things over with the roster. Eventually he had no choice but to sign off on a $400 per week base salary for performers when they weren't working, at least temporarily relieving some of the tension with the lower card talent. It represented the first time that Vince had ever offered anything resembling a guaranteed contract. It was a monumental occurrence, but it came at a time when his business could least afford it.

SURVIVOR SERIES was a well-established annual tradition for the WWF. The November supercard had first launched in 1987 as a direct assault on WCW predecessor Jim Crockett Promotions' biggest show of the year, *Starrcade*. Vince had been cute about implementing the show, threatening pay-per-view providers that they couldn't have *WrestleMania IV* unless they aired *Survivor Series* and canned *Starrcade*, the latter of which aired the same day as the WWF's new show. With business hot and *WrestleMania* on fire following the success of *WrestleMania III*, it was a threat the companies were not willing to take lightly. The result was a resounding win for Vince McMahon and the WWF. The majority of carriers ultimately rejected *Starrcade*, and *Survivor Series* pulled a 7.0 buy rate that translated to 325,000 buys.

Starrcade itself pulled a 3.3, which suggested nearly half the amount of viewers that *Survivor Series* had drawn, but this number was misleading. A buy rate is calculated based on the percentage of people with access to the pay-per-view service the show airs on who buy the show. If one-million people have access to the service and 100,000 purchase the show, it would garner a 10.0 buy rate, or ten percent. In the case of *Starrcade*, there were around 600,000 homes who could access the show, due to the WWF's machinations, so the actual numbers of orders was only in the region of 20,000. In contrast to that, *Survivor Series* had a potential audience of over 4.5 million.

The event quickly evolved into more than just a vindictive business move, with the yearly spectacular carrying with it the unique selling point of pitting two teams of five against each other (and in early editions, two teams of five tag teams, so a total of ten wrestlers on each side). The supercard continued to do blockbuster numbers for the next half a decade, but started to drop off considerably in line with the rest of the company's business in 1993.

Some had wondered if the team concept was becoming outdated, but with the onset of additional pay-per-views in 1995, *Survivor Series* needed that unique selling point more than ever to differentiate it from the plethora of other shows - WWF or otherwise. Prior to his departure, Bill Watts had proposed a twist on the tried and tested formula; a match mixing heels and babyfaces on the same team, competing against another team with a similar composition. Previously, it was almost unheard of to muddy the lines in such a manner, but Vince agreed to run with it and the "Wild Card Match" was born.

Pitting Shawn Michaels, Ahmed Johnson, Davey Boy Smith, and Sid against Yokozuna, Owen Hart, Razor Ramon, and Dean Douglas, the bout was as interesting politically as it was on the screen. The fraught tensions between many of the performers and the coming together of various rival cliques and factions, both as partners and opponents, made for a potentially volatile situation. For the road agents dealing with structuring the bout, keeping the egos of everyone involved happy was like being asked to solve the riddle of an international crisis.

Michaels was reluctant to work with Douglas, whom The Kliq had no desire to have any further involvement with. Yokozuna was at the head of the BSKs and had little time for Michaels, and he certainly wouldn't tolerate any of his prima-donna displays of petulance. Shawn had no problems with Smith or Hart though, because he respected them as workers. Davey was someone he would hang out with when The Kliq were not around, and pretty much everyone from any political leaning had a soft spot for notorious practical joker Owen. But one man Michaels wasn't so keen on was newcomer Johnson.

Johnson was pegged by Bill Watts as the WWF's answer to The Junkyard Dog (who had the best run of his career under Watts) or Ron Simmons (the first black WCW Champion, another decision made by Watts). He was to receive a huge promotional push and become a black hero, something Watts had felt the lily-white WWF was sorely lacking. As it was Johnson's televised in-ring debut, there was no question he had to be presented well and protected in how he was booked. It would have been entirely counterproductive to have him get beat. Quite the opposite; Johnson had to win and he had to win well. Michaels was wary of him, considering him a threat to his spot, as he looked like he was chiselled out of stone and yet could move like a cat.[52]

---

[52] Though as one member of the locker-room later quipped, he might have moved as quick a cat, but he did so with all the grace of an elephant.

Smith and Owen were not part of a named clique, they, along with Bret Hart, were simply family members who occasionally rode together and watched each other's backs. Unlike the other groups, they were far from exclusive road partners, and would often hang out and travel with others. Generally well liked by the majority of the locker-room, Davey and Owen didn't have heat with anyone coming into the match.

The soon to be departing Troy Martin did. As well as Michaels, serious tension still simmered between he and Scott Hall, and the potential for another verbal blow-up between the two was always on the horizon. They had exchanged oral barbs more than once, and a full-on fistfight always seemed to be just a moment away. Martin had also lost the respect of Yokozuna after the back injury incident in Germany, so he came into the match with guys who disliked him on both sides.

The novelty of the contest made it entertaining for the fans, and almost unbelievably it played out without any serious issues between the participants. Unsurprisingly given that his tenure with the company was drawing to a close, Dean Douglas was the first man scripted to be eliminated from the match. He was the victim of a pact amongst The Kliq that they would only work together, or with the boys in their favour. Douglas quickly fell to Shawn Michaels, who made sure to secure a decisive and clean win over Martin before his departure, in one last snub to the former 'Franchise'. But Martin couldn't care less, he just wanted to get out of the WWF as quickly as possible.

The Kliq had engineered the match so they had a hand in nearly every other elimination, and while Yokozuna was covered by Johnson for the match winning pinfall, it was only after having absorbed a Michaels superkick to the chin. The three men who stood tall as the victors were little surprise; Ahmed Johnson was being pushed hard and fast, Davey Boy Smith was working with the WWF Champion again at *In Your House 5* the next month, and Shawn Michaels was about to have a promotional rocket strapped to his back.

The match was Michaels' first televised outing since the Syracuse incident a month earlier, but he hadn't missed a beat. There was an unspoken concern amongst some in the booking office about what reaction Michaels would get, and whether his credibility had been shattered, or if fans would perceive him as being a phony. They didn't. Michaels was more popular than ever, and the portrayal of the Syracuse assault on Titan television had actually helped generate interest in his subsequent storyline quest for the WWF Championship, just as Vince McMahon had intended it would.

PLACATION WAS just as necessary amongst the undercard as it was the top stars, plainly demonstrated by the decision to add Bob Holly to the show-opening four-on-four match. The originally scheduled bout called for Chris Candido, Louie Spicolli, a repatriated Tom Prichard, and the freshly heel Sean Waltman, to work against a recently returned Marty Jannetty, Jinsei Shinzaki, the increasingly out of favour Barry Horowitz, and newcomer Allen 'Avatar' Sarven, better known in wrestling circles as Al Snow.

Sarven had been a hot commodity prior to his arrival at Titan, with both the WWF and WCW having made plays to sign him after he had impressed in both ECW and Smoky Mountain Wrestling. A try-out match with WCW went well and he received plaudits from the boys, but the office had treated him poorly and he wasn't impressed with how they operated. Short on talent who could work a dependable match with anybody, Vince had laid it on thick for Sarven by giving him a tour of the Titan offices and having him taken care of with transport. Then he passionately pitched his latest sure-fire money-drawing idea: Sarven would be known as Avatar, a *Power Ranger.*

Despite the absurdity of the gimmick, Sarven was impressed with the professionalism of the WWF's courting, and signed on with them. But rather than giving him the usual pre-debut vignettes as was customary for new, unknown talent, Vince instead thrust him straight onto a live *Monday Night Raw* from Brandon, Manitoba on October 23rd. Sarven, as Avatar, donned a mask as the bell rung after having entered the ring without one, confusing onlookers who had never seen anything like it before. Many observed that his new look was strikingly similar to one of Milton Bradley's *Karate Fighters,* one of the WWF's chief sponsors at the time. Others whose pro wrestling knowledge stretched beyond the WWF, pointed out that he looked identical to Japanese performer Hayabusa, and acted just like him too.

The match was designed to be a *squash* (walkover) in which Avatar could display his prowess whilst getting his new moves and mannerisms over, but the enhancement talent he was working with, Brian Walsh, didn't cooperate. Instead of making Avatar look impressive, Walsh shrugged off his offence and sold his moves badly, then Sarven compounded his problems by slipping off the ropes when attempting a high flying move. After another few minutes of awkward, mistimed exchanges, the supposedly babyface Avatar scored the win to a chorus of boos. It was one of the most underwhelming WWF introductions anyone could remember.

Avatar was already scheduled to be part of the *Survivor Series* opening multi-man bout, but his poor debut occurred at the same time that Bob Holly was complaining to management that he wasn't getting enough dates since the discontinuation of 'B' shows, and that he was considering leaving the company. Holly was considered a reliable hand and a good opponent for newcomers to work with, so Vince didn't want to lose him. Having already completely lost interest in the Avatar character, he told Sarven that he was no longer on the pay-per-view. He explained that he was replacing him with Bob Holly due to his longer tenure with the company, and that they would sit down and re-evaluate his persona in due course.[53]

Despite being shoehorned in, Holly was granted a rare televised pinfall over an opponent in the match. He was allowed to eliminate the soon to be repackaged Tom Prichard from the contest, before succumbing to Prichard's future tag partner Skip mere seconds later. The last man left standing was Waltman, with The Kliq underachiever seemingly finally set for a run higher up the card than he had previously enjoyed. His victory was designed to strengthen his standing in the eyes of the fans before he moved into a feud with his real-life best friend, Scott Hall.

REAL-LIFE friends working together was a common theme throughout the show; The Undertaker teamed with three of his BSK allies (Savio Vega, Henry Godwinn and Fatu) in his first match since fracturing his orbital bone, resulting in a whitewash win over a heel squadron consisting of Jerry Lawler, Isaac Yankem, Hunter Hearst Helmsley, and the man who put him on the shelf, Mabel.

The WWF also teamed up with the All Japan Women promotion to bring in a number of exciting performers to work with WWF Women's Champion Alundra Blayze, pitting them against each other in only the second all-female *Survivor Series* elimination match. Unfortunately the contest didn't come close to the sky high expectations that AJW followers had come to expect. Dave Meltzer expressed his surprise at how poorly the match came across:

---

[53] Sarven eventually came back in 1996 as Leif Cassidy, a seventies throwback character who was paired with Marty Jannetty to form a new version of popular eighties and nineties tag team The Rockers. The immediate problem he had was that Jannetty's partner in the original team had been Shawn Michaels, and fans didn't buy him as a replacement one iota. Sarven eventually returned to ECW for seasoning, finally getting over as pre-Avatar gimmick Al Snow, a character that etched the words, "Help Me!" backwards on his forehead with makeup, and talked to a mannequin head. The gimmick was brought to the WWF in 1998.

The All Japan women as a group are remarkably consistent, but I don't think I've seen a match involving this level of talent be as bad as this one in years.[54]

Elsewhere on the card, Vince again turned to a star from the company's more successful days, this time in the form of Curt 'Mr. Perfect' Hennig, who was introduced to a loud ovation at the start of the show. Hennig was not back to wrestle, as he was still reaping the benefits of a Lloyds of London insurance policy, which covered a long-standing back injury caused by years of reckless and extravagant bumping. Instead he was given commentating duties, sitting alongside McMahon and Jim Ross and providing colourful analysis. *Power Slam* magazine editor Fin Martin was not impressed, writing:

In the space of two matches, Hennig proved beyond any reasonable doubt that he rarely, if ever, tuned into WWF television unless he is under the employ of the company, he does not approve of (and is probably intimidated by) women working as wrestlers, and researching the product he is obligated to describe is not a priority. What a glorious comeback.

Perhaps surprisingly given their usual attitudes, Hennig was welcomed back with open arms by The Kliq. "In our car he was a God," gushed Kevin Nash, "He smartened up Shawn, he smartened up Scott. He was their guru," he added. Hennig's return was eventually supposed to result in a program between himself and Kliq member, Hunter Hearst Helmsley. Instead, Hennig jumped ship to WCW before that transpired, and didn't wrestle again for the WWF until the *Royal Rumble* in 2002, a year before his untimely death from acute cocaine intoxication.

BRET HART had suspected for months that he was going to be the man to dethrone Kevin Nash for the WWF Championship. The Diesel character hadn't connected with the audience like Vince and his staff had hoped, and some of the numbers with him on top were embarrassing. Bill Watts had made clear his intentions to put the belt on Hart, and even after he left the

---

[54] In a less than coincidental move, WCW used Japanese female performers in its *World War 3* pay-per-view just a week later, one of them former WWF Women's Champion Bull Nakano. Unlike the *Survivor Series* match, this was a triumph, with Meltzer describing it as "excellent".

company the seeds had already been sown in McMahon's mind that Bret was the right choice to carry the strap.

As far as Hart was concerned, it was about time. He was finally satisfied that his hard work and professionalism throughout a turbulent year had not gone unnoticed, but he was slightly troubled when Vince immediately told him that he would be losing the belt to Shawn Michaels four months later at *WrestleMania XII*. For Hart, it made the news of the impending reign bittersweet. He was going to be an extended caretaker champion to transition the belt to Michaels rather than the true top guy, a role he was firmly convinced he had earned. "I knew Shawn wasn't the guy to fill my shoes, and I was damn sure that he wouldn't draw any better than I did," Bret grumbled.

McMahon had actually made the decision to go with Hart back in August following a string of unsuccessful shows with Nash on top. The horrible *SummerSlam* number and the appalling *In Your House 4* the previous month in Winnipeg had only strengthened his resolve to switch the title. McMahon was apprehensive about informing Nash, because when he had first gave him the belt he promised him a long run, and he expected the big man to be furious. With Jim Ross looking on, McMahon gave Nash an elaborate fictitious pitch about wanting him to work with Mike Tyson on a charity show in Central Park, before casually dropping in that he was going to be dropping the belt to Bret, who would then lose it to Shawn.

McMahon was trying to use distraction tactics and the promise of something bigger to soften the blow, but Nash could see right through it. To him, this was simply Vince's way of coping with having to break bad news, but he decided that if the chairman felt the need to blow smoke in order to make himself feel better about doing that, then he would go along with it.

"Is there a problem?" McMahon asked Nash, after seeing the look of surprise on his face at the news. "No, I don't care, I'll drop it," responded Nash, who was well aware that the numbers were plummeting and understood the decision to change direction. He didn't even mind losing the belt to Hart, despite him not being a Kliq guy, because he knew that Bret would merely be keeping it warm for his best friend.

Nash also knew that just as he had been ten months earlier at the *Royal Rumble*, Hart was the perfect opponent for him to have a good match with, something he was desperately in need of. In the days leading up to the bout the two talked on the phone at length about what they could do to make the contest memorable, and found to their collective surprise that they were on the same page.

Had the match taken place a few weeks earlier it might not have been so smooth, because Nash had grown annoyed with Hart for being what he described as, "Difficult," in the months before the face-off. Talking about his irritation with Hart during a particular Kliq road trip, Nash got himself so worked up that he decided he was no longer willing to drop the strap to him. "Motherfucking *what*?" snapped Shawn Michaels, as his trademark temper immediately flared. Michaels then proceeded to selfishly berate Nash in a way hitherto unseen by his best friend, demanding that he lose to Hart because he was next in line for the belt, and that not doing so would ruin all of his future plans. Nash was taken aback by how vicious his friend was being towards him, but cooled off on his decision and agreed to do business. It wasn't the first time that Shawn had put his own interests ahead of even those he considered to be his closest allies, and it wouldn't be the last. But after all, as Kliq buddy Scott Hall would later say, "It's show-business, not show-friends."

When the time came for the "Anything Goes" bout between the two, Hart strode to the ring clad in the same all-pink tights that he had also worn in famous matches against Roddy Piper and Yokozuna over the years, and he got a much more positive reaction than the champion. Unlike at *Royal Rumble*, he didn't need to avoid garnering crowd favour here; a heel reaction for Nash - and more importantly a sympathetic reaction for Hart - was what the two wanted for the finish they had planned.

Nash started out the aggressor, dropping Hart onto the ringside barriers before spending a few minutes beating him up, then established further dominance by hurling Hart into the ringside steps. Nash grabbed a chair, so Hart bent over to give him his back as a target, and Nash belted him with a hard shot to the spine. The combat more closely resembled what one might have expected to see at an ECW show than on Vince's television, as the WWF was still marketing itself as family-friendly, but the brutality was having the desired effect in telling the story. When Nash subsequently called for his jack knife powerbomb finishing move, the boos rained down on him. The violent early assault had done the trick; the crowd were exactly where the performers wanted them.

Hart blocked the powerbomb by grabbing Nash's leg and then began to capitalise on the injured body part - a skill 'the Hitman' was adept at portraying. He assaulted the champion's limb, cutting him down and working him over on the ground. Then in an innovative spot, Hart tied Nash's leg to the ringpost with a camera cable. The idea actually came from a rib that Owen Hart once played on Bret during a house show match, where he tied his brother up and genuinely trapped him.

Hart upped his own aggression levels with repeated chair shots to Nash's prone knee, each one greeted with an audible, "Ooh," from the crowd amid growing surprise that Hart was being so uncompromising in his onslaught. Nash was now the proverbial one legged man in an ass kicking contest, but as nothing was off limits he dropped Hart testicles-first over the ropes, and then launched him from the buckles across the ring. That gave Nash time to escape the cable, but it proved to be more difficult than he had expected. "It was almost a shoot," he remembered, "I couldn't get that thing off my fucking leg for nuthin'."

After finally defeating the wires, Nash turned his attention back to beating Hart and the see-saw battle continued with the champion in control. Earlier in the bout, both guys had removed turnbuckle pads in opposite corners as part of their posturing pre-match mind games, and Nash used that to his advantage, throwing Hart hard, chest-first into the exposed steel. With that the crowd, who had started to grow unsure of Hart following the leg attack, were back behind 'the Hitman' fully. The next stage of the contest belonged to Hart, who embarked on his routine finishing sequence after driving Nash's head into the exposed turnbuckle, which served as a storyline receipt for Nash having done the same to him. When Nash ended up escaping to the outside of the ring, Bret followed immediately with a slingshot plancha, but Nash moved, causing Hart to land hard on the outside.

Prior to the bout, Bret and Nash had realised that they would need something special to differentiate the match from their two previous outings on pay-per-view, and while things like blood shedding and weapon use were still not actively encouraged by the WWF, the level of realism and violence being presented had undeniably been ramped up throughout the company in recent weeks. That much was evident to them simply based on the type of match they had been directed to have by Vince that evening.

The pair found their answer in the bingo hall of ECW, and just a month after Jerry Lawler's bloody indiscretion on *Monday Night Raw*, they lifted a violent spot straight from Sabu, the nephew of one of wrestling's great heels, The Sheik. Sabu made up for a lack of wrestling skill with a willingness to put his body through near torture, punctuated by a series of nasty, deep scars that criss-crossed his torso. His trademark was breaking tables, usually with his own body, and that particular stunt was perfect for what Hart and Nash wanted to achieve, but was unheard of in the WWF.

As Hart was trying to return to the ring following the missed plancha, Nash charged him off the apron and through the Spanish announcers' table situated at ringside. It almost seemed like an accident, which was rather the intention. The response in the arena was immediate shock, with fans charging to the barricade to witness the aftermath of the destruction for themselves. The majority had never seen ECW before, and many had never even heard of Paul Heyman's groundbreaking promotion, so the stunt came as a complete shock. Fans believed they had just witnessed something totally off script.

When Nash brought Hart back into the ring it looked like he had the match in hand, and viewers knew that all he needed to do was finish him off with the jack knife. Instead of doing that, Nash allowed his character to show a moment of weakness by expressing sympathy for Hart's plight. The message being conveyed was that putting Hart through the table had been an accident, and that Diesel felt remorse. It was that indecision that would ultimately cost him his title, as Hart caught him with a surprise small package and scored what was presented as a lucky pin.

"Fucking motherfucker," angrily mouthed Nash after the match, directly into the camera, laconically conveying Diesel's frustrations with his own compassion in a decidedly non-family-friendly way. The Diesel character showed a further shift in attitude immediately afterwards, dropping Hart with two hard powerbombs as the announcers talked about his heinous actions and ignored Hart's title win entirely, not even mentioning it once in passing. Away from the storyline, Nash then allowed some of the real-life residual resentment for the pair's previous issues to spill out, "Don't forget who did you the fucking favour," he spat at Hart as he threw him the WWF Championship belt.

The match was a success; it achieved everything it had set out to and more, and both the wrestlers and Vince McMahon knew that the table spot was sure to leave people talking. There had never been anything like it in the World Wrestling Federation prior, and some people saw it as proof that Vince was willing to push the envelope further and further in order to compete with the threat posed by WCW.

One of those people was Mike Ortman, who happened to be in attendance that night, watching the show with some Canadian business partners who were still apprehensive about working with the WWF. Tensions had escalated recently because the Canadian television (and pay-per-view) services were in the process of banning programming containing excessive violence and gratuitous adult content from airing before 9pm. Ortman knew that if the WWF was moved to the late evening timeslot it would be a major blow to them, as it would undermine their attempts to woo new sponsors and present their product as suitable for all ages, including to the demographic marketing executives sought the most: children.

The table stunt that Hart and Nash had pulled left him frustrated. And had he really just seen the word, "fuck," come out of Nash's mouth? He hurriedly tried to defend the profanity and the newfound levels of violence to the partners as being a one-off, promising that nothing like it would ever air on free television. When Ortman brought up the matter with Vince later that night, the chairman casually dismissed it as simply two guys getting carried away, and he promised that it wouldn't happen again. Ortman didn't know whether to believe the explanation, though little did he realise that McMahon was openly lying to his face, having green-lighted both the table spot and the swearing himself.

Bret Hart had actually suggested the table bump months earlier to Vince, and had then listened with amusement when McMahon called him up a few days after their conversation and laid out the whole thing to him again as if it were his own idea. The swearing had already been cleared with him too by Nash, with the cameraman and director both under orders to film and show the potty-mouthed tirade rather than cut away from it. Vince had known for months about the stunts he was going to pull, intentionally and gleefully defying instructions from his aides, the government, and the networks to tone things down. Whether it be for the benefit of his product or not, Vince simply insisted on doing things his own way.

Ortman would have realised he was fighting a losing battle had he been in attendance for the pre-*Survivor Series* meeting that McMahon had summoned his roster to. In it, he informed them that from now on the WWF was going to be tending towards a more adult audience than in the past, and the content of their shows would reflect that. In Titan's internal struggle between Ortman's need for morality and McMahon's refusal to be constrained, there would only be one outcome.

THIRTEEN

THE WWF CONTINUED TO PUSH the envelope the night following *Survivor Series*, with Kevin Nash debuting the new pissed off and edgier Diesel persona on television, interrupting a match between Chris Candido and Savio Vega to cut a candid promo:

A lot of people are probably wondering where 'Big Daddy Cool's' head is at right now. You know, I thought about it and I thought I would maybe come out here and apologise, for what I did to Bret and for what I did to all my dear fans. I don't think so! You know, last night when I went back to my hotel room I wondered if I'd be able to get any sleep; for the first time in a year, I slept like a baby. When I woke up this morning and I looked in the mirror, do you know what I saw? I saw a smile on my face. It's the first time I saw myself smile in a year, as I saw myself, not some corporate puppet that you tried to create, Vince. You missed the ball on this one baby, you missed the ball. After I won the title, twenty-four hours later I'm up at Titan Tower with the marketing suits, the merchandising suits; 'Hey Diesel, we need you to smile a little bit, we need you to be a little more politically correct, a little more corporate.' Well baby, what you saw last night was the tip of the iceberg. 'Big Daddy Cool' is back; that same guy you saw in Providence at the *Royal Rumble* a couple of years ago. The only thing that matters to me right now is my family, my friends - that includes you, Shawn Michaels - and I'm not saying I'm not gonna smack hands, but it better have a black glove on it baby, so I know you're with me. Whether you like me, love me or hate me, that's the way its gonna be. I'm back!

The speech was the first of its kind on WWF television, and an obvious attempt by Vince to update his product for the modern audience. While no lines were crossed in relation to *The Principles* document, it still seemed to Mike Ortman that they were on potentially shaky ground. According to Nash, the rant was based on his real-life frustrations with the way he had been used as champion, and while he delivered it in character, it was as close to a shoot as the WWF viewers had ever seen on the show. Vince was becoming more and more prepared to try anything to compete with WCW, and he began willingly blurring the lines of reality and fiction.

ANOTHER INCIDENT on *Raw* that night had fans, company staff and even the other boys, completely fooled. Following his well-reported concussion as a result of the Syracuse incident in October, Shawn Michaels had returned to action at *Survivor Series* the following month. The storyline was that he would have to take things easy, as another blow to the head could end his career. Michaels made it through the pay-per-view with no problems, so fans assumed he was now fine and back at one-hundred percent. That night on *Monday Night Raw* he wrestled Owen Hart in a match that was the usual highly competitive, athletic and well-worked bout between the two. That was until a spot towards the end of the bout, where Owen kicked Shawn in the back of his head with a move called an enzuigiri.

At first there didn't seem to be any problems, but then Michaels clutched his head and feigned dizziness, before collapsing to his knees and acting like he had passed out. Immediately there was panic behind the scenes, even more so when the broadcast went to dead air as the announcers rushed to check on him. Vince hadn't before dared to attempt such a stunt, because he feared viewers would think the show was experiencing technical difficulties. As such, everyone in the back assumed the stunt to be real. Other than The Kliq, the only people who knew that it was all an elaborate work were Owen, Vince, and commentators Jim Ross and Jerry Lawler.

Michaels had to fight hard to get dead air on the show; Vince was extremely reluctant to have nobody calling what was happening for the viewers at home. Shawn was typically persistent, "It needs to be *real!*" he implored the chairman, "Calling the action is wrestling, it's a wrestling angle. If a guy passed out in the ring, wouldn't you freak?" McMahon had to concede that he would, but it was still a decision he didn't take lightly. He remained concerned that fans would turn over to *Nitro*, but his fears were unfounded. The dead air made the angle seem all the more legitimate and his viewers were captivated. The majority knew that wrestling wasn't real, but this? This they *knew* was real.

To his credit, Michaels played the angle to the hilt, even being taken to hospital for scans while Paul Levesque played the role of concerned friend. Given that Levesque was an on-screen heel, the illusory nature of wrestling was further fogged and convinced any remaining naysayers that they had witnessed a shoot. Even the doctors bought into the façade. "We pretty much fooled everybody," Shawn later boasted. While *Nitro* beat *Raw* in the ratings that night, the true test of the angle's effectiveness would be seen the following week. It was hoped fans would tune in to see how the drama unfolded. As expected, the next week produced a positive result, a win for

Raw, with viewers desperate for an update on the condition of Michaels. They were emotionally invested in the storyline.

As good as the initial angle was, the way the story subsequently played out on television rather exposed it as being just that; an angle. Despite the ploy, *Nitro* was back on top the following week. Nevertheless, this was still new ground for Vince, and he would get better at producing reality-based television as he further abandoned his own long-standing principles, and pushed the boundaries of what was expected on his wrestling show.

The WWF was starting to forge a new identity for itself, and the fresh feel of the content was garnering some critical acclaim. But less good news was the buy rate for *Survivor Series*. Coming in at a 0.57, it represented a huge drop from the previous year's number. Despite being similar to the other terrible buy rates the group had managed throughout the year, Vince was sanguine about the number. He had already made peace with the Diesel experiment failing to draw, and expected that things would turn around once the company's new, edgier direction was fully implemented. *Survivor Series* was merely a stepping stone in that direction.

THE WEEKLY ratings war between *Raw* and *Nitro* rumbled on for the remainder of the year, with the two companies exchanging victories from one week to the next, and neither side establishing a significant advantage. Just as Eric Bischoff was searching for another stunt to shift the momentum towards WCW, one fell right into his lap in December when he received a call from Debra Miceli, the recently released WWF Women's Champion Alundra Blayze.

Miceli informed Bischoff that she had been terminated from her WWF contract due to the company's perilous financial situation - the news of which alone was like music to his ears - and that she wanted to come back to WCW, where she had previously performed under the moniker 'Madusa'. Eric was doubly thrilled when she told him that Vince had fired her without her dropping the title. Sensing a once-in-a-lifetime opportunity to do something extraordinary, Bischoff salivated at the prospect of the plan he was formulating.

"Do you still have the belt?" he asked her.

"Erm, Yeah," she responded, wondering what he had in mind.

"Why don't you bring that along with you [to *Nitro*] too..." he insisted.

Like Luger, Miceli was reluctant because of the bridges she would burn with her ex-employees, but for Bischoff this was war, and it was no belt, no deal. Not wanting to be out of work, Miceli came to the same conclusion as Lex Luger, that she owed Vince nothing since he had fired her, and so she agreed to the terms. On the December 18th *Nitro*, she showed up unannounced at the commentator's desk where Bischoff was sitting. After running down the Alundra Blayze character, Miceli, under orders from Bischoff, dumped the belt in a trash can. If giving away the WWF's results had been a dirty trick, having one of his performers denigrate their championship belt live on television was akin to sacrilege.

On-screen Bischoff feigned shock, but inside he was thrilled with how the stunt had played out. He had created another "moment" on *Nitro*, and when the ratings came in he had further cause for celebration. *Nitro* had won again, their third victory in a row, with a 2.7 to *Raw*'s measly 2.3. Other than the unopposed first show, it was on par with the best rating they had done to date. The deed had perfectly encapsulated the "anything can happen" nature of the show that Bischoff so desperately craved. Fans who were watching *Nitro* stayed with it rather than flicking over to *Raw*, wondering just what on earth would happen next.

Meanwhile over in Newark where *Monday Night Raw* was airing live, Vince McMahon was given the news of the stunt from a technician who had been keeping tabs on the rival show in the production truck. He was stunned, but not as angry as many expected.[55] Rather than vowing to tear WCW apart, Vince seemed despondent, and on commentary during the broadcast he was obviously distracted. It seemed to Vince that every week Bischoff and *Nitro* were attacking the WWF, and at that point he had no answers as to how he could combat them.

"WCW had us by the balls, that was in the back of Vince's mind," said Tom Prichard, who also recalled, "Everyone was pissed at Madusa. Back then you would get pissed at people all the time for the things they did, but the truth is, most would have done the same thing for the money."

Jim Cornette shared similar sentiments, "The locker-room thought Madusa was a fucking douche bag, but the fact is, Vince was stupid enough to fire her without getting the belt back first. It wasn't really a huge thing, it was just insulting. The only thing it did was prove that Eric Bischoff was a skunky little fucker."

NOT EVERY decision that Eric Bischoff made in 1995 was a good one. Firing Steven James Williams was one in particular that haunted him for the rest of his WCW tenure. Williams resurfaced in the WWF, and eventually

---

[55] Though, it would have been somewhat hypocritical for Vince to have been too annoyed by the stunt. In 1991 he had gleefully signed Ric Flair away from WCW while he was still reigning as their World Heavyweight champion, and went so far as to put the Nature Boy on television wearing the gold, using it as part of an angle.

transformed into one of wrestling's biggest ever stars: 'Stone Cold' Steve Austin.

Austin, a gruff Texan with an ill-fitting pretty boy gimmick, had been with the Atlanta group since 1991, prior to Bischoff's arrival. Initially playing a loose imitation of Ric Flair with a sequined robe, flowing blonde hair, and the nickname 'Stunning', Austin had a reputation for being a solid in-ring mechanic, but the prevailing belief within the office was that he lacked charisma. He changed perceptions when he was forced into a union with Brian Pillman, and the two took it upon themselves to do everything they could to make the thrown-together tandem work. Competing as the Hollywood Blonds, Austin and Pillman bounced ideas off one another as they travelled the road together. They became good friends upon realising that they shared a lot of the same beliefs about how wrestling should be, and similar frustrations regarding their utilisation.

With little help from an office that had zero faith in them, the Hollywood Blonds did get over through sheer force of will. To say the pair were surprised when WCW decided to split them up without warning would be an understatement; Austin was positively incandescent about having the rug pulled from beneath the most successful and satisfying run of his career to that point.

He was placated somewhat by a series of well-received matches against Ricky Steamboat that showcased his abilities well, and a run with the United States Championship that gave him hope for a future spot in the company's main events. The U.S. belt was seen as a stepping stone of sorts, a way to test someone before they transitioned to the next level. But for Austin, that step up never came. Instead he was forced to suffer a humiliating thirty-five second defeat to washed up eighties star 'Hacksaw' Jim Duggan, and was then quietly moved down the card as WCW was overtaken by the influx of former WWF wrestlers, spearheaded by Hulk Hogan and his cronies.

Austin was not particularly fond of Hogan, because he had pitched an idea to Eric Bischoff for a program with WCW's newest acquisition prior to his arrival, but Bischoff had dismissed the request and bluntly stated that Hogan only wanted to work with Ric Flair. Rather than suggesting it might be something they would do at a later date, Bischoff blew off the suggestion completely, leaving Austin angry and frustrated that his hard work wasn't being appreciated.

During a match in Japan, Austin suffered a torn triceps after performing a routine splash, leaving him sidelined as he underwent surgery to reattach it. Realising that being out of sight meant being out of mind, Austin decided to show up at a set of television tapings to keep his name in the consciousness and to catch up with the boys. He was casually strolling through the arena, understating the seriousness of his injury, when he bumped into WCW's head booker Kevin Sullivan. The two exchanged polite pleasantries, with Austin making sure to point out that he was injured but working hard on his recovery, and hoped to be back soon.

Not three days went by before he received a call from Bischoff's personal assistant Janie Engle, with the instruction to contact Eric urgently. When he got hold of him, Bischoff informed Steve that due to the amount he was being paid and because of how long he had been out injured, the company was exercising its right to terminate his deal thanks to a ninety-day incapacity clause buried away in the small print of his contract. It was a clause that Bischoff would also use to fire another of WCW's "home-grown" stars, Leon 'Vader' White, later in the year.

To Steve, the timing of the call following his encounter with Sullivan was no coincidence. Showing up at the tapings had led to Bischoff being reminded that he was paying Austin to sit at home and do nothing, the opposite result to what Steve had hoped for. But what stuck in Austin's craw the most was the manner of the dismissal. "The thing that really pissed me off was the way I was fired," he groused, "I mean, treat me like a damn decent human being and invite me down there and say, 'Steve, we know you're hurt and we're sorry about that, but we ain't got nothing for you.' The way it went down was totally disrespectful."

All of a sudden Austin was out of work and angry about it, but he was given the chance to channel his anger into a new character, courtesy of Paul Heyman's ECW outfit. Austin's cuss-filled rants against his former boss were a perfect fit for the outlaw image that Heyman's promotion was trying to portray, and within a few months he was the hottest free agent in wrestling.

It was Kevin Nash who first went to bat for Austin in the WWF, as the two had been friends for years having travelled the road together in WCW. Nash knew that Austin was money and implored Vince to sign him, but McMahon was reluctant. Like Bischoff, he viewed Steve as a solid performer but one lacking in charisma. Others who had seen far more of his work than McMahon knew differently.

Jim Ross was employed as the head of talent relations when talk of signing Austin came up, and he too offered his support for the idea of bringing Steve in. Like Nash, he knew him from his time in WCW and had always been a fan of his work. McMahon still viewed Austin as an impressive technical wrestler but nothing more, meaning he had a limited upside that ended in the midcard. He didn't think he had the intangibles required to be a top hand in the WWF.

Nevertheless, Vince needed new talent so finally caved in to the pressure and unenthusiastically agreed to give Austin a chance. McMahon called Austin at his Texas home, "Listen," he started in his usual assured tone, "I've got an idea for you, tell me what you think. I want to bring you into the WWF as 'The Ringmaster', you know, like a master of the ring."[56] He continued, "Ted DiBiase is going to be your manager, and we're going to make you the Million Dollar Champion."

After listening to the pitch and clicking the phone receiver back into place, Austin muttered a silent cuss to himself and thought Vince's proposal over. On one hand it was a job with the World Wrestling Federation and a steady income, but on the other they wanted to muzzle him by putting him with a mouthpiece, and discount everything he had done in his career to date. The Ringmaster? It sounded to him like a circus act. He was loathe to void the last five years of his work to pitch up in New York and be lumbered with a dead-end gimmick. What was wrong with just being Steve Austin?, he protested.

Almost as reluctantly as Vince had initially been to offer him a position, Steve was equally unconvinced about signing on with Titan, but a job was a job and he figured it would be easier to fight the thing from the inside once he had a contract than to argue beforehand and potentially lose the opportunity. Not only that, but it was a way to protect himself should there be a recurrence of his triceps injury, as the company would pay for his surgery. With trepidation in his mind, Austin signed the deal and started working for the group in December.

While he was tolerant of the name change for the time being, one thing he wouldn't yield on was his attire. The office had told him that he couldn't wear his preferred black as that was "Diesel's colour," so they asked him to don an emerald green singlet. Green was the colour of money, they said, and with 'The Million Dollar Man' Ted DiBiase being The Ringmaster's manager, it was logical to them. Incredulous at being told what to wear having already given up his name, Austin said no to that right away, telling the office in no uncertain terms that while he would compromise on the colour, he wouldn't ever wear a singlet.

Austin then asked about boots, expecting to be presided over on that too, but was taken aback when Vince told him it didn't matter and that he

---

[56] The name wasn't one that Vince had just come up with off-hand; he had been wanting to use the gimmick for years. He had initially pegged it for Bryan Clarke back in 1993, but changed his mind and gave him the Adam Bomb persona instead.

should just wear whatever he wanted. The response caused Steve to wonder what he had gotten himself in to by coming to the WWF. Here was this supposed creative genius who didn't appear to rate his speaking ability all that highly, who was changing his look and changing his name, yet it didn't appear he had put much thought into the character at all. To Austin, it seemed apathetic, and he wondered if he would have been better off staying with ECW. The money may have been lower, but at least he would have been creatively satisfied.

Austin persevered, but he had yet more problems with the office in the early days, namely agents telling him that he needed to do more in the ring and pick up the pace in his matches. Ted DiBiase recalled a conversation where Austin had asked him if he should listen to their advice, because he thought it was ridiculous. DiBiase agreed with Steve and told him not to change anything, as the way he performed carried an air of believability that few possessed. DiBiase advised that he would eventually get over based on the fact he was different to everyone else, even if it took more time. It would turn out to be a prophetic vision.

TWO DAYS before December's *In Your House 5*, the WWF sent a group of its performers to the freezing region of Calgary, Canada, for a one night only revival of Stampede Wrestling, held to celebrate Stu Hart's eightieth birthday. Vince didn't make a habit of allowing his talent to work outside dates, but this was an exception due to his reverence for the Hart family patriarch.

It was a policy that Scott Hall, who wrestled on the show that night in Calgary, was well aware of. His contract was due for renewal with Titan but he was reluctant to sign a deal. He remembered the words Chief Jay Strongbow had once told him, "Kid, in this business you can either make friends or you can make money." Hall already had plenty of close friends; now he wanted to make money. He didn't want to leave the WWF, but at thirty-seven years-old he realised that his time to make his fortune in the business was rapidly eluding him.

Hall knew that the company was struggling financially and couldn't afford to renew his deal at a higher rate, so he asked that Vince permit him to work some dates in Japan to supplement his income whilst allowing him to stay on with Titan. Vince refused, as he was not willing, nor had he ever been willing, to let one of his performers regularly work elsewhere. Even though there remained another few months for Hall to consider his options before a decision was needed on his deal, this rebuttal further increased his frustrations, moving his mind closer and closer to the exit door.

Elsewhere on the Calgary show, subtitled *Showdown at the Corral*, there was an historic but unheralded meeting between infrequently used WWF wrestler Louie 'Rad Radford' Spicolli, and WCW's newly acquired Stampede original, Chris Benoit. It was the first inter-promotional match of its kind in the Monday Night War era, and the fact that it was able to happen at all was another testament to the respect that the great Stu Hart commanded within the industry.

Booking a finish was somewhat more difficult, but a sticky situation was averted with a Vince hallmark; the screwjob finish. Benoit nailed a superplex and covered for the three, but Spicolli clearly got a shoulder up at two, only for the ref to keep counting and award the match to Benoit. Vince had ran the exact same play to transition the WWF Championship from Hulk Hogan to Andre the Giant in 1988. As a result, everyone was happy. WCW had their guy win, the WWF could point to shoddy refereeing as an excuse for their guy losing, and the Stampede crowd saw one of their own score the victory.

The main event was identical to the one set for the WWF pay-per-view in two days time, seeing Bret Hart pitted against his brother-in-law, Davey Boy Smith. Originally, the card had Shawn Michaels opposite Hart, but he had been pulled from the event in order to sell his concussion angle. As such, 'The British Bulldog', another former star for Stampede years earlier, took his place.

Hart decided to use the bout as an opportunity to refine some spots he planned to use at *In Your House*, though he was still struggling to come up with a finish to that match. He knew he was emerging victorious in both contests, but the WWF storyline between he and Davey had played out in such a way that his trademark sharpshooter hold wasn't appropriate to conclude the tie with.

Not only was Smith being presented on television as someone whom Hart had never beaten in singles competition, but Smith had won their only previous high-profile singles match at *SummerSlam* in 1992 via a surprise pinfall, following a blistering back-and-forth contest. Hart wanted something similar that he could catch Smith with, because the use of his submission hold as the finish would mean a match-long struggle, and a focussed assault on Smith's legs. After the failure of the Nash-Smith match at *In Your House 4*, where Smith employed that same tactic, Bret realised it would be a mistake to go down that route.

As Hart was amongst peers he respected, and who in turn all had a great deal of veneration for him, he asked the locker-room if anyone had any ideas about what he could use. From the corner of the room came the shy, unassuming voice of young Winnipeg native Chris Irvine, one of the latest students from the famous Hart family dungeon.

Irvine, who had worked extensively in Mexico and Japan, remembered a manoeuvre he had seen performed by Negro Casas called *la magistral*, a flashy variant of a cradle pinfall, which he then demonstrated for Hart. 'The Hitman' knew a good move when he saw one and realised it would be perfect for what he wanted with Davey. He tried it that night and pulled it off with his typical faultless precision, so decided to use it at the upcoming pay-per-view show.

Irvine was thrilled that Hart, the WWF Champion, an icon in Canada and across the wrestling world, would be willing to take advice from an unknown rookie. He thought it was a classy act, later stating how it inspired him to persist in the business. Ultimately it paid off, and Irvine became one of the biggest names in the business as the highly decorated, multiple-time World Champion, Chris Jericho.

THE DEPARTURE of Bill Watts had left a void in the Titan offices. The role was a notoriously tough one to succeed in due to the dictatorship of McMahon, but the chairman still had plenty of people on his staff willing to take the poisoned chalice.

One of them was Gerald Brisco, who fit the typical depiction of a glad-handing yes-man down to a tee. Brisco had been an accomplished amateur wrestler in his youth before transitioning to the pro ranks alongside his brother Jack. Both were mainstays in the old NWA and top stars there, then later in their careers they acquired a minority interest in NWA affiliate Georgia Championship Wrestling and assisted in running the company.

McMahon came calling in 1984 during his expansion and offered to buy out the brothers (and another partner, Jim Herd) to become the majority shareholder in the company, so he could acquire its timeslot on *TBS* for the WWF. After Vince broke a variety of promises to the station that he would only present first-run programming, the relationship between *TBS* and the WWF broke down. Ultimately it led to the bad blood between McMahon and Ted Turner, one of the catalysts for the Monday Night Wars a decade later. McMahon had a kinship with Brisco for opening the doors of GCW to him, and he was a trusted aide who could be relied upon to tell him what he wanted to hear.

Towards the end of the year, a sudden influx of talent from the recently folded Smoky Mountain Wrestling, caused some outsiders to suspect that its owner Jim Cornette had been hired to work on the booking team, but that wasn't the case.[57] As Cornette would divulge, deals were already in place for Smoky Mountain talent to appear in the WWF, as the *Royal Rumble* was coming up and the company were going to have trouble filling the thirty slots in the match, so were working with outside groups to temporarily swell the ranks. The eventual closure of SMW simply meant that some were given full-time contracts, as they had nowhere else to work.

One of them was Tom Prichard, who had been associated with Cornette throughout his WWF tenure as part of the Heavenly Bodies tag team. Vince felt his persona needed refreshing, so wanted to repackage him as a Body Donna and have him resemble Chris Candido, under the handle Zip.[58] Prichard remembers that he received a call from his brother Bruce, who was one of the top brass in the WWF office. "Do you want to shave your hair and dye it white?" Bruce asked, fiendishly delighted to be the one to inform him. "Absolutely not! No, no I don't!" replied Tom, aghast. With that, Bruce hung up. Tom realised he had no choice but to comply otherwise he wouldn't get the gig, and so he relented. "It was just hair," he later reflected, "It sucked though, every minute of it sucked. Even cashing the cheques sucked, because they weren't that great."

Jonathan Rechner had enjoyed some minor success as Boo Bradley in Smoky Mountain, and made his Titan debut at December's edition of *In Your House*. The role he played was hardly what Cornette had envisioned when he suggested the rugged brawler to McMahon. With Christmas fast approaching, Vince had an idea for the ultimate seasonal heel: an *evil* Santa Claus. Thus Xanta Klaus, St. Nick's evil twin brother, debuted on the show. Flanked by Ted DiBiase, Xanta Klaus beat the stuffing out of Savio Vega with a sack full of gifts, as children in the audience cried. Like the evil clown Doink had been three years earlier, the gimmick was a darker side of Vince showing through.

Not only was the shelf-life for such a persona extremely limited, but Rechner didn't help himself with his backstage demeanour. "He was like a special needs kid," explained Cornette, "He would work his ass off, but he was simple minded and you had to give him a lot of attention and direction. He went into the WWF with that same attitude, needing to have everything explained to him. It annoyed people pretty fast and Vince quickly booted him."

---

[57] Two months later in February 1996, Cornette was added to the booking team, a position he retained for the better part of two years.

[58] Originally he was going to be called "Flip", but the name was already copyrighted by someone else, so it was changed to Zip.

Buddy Landel was another Smoky Mountain alumni brought in at *In Your House 5*. The blonde 'Nature Boy' made his entrance to the ring in a sequinned robe, walking out to Jim Johnston's facsimile version of the opening refrains of Richard Strauss classic *Also sprach Zarathustra* - the same song that Ric Flair had used as entrance music during his WWF run - leaving no mistake as to who Landel was parodying. Except that he wasn't presented as a parody act; he was supposed to be the new, younger, *better* Ric Flair. Nobody bought it. Landel wasn't helped by the booking, as he was demolished by Ahmed Johnson in less than a minute at *In Your House 5*, having been introduced by the departing Dean Douglas.

Just over a week later when the show was broadcast in its entirety (but with "questionable content" cut out) on a UK special called *Christmas Mania*, Vince instructed host Dok Hendrix to blast Martin with one final parting shot. After noting that Dean Douglas was unable to compete in the match and Landel was subbing for him, the former Michael Hayes sardonically quipped, "Douglas is gone... but nobody really liked him anyway."

For Landel, it was his only WWF pay-per-view appearance. He slipped and fell on ice in a freak accident two days later when leaving a television taping, tearing his quad, which put him on the shelf for months. Outside of a two-shot stint doing jobs on *Shotgun* in 1999, he never worked for the company again, but McMahon did at least soften the blow by sending him a large bonus cheque for his three days work.

One notable happening from the match saw Jeff Jarrett return from his self-imposed exile to set up a program with Ahmed Johnson. Having been introduced by Memphis ally Jerry Lawler, Jarrett joined 'the King' and McMahon behind the commentary desk for the brief bout, then blasted Johnson after the match. Even though part of the reason Jarrett had left was because he was unhappy with his position on the card, it was clear that he was going to be used as fodder in Johnson's mega push.

Vince couldn't push Jarrett until he had first punished him; he felt that doing so would give the wrong message to his roster. Because Jarrett had spat his dummy out so publicly in July when things hadn't gone his way, many would assume that his return was due to Vince caving in to his demands. If McMahon had given Jarrett an elevated position on the shows then such a belief would be furthered. Not to mention that his employees would view it as a sign of weakness and potentially try similar hardball tactics. By burying Jarrett in such a way upon his return, McMahon sent out a very clear message to his talent base that petulantly walking out on the company may be forgiven, but wouldn't as soon be forgotten.

WITH THE numbers perpetually falling for the *In Your House* shows, Vince wanted to load *In Your House 5* with as many novel attractions as he could. One of them was the promise by Diesel to get revenge on Owen Hart for causing Shawn Michaels' collapse in the ring, which Owen had bragged about on television for weeks. Rather than keeping Owen strong for a program with Shawn down the line when he eventually dethroned Owen's brother Bret for the WWF title, The Kliq treated Owen like dirt. He won the match via disqualification, but was pounded by Nash for the four minute duration, reducing his credibility to that of an enhancement worker. The beating scooped away all of Owen's newly returned heat, and he dropped back to the midcard shortly thereafter.

Another Kliq member, Paul Levesque, had a less enjoyable evening. He was booked in one of the two stipulation matches that Vince had hoped would draw people to watch the show, a unique first-time ever "Arkansas Hog Pen Match" with Mark Canterbury. The winner would be the first man to throw his opponent into a fenced-off area that contained mud, real live hogs and a silo's worth of pig excrement. This was Vince's match-making at its most banal, with the supposed appeal being the chance to see hillbilly Henry Godwinn cover snobby blue-blood Hunter Hearst Helmsley in pig faeces.

The bout was a bizarre real-life manifestation of Vince's own internal battle, pitching his trailer park upbringing against his current affluent status; his past against his present. Despite his own wealth, Vince admitted to a loathing of rich people, especially those who flaunted their status and thought they were superior to others because of it. McMahon's refusal to make peace with his formative years, or his current lofty status of relative prosperity, perhaps somewhat explained his contradictory personality and his unpredictable Jekyll and Hyde demeanour.

With that in mind, the result of the bout was perhaps of little surprise. Hunter Hearst Helmsley won, but Vince couldn't resist booking the heel getting his comeuppance and so Helmsley was sent hard into the mud, where he rolled around in the filth for the amusement of the chairman. The on-screen personification of Vince McMahon was victorious, but he was made to pay for his success. During the course of the bout, Paul Levesque had sustained a large gash on his back that was seeping blood (which would remain visible throughout his career), and having it smeared in pig excrement was probably not something he envisioned when he had first signed on with the company. But, such was the sense of humour of McMahon.

Another stipulation match saw The Undertaker look for storyline revenge against Mabel for the injury he had caused him back in October. Calaway was showing off a frightening new addition to his character; a white mask that protected his fragile eye bone, but resembled something from *The Phantom of the Opera*. It added an exciting new element to the persona, but Calaway found it uncomfortable to work behind and it was dropped the following month. The match the pair were booked in was a "Casket Match", with the idea being to stuff one's opponent into a ringside coffin to win. The Undertaker duly achieved the victory, and Nelson Frazier was effectively through with the promotion.

BRET HART was annoyed that his title win at *Survivor Series* had seemingly only occurred as a catalyst for Kevin Nash's personality shift, and he had surprisingly little momentum as the new champion going into the *In Your House* match with Davey Boy Smith in Hershey. With Smith having left all of the planning to Hart, and an idea for a heel turn involving Bret's sister and Davey's wife, Diana nixed, 'the Hitman' was running out of ideas for how to make the match memorable.

Bret was determined to show Vince that he was the superior candidate to be the company's top guy, not Shawn, Nash, or anyone else. He vowed to have another classic with Smith, and he knew just what he needed to do in order to achieve that; he needed to bleed. With blading still banned, Bret realised that he would have to be careful not to get caught committing the act, lest he face a large fine and a furious boss.

The match unfolded in a solid manner, but the fans weren't biting like they had at Wembley in 1992 when the pair met at *SummerSlam*. Bret instinctively knew when the time was right to "get colour", and he gently spat a concealed blade out of his mouth into his sweaty hands in preparation for the moment. As Hart instructed, Davey hurtled him into the steel ring steps and Bret cut himself high in his hairline so as to make the wound appear genuine. Blood poured from him in torrents, and from that point onwards the crowd were ensnared for the remainder of the match.

Commentating at ringside, McMahon tried to downplay the claret, instructing his director to use wide shots without focusing on the wound, while apologising on the air for the bloodshed. But he also heard the visceral response from the crowd, who were reacting in a big way to Hart's crimson mask; clearly they loved the return of bleeding to WWF programming. It elevated a good match into one of the most thrilling contests of the year.

It mattered little to Michael Ortman that the match was being praised for its quality, because he was no longer just irritated by the WWF's recent actions, he was downright annoyed by them. Once again, McMahon went on the defensive and protested innocence, claiming that the cut Bret had received was legitimately caused by the ring steps. The story was corroborated by the state commission doctor, who had also been masterfully hoaxed by Hart.

Unlike at *Survivor Series,* but as with the Jerry Lawler incident, Vince genuinely didn't know that one of his boys had taken it upon themselves to defy company policy. Jim Cornette defends both Lawler's and Hart's actions, noting that they were just trying to help the company by doing things they knew would get over. While Vince may have been ignorant to what was going on, he certainly wasn't innocent when he made the decision to put the whole Hart-Smith match, in its entirety, on an episode of *Monday Night Raw* just a few weeks later.

The constant headaches in dealing with Vince soon proved to be too much for Ortman, who left the WWF early in 1996. Taking a much less stressful job working with *Fox Sports,* he eventually carved out a highly successful career working for *Comcast,* helping to expand their customer base six-fold during his near decade there.

IF BRET Hart was to be a difference maker to the numbers, it didn't show after *In Your House 5,* with his match against Smith only bringing a paltry 80,000 buys for a new company low 0.35 buy rate. The two had managed to draw that same number of people into one *building* for their classic encounter at *SummerSlam* back in 1992, a sharp contrast that showed just how much the business had declined. At the Wembley show, an electric, partisan crowd had roared home their national hero Smith en route to his victory over Hart, in one of the WWF's all-time great matches. That show had convinced nearly 300,000 people to part with their money (at a much higher cost) and order the event, despite taking place at a time when the bottom had just fallen out of the business amidst the swirl of sex and steroid allegations aimed towards the company .

In Your House 5 wasn't helped by a number of factors. Ultimate Fighting Championship's decision to promote their *Ultimate Ultimate* pay-per-view the night before had caused damage, as the crossover between audiences was very similar. The UFC show did just over 250,000 buys, far outperforming *In Your House 5.* The December WWF show had also featured the first price hike for the series, as Vince had been concerned that the events were bordering on unprofitable at $14.95. He increased the cost to $19.95, which meant in real terms an extra $2-3 per order went into the company coffers (with the remainder of the extra money going to the cable companies providing the service). For *In Your House 5*, that meant nearly $200,000 in extra revenue, a significant sum at a time when business was flat-lining.

AS THE year drew to a close, the state of the WWF's business was in a worse shape on paper than ever before, but Vince remained confident, unfazed by the fact. When he assessed his culled talent pool, he was satisfied that he had the pieces of the puzzle available to him in order to rebuild his ailing group - it was just a matter of how to arrange them.

1995 ended with Bret Hart sitting atop the WWF kingdom as its reigning champion for the third time in his career, but it was clear to everyone watching that the torch would soon be passed to Shawn Michaels. Despite a difficult year behind the scenes, Michaels had excelled in front of the cameras, and fans were rallying behind him as Titan's next great hope. The Michaels ascent to the top was already well underway as the year ended, and 1996 promised to be his coming of age.

A few months into 1996, things began to unravel for the WWF, thanks to the dissolution of The Kliq. Scott Hall had made no secret throughout 1995 that he was unhappy with his role in the company, and when Eric Bischoff came calling with an offer of guaranteed money that was too good to turn down, he took the deal. A few weeks later, Kevin Nash followed suit. Nash had realised that once he was dethroned as WWF Champion, his days were numbered. His size and persona dictated that he had to be a top guy or nothing at all, and he knew that Vince had no intention of going with him in that spot again, but out of respect, Nash asked him to match Turner's deal. McMahon couldn't afford it, and accepted Nash's resignation with a face of thunder. When Sean Waltman learned of the pair's decision, he quickly followed them out of the door, breaking up The Kliq for good.

One of Vince's biggest fears had been realised, and he was annoyed that having kowtowed to the group's whims all year long, they showed him no loyalty in return. 1995 had been dominated by The Kliq, often at the expense of other talented performers. Vince had invested time and money into the Razor Ramon, Diesel, and 1-2-3 Kid personas, and now WCW was going to be the one reaping the benefits rather than him. As usual he remained unmoved in front of the boys, but he was furious at the betrayal.

One serendipitous outcome of the trio's imminent departure was the eventual cessation of hostilities between The Kliq and the BSKs, who finally made peace during a tour of Germany in April, 1996. The two factions shared an evening of merriment and cleared the air, with the 'Krew' vowing to support Michaels as *the man* once his friends had departed the company.

Hall and Nash leaving also opened up a spot for Paul Levesque to rise up the card as a top level heel, albeit one that would continue to elude him for a time afterwards. The Kliq ruined the opportunity for him with one last act of selfishness during Hall and Nash's final night in the company. During a house show in Madison Square Garden, in a moment that would go down in wrestling folklore as *The Curtain Call*, heels Nash and Levesque shared an emotional goodbye alongside babyface opponents Michaels and Hall, with the four embracing in the ring and flashing their Kliq hand gesture to the crowd.

Vince, the agents and the boys were apoplectic about the kayfabe violation taking place in the hallowed grounds of the Garden, and there were instant calls for severe punishments to be dished out. But McMahon was unable to do anything to Hall and Nash, as they were gone from the company immediately after the show. Shawn Michaels was his WWF Champion, and after years of elevating him up to that level - and with a lack of other real options - McMahon wanted him to remain as such. That only left Paul Levesque.

Levesque's 1996 career path had already been laid out, with him booked to win that year's *King of the Ring* tournament before transitioning into a feud with Michaels. With Levesque the only member of The Kliq that McMahon could punish, he solely took all of the heat for the Garden incident. Not only was he forced to apologise to every member of the roster for his actions, but he also had his promised push instantly nixed.

The *King of the Ring* crown was instead given to Steve Austin, who had been allowed to morph from the moribund Ringmaster gimmick into a surly, no-nonsense redneck, now donned in his preferred all-black, with the sobriquet 'Stone Cold'. Austin defeated a recently returned Jake Roberts to win the tournament, then cut a legendary speech following the victory in which he mocked Roberts' newfound Christian values:

Talk about your Psalms, talk about John 3:16... Austin 3:16 says I just whipped your ass!

Within a few months, the phrase "Austin 3:16" had become intrinsically weaved into the rich tapestry of wrestling subculture, and as a result the Austin persona went into overdrive. He became one of the biggest money-drawing stars in the history of wrestling, directly responsible for the WWF's second boom period and hailed by many as the reason the company was able to survive and ultimately prosper. Each week in Atlanta, Eric Bischoff could only watch helplessly as the man he fired over the phone became the hottest property in the entire business.

The Kliq *had* succeeded in changing the business for the better, but only because the by-product of their insubordination was Austin being given a forum that he wouldn't have otherwise had. Ultimately the group provided the man who rebuilt the business, but rather than coming from within their ranks he was born from their own selfishness.

Throughout 1996, Vince would come under immense pressure to compete with WCW. He was desperate to take the WWF back to the heights it had enjoyed in the eighties, and was sick and tired of being restricted in his creative output. Soon he left all remaining morality by the wayside and burst out of his enforced corporate cage. He declared via a memo that, "The company's show may include elements which are consistent with the time period," or in other words, *The Principles* were no longer a consideration. McMahon was going to do whatever he wanted in his battle with Bischoff and Turner, whether *USA Network* officials, sponsors, business partners, and members of his own staff, liked it or not.

As time passed, that included the stringent drug testing policy being relaxed until it was quietly abolished, and resultantly the physical size of the roster soon visibly grew. 1996 would also see the product become more sexualised than ever before thanks to the unleashing of Tammy Sytch, and the newest *Baywatch*-esque model to wander through the doors of Titan Tower: Rena 'Sable' Merowitz. Later in the year, the WWF would air the word "fuck" on *Raw* as part of an edgy angle where Brian Pillman pulled a gun on Steve Austin at his home in Cincinnati. Furthermore, the acquisition of hardcore wrestling icon Mick 'Mankind' Foley upped the violence on WWF shows to never before seen levels. The ante was well and truly raised, and soon, there was little content that was off limits for the show.

To those who knew McMahon, none of these things were a surprise. Vince was a fighter and he wanted to have complete autonomy over his product. If he was going to war, he was fighting it on *his* terms.

REFERENCES

The following is a list of people quoted in the book, and where the quote is originally sourced, or credited to them by someone else.

Anoa'i, Rodney
179: (Attributed by Jim Cornette in author interview)
181: (Attributed) *Timeline the History of WWE 1995: As told by Kevin Nash*.
    Sean Oliver, Kayfabe Commentaries

Austin, Steve
122: *Steve Austin Show. "Episode #56 - X-Pac (Part 2)"* 2013,
    http://podcastone.com/Steve-Austin-Show
178: *Steve Austin Show. "Episode #22 - Showtime Eric Young"* 2013,
    http://podcastone.com/Steve-Austin-Show
209: *Stone Cold Steve Austin: The Bottom Line on the Most Popular Superstar of
    All Time*. WWE, 2011
209: Steve Austin, Dennis Bryant, Jim Ross. *The Stone Cold Truth*. WWF,
    2003

Beard, James
59: Wrestling Classics. http://wrestlingclassics.com/.ubb/cache
    SYJY8SE2/ubb_files/forums/Forum17/004095.cgi

Bearer, Paul
72, 113: *Straight Shootin' Series: Percy Pringle Volume 2*, Rob Feinstein, RF
    Video

Bellars, Stephanie
27: *Gorgeous George Shoot Interview*. Rob Feinstein, RF Video

Bigelow, Bam Bam
71, 115. 184: *Bam Bam Bigelow Shoot Interview*. Nick Knowledge, The
    Wrestling Universe Shoot Series, 2002
95: (Attributed) *Timeline the History of WWE 1995: As told by Kevin Nash*.
    Sean Oliver, Kayfabe Commentaries

Bischoff, Eric
100, 146, 148, 206: Eric Bischoff, Jeremy Roberts, *Eric Bischoff: Controversy Creates Cash*, WWE, 2007

Brisco, Gerald
43: (Attributed by Jim Cornette in author conducted interview)

Candido, Chris
113: (Attributed) *Straight Shootin' Series: Percy Pringle Volume 2*, Rob Feinstein, RF Video
114: *Chris Candido Shoot Interview*. Rob Feinstein, RF Video, 2005

Chatterton, Rita
4, 5: *Geraldo*. Geraldo Rivera, Tribune Entertainment, 1992

Cornette, Jim
19, 23, 27, 40, 43, 72, 103, 114, 131, 144, 145, 148, 150, 152, 153, 155, 163, 166, 179, 186, 191, 192, 207, 214: (Author conducted interview)

DeVito, Jr., Basil V.
71: Basil V. DeVito, Jr., Joe Layden. *WWF WrestleMania: The Official Insiders Story*. HarperEntertainment, 2001

Douglas, Shane
125, 126: Wrestling Epicenter. "*Shane Douglas Interview Online*." 2005, www.wrestlingepicenter.com/shows/ShaneDouglas/
126, 128, 180, 182: Beneath The Mat Dot Com. "*Shane Douglas Radio Interview*"
181: (Attributed) *Timeline the History of WWE 1995: As told by Kevin Nash*. Sean Oliver, Kayfabe Commentaries
126, 181, 182, 184: "Let's Talk with Shane Douglas". *Powerslam*. 20. Pg. 22-25

Frazier, Nelson
139, 141: *Nelson Frazier Shoot Interview*, Pro Wrestling Diary

Hall, Scott
76: Unknown source Scott Hall interview
96: (Attributed) *Timeline the History of WWE 1995: As told by Kevin Nash*. Sean Oliver, Kayfabe Commentaries

Harris, Ron
165: (Attributed by Jim Cornette in author conducted interview)

Hart, Bret
52, 76, 77, 82, 199: Bret Hart, *Hitman: My Real Life in the Cartoon World of Wrestling*, Grand Central Publishing, 2008
157: *Bret Hitman Hart: The Dungeon Collection*. WWE, 2013

Holly, Bob
49, 86, 92, 105, 133: Bob Holly, Ross Williams, *The Hardcore Truth: The Bob Holly Story*, ECW Press, 2013

Honky Tonk Man
115: *Face Off: Honky Tonk Man vs. Raven*. Rob Feinstein. RF Video

Horowitz, Barry
133: *Wrestlefest '06 Q & A Series*. Highspots.com

Jannetty, Marty
7: *Wrestling Observer Newsletter*. www.f4wonline.com. May 9, 1994.

Knight, Dennis
111: *The Godwinns Shoot Interview*. Rob Feinstein, RF Video

Lawler, Jerry
164: Jerry Lawler, *It's Good to be the King...Sometimes*. WWE, 2002

Levesque, Paul
170: *The Shawn Michaels Story: Heartbreak & Triumph*. WWF, 2007

Luger, Lex
148: *Lex Luger Shoot Interview*. Rob Feinstein, RF Video

Martin, Fin
177: "Championship Chaos". *Powerslam*. 17. Pg. 13
198: "Bret Bags the Big One". *Powerslam*. 18. Pg. 18

Mascari, Robert
172, 173, 174: (Author conducted interview)

McMahon, Stephanie
27: *The World's Greatest Wrestling Managers*. WWE, 2006
27: *WWE Countdown: Hottest Couples*, WWE, 2014

McMahon, Vince
5: *Donahue*. Phil Donahue, 1992
6: (Attributed) *Timeline the History of WWE 1994: As told by Sean Waltman*. Sean Oliver, Kayfabe Commentaries
10: *Jake The Snake Roberts: Pick Your Poison*. WWE, 2005
11: *The Ultimate Legend*. WWF, 2014
75: Unknown source Scott Hall interview
63, 82, 136, 170, 171: (Attributed) Shawn Michaels, Aaron Feigenbaum. *Heartbreak & Triumph: The Shawn Michaels Story*. WWE, 2006
66: (Attributed) Basil V. DeVito, Jr., Joe Layden. *WWF WrestleMania: The Official Insiders Story*. HarperEntertainment, 2001
81, 199: (Attributed) *Timeline the History of WWE 1995: As told by Kevin Nash*. Sean Oliver, Kayfabe Commentaries
86: *The True Story of WrestleMania*. WWE, 2011
125: (Attributed) "Let's Talk with Shane Douglas". *Powerslam*. 20. Pg. 22-25
131, 167: (Attributed) Bill Watts, Scott Williams. *The Cowboy and the Cross: The Bill Watts Story: Rebellion, Wrestling and Redemption*. ECW Press, 2006
187: (Attributed by Jim Cornette in author conducted interview)
190: (Attributed) Wrestling Epicenter. "*Shane Douglas Interview Online*." 2005, www.wrestlingepicenter.com/shows/ShaneDouglas
210: (Attributed) *Stone Cold Steve Austin: The Bottom Line on the Most Popular Superstar of All Time*. WWE, 2011

Miceli, Debra
206: (Attributed) Eric Bischoff, Jeremy Roberts, *Eric Bischoff: Controversy Creates Cash*, WWE, 2007

Michaels, Shawn
34, 80, 81, 87, 127, 136, 167, 168, 172, 182, 184, 185, 205: Shawn Michaels, Aaron Feigenbaum. *Heartbreak & Triumph: The Shawn Michaels Story*. WWE, 2006
38: (Attributed) *Triple H: Thy Kingdom Come*. WWE, 2013
95, 96, 200: (Attributed) *Timeline the History of WWE 1995: As told by Kevin Nash*. Sean Oliver, Kayfabe Commentaries
182: *Shawn Michaels Shoot Interview*, Rob Feinstein, RF Video

Ross, Jim
43: *The Shawn Michaels Story: Heartbreak & Triumph.* WWE, 2007
170: *The Legends of Wrestling: Territories.* WWE, 2008

Runnels, Dustin
177: Dustin Runnels, Mark Vancil, *Cross Rhodes: Goldust, Out of the Darkness.* WWE, 2010

Savage, Randy
21, 22, 23, 24: (Attributed by Lanny Poffo in author conducted interview)
29: *Randy Savage Interview*, Blake Norton, IGN

Smith, Davey Boy
112: (Attributed) *Steve Austin Show. "Episode #56 - X-Pac (Part 2)"* 2013, http://podcastone.com/Steve-Austin-Show

Steele, George
113: (Attributed by Tom Prichard in author conducted interview)

Strongbow, Chief Jay
22: (Attributed by Lanny Poffo in author conducted interview)
211: (Attributed) *nWo Back in Black*, WWF, 2002

Sytch, Tammy
110: *YouShoot: Tammy Sytch.* Sean Oliver, Kayfabe Commentaries

Turner, Ted
100: (Attributed) *The Monday Night War.* WWE, 2004

Waltman, Sean
44: Adam Kleinberg, Adam Nudelman, *Mysteries of Wrestling: Solved.* ECW Press, 2005
112: *YouShoot: Sean Waltman.* Sean Oliver, Kayfabe Commentaries
112: *Steve Austin Show. "Episode #56 - X-Pac (Part 2)"* 2013, http://podcastone.com/Steve-Austin-Show
182: (Attributed) Shawn Michaels, Aaron Feigenbaum. *Heartbreak & Triumph: The Shawn Michaels Story.* WWE, 2006

Watts, Bill
10: (Attributed) *Jake The Snake Roberts: Pick Your Poison.* WWE, 2005
131, 167: Bill Watts, Scott Williams. *The Cowboy and the Cross: The Bill Watts Story: Rebellion, Wrestling and Redemption.* ECW Press, 2006
167: (Attributed by Jim Cornette in author conducted interview)

Wiand, Stephanie
121: (Author conducted interview)

- Facts regarding the Shawn Michaels Syracuse incident come from witness interviews conducted by the writer, written affidavits provided at the time by the defendant Douglas Griffith, Shawn Michaels, Donna Jones, and court reports regarding the case's dismissal.

All television rating data provided by Nielsen Media Research

All pay-per-view buyrate data provided by the Wrestling Observer Newsletter.

The following issues of the Wrestling Observer Newsletter were used for research purposed to help compile this tome:

February 4 1991, March 11 1991, March 1 1993, March 22 1993, March 29 1993, April 12 1993, April 26 1993, June 28 1993, July 5 1993, March 28 1994, May 9 1994, May 16 1994, May 30 1994, June 27 1995, July 4 1994, July 11 1994, September 5 1994, September 12 1994, September 19 1994, November 14 1994, November 21 1994, January 2 1995, January 9 1995, January 16 1996, January 23 1995, January 30 1995, February 6 1995, February 13 1995, February 20 1995, March 6 1995, March 7 1995, March 13 1995, March 20 1995, March 27 1995, April 10 1995, April 17 1995, April 24 1995, April 29 1995, May 1 1995, May 8 1995, May 15 1995, May 22 1995, May 29 1995, June 5 995, June 12 1995, June 19 1995, June 26 1995, July 3 1995, July 10 1995, July 17 1995, July 24 1995, July 31 1995, August 7 1995, August 14 1995, August 21 1995, August 28 1995, September 4 1995, September 11 1995, September 18 1995, September 25 1995, October 2 1995, October 9 1995, October 16 1995, October 23 1995, October 30 1995, November 6 1995, November 13 1995, November 17 1995, November 20 1995, December 4 1995, December 11 1995, December 18 1995, December 26 1995

ACKNOWLEDGEMENTS

Thanks to the following, without whom this book would not have been possible: Benjamin Richardson for his fastidious proofing, fact-checking, reworking and reimagining of many of the words in these pages. Not to mention the breathtaking cover art. Jim Cornette, for agreeing to go over the stories from the year in fine detail, with an enormous amount of patience. His character references and insight into the inner workings of the WWF were invaluable. I am also exceedingly grateful that he thought enough of the bits and pieces he read that he was willing to put his name to it and write the foreword. Dave Meltzer, for his incredible weekly Wrestling Observer Newsletter, a vital source of information, facts and stats. Robert Mascari, for agreeing to scour his archives and provide me with information about a case from twenty years ago, as well as discussing the many questions I had regarding it at length. Tom Prichard for the hours we spent discussing various topics that feature in these pages. Lanny Poffo for fielding some fairly intense questions about his brother and for helping me get to the bottom of a long-intriguing situation. Stephanie Wiand for giving me the time of day regarding a subject that no longer interests her. Alex Shane for his interest in the project and role as a sounding board. Steve Halfpenny for assisting in naming the book and for his various insights and ever present opinions. Jon Apsey, who was a key influence early on in getting the project off the ground, particularly in establishing the narrative and helping the book find its "voice". My wife and children for being supportive of my need to have quiet time in order to get the jumble of ideas from my head and onto the page, with minimal complaint. My parents for encouraging me to pursue my various endeavours. Lee Maughan and Arnold Furious, my colleagues at History of Wrestling who willingly allowed me to venture out into the deep seas of this project alone, but were always available to lend a hand.

INDEX

INDEX

INDEX

INDEX

INDEX

INDEX

INDEX